Pathways to God
Torah, Society, and State

Rabbi Nachum L. Rabinovitch

Pathways to God

Torah, Society, and State

Translated by Elli Fischer

Me'aliyot Press
Maggid Books

Pathways to God
Torah, Society, and State

First English Edition, 2025

Maggid Books
An imprint of Koren Publishers Jerusalem Ltd.

POB 8531, New Milford, CT 06776-8531, USA
& POB 4044, Jerusalem 9104001, Israel
www.korenpub.com

The publication of this book was made possible
through the generous support of *The Jewish Book Trust.*

This translation was published posthumously
and was not reviewed by the author.

ISBN 978-1-59264-622-7, *hardcover*

Printed and bound in the United States

In memory of our beloved Sabba,

HaRav Nachum Eliezer Rabinovitch zt"l

הרב נחום אליעזר רבינוביץ זצ״ל

Spiritual giant, outstanding scholar, leader, and teacher to so many across the globe, as well as being our caring, loving, and devoted grandfather and great-grandfather.

Always ready to listen,
ever kind and sensitive.

Deeply loved and missed by us all,

הנכדים והנינים, האוהבים ומתגעגעים

Dedicated in memory of our dear parents

ישראל בן יוסף יהודה אריה זצ״ל

מאשה בת חיים הכהן ז״ל

דוד מאיר בן משה זצ״ל

who, whilst facing considerable challenges,
embodied heartfelt and unwavering dedication to values
of Torah and ḥesed with humility, sensitivity, and kindness.

May the Truth of Torah continue to spring
forth from their rich legacy.

Chaim and Renee Fromowitz
and family

In memory of

HaRav Hagon HaGadol
Rav Nachum Eliezer Rabinovitch

In honor of
Annette Basri

Contents

Editor's Preface

We are pleased to present this, the second volume of Rabbi Nachum L. Rabinovitch's writings in the Maggid Modern Classics series. The English translation of Rabbi Rabinovitch's original Hebrew work, *Mesilot BiLvavam* (Me'aliyot, 2015), is presented in two volumes, following the work's original division into two sections focusing on the individual and society: *Pathways to Their Hearts: Torah Perspectives on the Individual* (Maggid and Me'aliyot, 2023), and the present volume, *Pathways to God: Torah, Society, and State.*

A translation of Rabbi Rabinovitch's original prologue to the Hebrew edition, including his acknowledgments and personal notes, appears in the previous volume.

This second volume too would not have been possible without the efforts of Ayal Fishler of Me'aliyot Press; the leadership of Yeshivat Birkat Moshe; and Guido Rauch, to whom we are grateful for his partnership and his support for this important book.

We wish to add our thanks to translator Rabbi Elli Fischer, as well as the publishing team at Koren Jerusalem: publisher Matthew Miller, editorial director Rabbi Reuven Ziegler, Dr. Yoel Finkelman,

Aryeh Grossman, Ita Olesker, Rina Ben Gal, Nechama Unterman, and Tani Bayer. We thank them for their professionalism and assistance in seeing this volume to print.

This translation was published posthumously and was not reviewed by the author.

Note to the Reader

All citations of Maimonides' works are to the following editions, unless otherwise indicated:

- *Commentary to the Mishna*: Qafih edition (Jerusalem: Mossad Harav Kook, 1963–1969).
- Introductory essays within the *Commentary on the Mishna* (with the exception of *Eight Chapters*): Shilat edition (Jerusalem: Me'aliyot, 1992).
- *Sefer HaMitzvot*: Qafih edition (Jerusalem: Mossad Harav
- Kook, 1971).
- *Mishneh Torah*: Where available, the citations are from my edition, *Yad Peshuta* (Ma'aleh Adumim: Me'aliyot, 1990–2011).
- Otherwise, we use the text of the *Mishneh Torah* Project edition: Y. Makbili, ed. (Haifa: Or Vishua, 2009).
- *Guide of the Perplexed*: Pines translation (Chicago: University of Chicago Press, 1963).
- *Iggerot HaRambam* (with the exception of the *Epistle to Yemen*): Shilat edition (Jerusalem: Me'aliyot, 5750).

- *Responsa of Maimonides*: Blau edition (Jerusalem: Mekitzei
- Nirdamim, 1958–1960).
- *The Eight Chapters of Maimonides on Ethics: Shemonah Perakim:* Gorfinkle translation and edition (New York: Columbia University Press, 1912).
- *Moses Maimonides' Epistle to Yemen*: Cohen (trans.) and Halkin edition (New York: American Academy for Jewish Research, 1952).

Whenever "*Hilkhot X*" is cited, the reference is to *Mishneh Torah*. References to talmudic tractates in the Yerushalmi are prefaced with Y; if there is no prefacing letter, the reference is to the Babylonian Talmud.

Chapter 1

On the Holocaust and Rebirth

"Let Me Know Your Ways"

The painful problems of exile and suffering have been with us since Israel became a nation. The Sages explained that when Moses said, "Now, if I have truly gained Your favor, please let me know Your ways" (Ex. 33:13), his intent was as follows:

> He said before Him: "Master of the World! Why are there innocent people who prosper and innocent people who suffer, evildoers who prosper and evildoers who suffer?"[1]

Moses was tired of easy answers. When "he went out to his brothers and saw their suffering" (Ex. 2:11), his spirit was overwhelmed: Why did Israel, more than any other nation, deserve enslavement and forced labor? Although this was preordained by God in a prophecy to Abraham, "Know well that your offspring shall be strangers in a land not theirs, and they shall be enslaved and oppressed four hundred years" (Gen. 15:13), still, this prediction is itself a source of anguish. Is this the proper reward for Abraham, who withstood ten trials? Moses raises

1. Berakhot 7a.

a challenging question: "Why did You bring harm upon this people?" (Ex. 5:22). The same question reverberates through history, to our own times: "Why, O Lord, do You stand far off, do You hide in times of trouble?" (Ps. 10:1).

The problem of evil has challenged the thought and faith of gentile thinkers as well. Since they accepted the prophet's word, that God alone "forms light and creates darkness, makes peace and creates evil" (Is. 45:7), they were faced with the frightening question: "Shall not the Judge of all the earth deal justly?" (Gen. 18:25). This gave rise to an entire philosophical discipline known as "theodicy," whose purpose is to justify God, as it were, and explain why He created evil.

Neither the prophets nor the Sages make themselves out to be God's advocates. Jeremiah, the prophet of fury and devastation who rebuked Israel for its sins and prophetically foresaw the destruction of the Temple, the exile of the people, and rivers of spilled blood, is the one who grieved over his shattered people and said: "We have transgressed and rebelled, and You have not forgiven" (Lam. 3:42). It is true that we sinned, but You, Master of the Universe, how could You not forgive? "See, O Lord, and behold, to whom You have done this" (ibid. 2:20). The prophets "knew of the Holy One, blessed be He, that He is truthful; therefore, they did not speak falsely about Him" (Yoma 69b). Why should man give futile answers? "Let him sit alone and be silent when the Lord disciplines him" (Lam. 3:28). There are some things that mortal man cannot speak of, and he must instead "place his mouth in the dust" (ibid. 29).

God is also displeased with His various advocates. We see this from Job's friends, each of whom tried to justify, in his own way, the horrific tragedies that befell Job. One said that suffering befalls man in retribution for his sins. Another said that suffering befalls him so that he will receive more reward. And so forth. But Scripture explicitly rejects their approaches, summing up: "The Lord said to Eliphaz the Temanite, 'I am incensed at you and your two friends, for you have not spoken the truth about Me as did My servant Job'" (Job 42:7). "You have not spoken the truth" – God does not want those who, in their incomplete understanding, do not even grasp the terrifying dimensions of the question and, with their limited intelligence, propose answers that are very far from the truth.

"Moses Hid His Face"

The Gemara's [Talmud's] approach to Moses' request, "Let me know Your ways," is both surprising and profound. The Gemara explains the essence of the prophetic vision in which God first revealed Himself to Moses. Commenting on the verses "He gazed, and there was a bush all aflame, yet the bush was not consumed ... and Moses hid his face, for he was afraid to look at God" (Ex. 3:2, 6), the Gemara says:

> R. Shmuel b. Naḥmani said in the name of R. Yonatan: In the merit of three things, [Moses] was granted three things. As a reward for "Moses hid his face," he merited that his face shone; as a reward for "for he was afraid," he merited "they were afraid to approach him" (Ex. 34:30); as a reward for "to look at," he merited "he looks at an image of the Lord" (Num. 12:8).[2]

A superficial reading shows that the first two of the three things that Moses was granted were *quid pro quo*: Because "Moses hid his face," "the skin of his face was radiant" (Ex. 34:29); because "he was afraid" to approach God, they – the elders and all of Israel – "were afraid to approach him" when they saw the aura of radiance that enveloped him.

But what is the meaning of the third element? As a reward for not looking at God, he merited to "look at an image of the Lord"? If it is virtuous to refrain from gazing upon a prophetic manifestation of the Divine, then how can the reward for such restraint be to "look at an image of the Lord"? It is improper to look! And if this is considered a precious reward, why did he refrain in the first place? What was he afraid of? And why does he deserve reward for his fear and restraint?

God wanted to reveal to Moses the solution to the question that had been troubling him his whole life. The verse that tells how Moses refrains from gazing uses the name Elokim, which represents God's attribute of justice: "For he was afraid to look at God [Elokim]." God wanted to raise Moses above and beyond all other creatures, so that he could fathom the secret of the name Elokim and see human suffering not from the human perspective, but from the Creator's perspective. He

2. Berakhot 7a.

was given the chance to peer behind the curtain that prevents the human mind from understanding the ways of divine providence.

But Moses refused: "Moses hid his face, for he was afraid to look at God." Moses, who was plagued by this question his whole life, recoiled and refused to look. Why? "He was afraid." Afraid of what? He was offered an answer to the ultimate question faced by believers in the one true God! And at the moment that he was given this opportunity to break through the limits of the human intellect – he hid his face. Why?

The Human Intellect and the Attribute of Justice

However, this is precisely the point. Moses understood that there can be no human heart without the human mind. Even in our everyday experiences, we see that when we understand the purpose of another's pain, we do not empathize quite as much. To use an almost childish example, parents will let a doctor stick their baby with a needle in order to vaccinate him. They hear the child's cries of pain and fear, yet the pangs in the parents' hearts do not override their satisfaction over the fact that their child is being inoculated against all sorts of terrible diseases.

A more serious example is the phenomenon, well-known in the medical profession, of competent physicians who become so hardened that they no longer look at the patient as a human being in distress. Their initial intentions are good – they want to help patients and find new and better treatments for their diseases – but ultimately their work is liable to coarsen their personalities, render them deaf to the distress and suffering of fellow human beings, and cause them to treat patients like laboratory specimens. It goes without saying that military and political leaders throughout history are prone to exhibiting the same traits; they speak of "the price of victory" and assess what "price" should be deemed reasonable. Even Queen Esther explained to the king: "Had we only been sold as bondmen and bondwomen, I would have kept silent" (Est. 7:4), but the extermination of an entire people is too high a price, and "we have been sold, my people and I, to be destroyed, massacred, and exterminated." What emperor worthy of the name is not convinced that it is worthwhile to sacrifice tens of thousands of his countrymen on the altar of victory? The risk is even greater when the leader has good intentions. Were he to know in advance that he would indeed achieve the "good" of his goal, no price would be too high, and his heart would turn to stone.

Moses knew that it would be impossible to exceed the limitations of the human intellect and still maintain his human heart, his empathy for others. That is why Moses was afraid to look upon God. When he saw the taskmasters beating his brothers when they failed to meet their brick quota, when he saw Egyptians taking Israelite babies and pushing them into gaps in the wall in lieu of missing bricks, his heart broke. From the depths of his soul, he boldly demanded of God: "Why did You bring harm upon this people?" He sensed the outrage with every fiber of his being, and he rose up to salvage what he could. But if he were to lose his human heart, he would no longer be human, God forbid. This is what Moses feared!

The contrived explanations of intellectual midgets paralyze and marginalize human emotion, causing apathy and even cruelty. Certainly, then, had man been allowed to understand the ways of God's attribute of justice, it would have been at the expense of his humanity. Therefore, "Moses hid his face," and the prophet says almost a thousand years later: "Let him sit alone and be silent." The human intellect has no access to the attribute of justice. That gate is closed and locked before man. "You have clothed Yourself in anger and pursued us; You have slain without pity. You have screened Yourself off with a cloud, that no prayer may pass through" (Lam. 3:43–44).

From Moshe Rabbeinu we turn to Moshe ben Maimon, Maimonides, who was also greatly troubled by the question of evil. After surveying all the common explanations for why "the greatest and heaviest misfortunes befall the most perfect individual, who was the most unblemished of them in righteousness," his definitive conclusion is: "It is obligatory to stop at this point and believe that nothing is hidden from Him."[3]

The Wicked Who Prosper: The Attribute of Kindness

When a person becomes aware of the limits on human understanding, he shares Moses' response of being "afraid to look at Elokim." Moses

3. *Moreh Nevukhim* III:23, pp. 491, 496.

also deserves reward for this act of restraint. The reward for not looking at Elokim is that "he looks at an image of the Lord" – here the verse uses the Tetragrammaton, which symbolizes God's attribute of mercy.

There are two aspects of the problem of justice in this world. On the one hand there are the innocent who suffer. Why is there so much suffering in the world? Why is never-ending fury poured out on the Jewish people? Why have men, women, and children been exterminated, babies who never knew sin, pure souls that could have illuminated the world with their radiance? "Why do You hide Your face, ignoring our affliction and distress?" (Ps. 44:25). If there is an explanation for evil, it is forbidden to hear it, just as Moses refused to listen. And even if there is still hope for good, it does not compensate for evil. Regarding Isaiah's prophecy of comfort, R. Yoḥanan said:

> Woe to the nations who have no remedy, for it says: "Instead of copper I will bring gold, instead of iron I will bring silver; instead of wood, copper; and instead of stone, iron" (Is. 60:17). But what can one bring instead of R. Akiva and his companions? Of them it is said: "Though I cleanse, their blood I will not cleanse" (Joel 4:21).[4]

This does not apply only to R. Akiva; every infant whose life was cut short by evildoers is irreplaceable. What can be brought to replace a million children who were murdered during the Holocaust?

There is another facet of the problem of theodicy: the wicked who prosper. The world is filled with limitless kindness. All existence abounds with goodness, and evildoers, too, enjoy the world's bounty. Moses' reward was, "he looks at an image of the Lord." He was privileged to tear off all masks and reveal the positive in each and every person. He was thus able to see and understand why there is so much compassion in the world.

Although we have not achieved the same degree of insight as Moses, we can nevertheless adopt his approach in this respect. It is impossible for us to fathom the secret of the manifestation of the

4. Rosh HaShana 23a.

Tetragrammaton, and we cannot grasp the attribute of divine mercy in all its glory and grandeur. However, there is something we certainly can do: if we are honest with ourselves and we soberly examine everything that befalls us, we will acknowledge the amazing and unexpected reversal of our condition during the past half century. During the Holocaust there were many who thought – with apparent justification – that the end of the Jewish people had arrived. How close was the "Final Solution" to really being final!

We must open our eyes and see what has happened to us. In the words of the prophet: "Raise your eyes and look around; they have all gathered and come to you" (Is. 60:4).

We cannot explain the hiding of God's countenance during the Holocaust. We cannot understand "why...You hide in times of trouble" (Ps. 10:1). A man of faith must also be a man of truth, and so he does not mock the unseen God with false descriptions. There can be no restitution in this world for the rivers of blood that were shed in sanctification of God's name. When a believer stands before the terrifying mystery of innumerable martyrs, when the gates of heaven are sealed shut in the face of heartrending pleas for mercy and furious demands for justice, the man of faith can do nothing but "sit alone and be silent...place his mouth in the dust" (Lam. 3:28–29).

The establishment of the State of Israel does not compensate for the horrors of the Holocaust, and it certainly does not make restitution for the accumulated pain of seventy-five generations steeped in suffering.

But was it really our own strength and might that brought about our success? Were all the experts who predicted a decisive Arab victory during the War of Independence mistaken and blind? Later, did the commanders who mapped out the strategy for the Six Day War ever foresee such an overwhelming victory? Were there even contingency plans that addressed such an optimistic forecast? Not only did they not expect it – it was beyond their wildest dreams!

Of all the generations that pined and yearned and longed and even sacrificed for Zion – are we really the best and most worthy? Who would be so bold as to claim that we have deserved the amazing kindness that God has bestowed upon us, as it is written: "With vast mercy I will gather you" (Is. 54:7)? It is all a result of God's attribute of mercy.

One who is guided by truth knows that it was not due to our righteousness that God has granted us such kindness. Rather, God's attribute of mercy has been manifested on our behalf, and we should meditate upon it: "He looks at an image of the Lord."

Chapter 2

The Religious Significance of the State of Israel, Part I

Introduction

From the end of the Hasmonean dynasty until our day, there has been no Jewish kingdom. Even when there was a Jewish kingdom, it was rarely governed in accordance with the Torah. The Hasmonean kings, whose progenitors were called "most pious" by the sages of yore,[1] ultimately failed, to the extent that the very concept of a Jewish kingdom has been removed from this world and hidden away until the End of Days, when the world will be mended under divine sovereignty in anticipation of the messianic age. The King Messiah, may he speedily arrive, will establish a righteous kingdom.[2] Some people therefore erroneously maintain that Jewish independence has no spiritual significance until that time.

We have undergone a long period of two thousand years with no independence and no state. It is no wonder, then, that when the State of Israel was established, many of our best and brightest did not know how to greet it. We were suddenly faced with the new halakhic challenges of having a state – challenges that our predecessors could

1. See Nahmanides on Genesis 49:10.
2. See below, the chapter titled "The Structure of the State According to the Torah, Part I: Principles."

not have imagined. Quite suddenly, we were bound to observe mitzvot [commandments] that had faded from practice and whose rationales had long been forgotten. We are the orphaned generation that survived the great conflagration of the Holocaust, and since the destruction of our communities, the character of the Jewish public sphere is no longer Torah-oriented. We, who adhere at least to the mitzvot incumbent upon individuals, endure as a mere fragment; most of the surviving remnant of the Jewish people is regrettably distant from any concept of Torah and mitzvot. Yet it is we, the members of this impoverished generation, who are faced with this tremendous challenge that had no equal for two thousand years: a Jewish state in the Land of Israel, the Jewish collective in its land!

It is easy to understand the mindset of those who fear this challenge and have reservations about the state, out of a tendency, perhaps even unconscious, to avoid tests that we have not faced since ancient times, which our ancestors in the distant past did not know how to withstand or leave any guidelines about how to confront. Seemingly straightforward halakhot that pertain to life in the Land of Israel, like the laws of tithes, priestly gifts, the Sabbatical year, and others, are addressed at length in the Talmud and codes, yet it is not easy to arrive at definitive rulings about them since they were not practiced for so long. Certainly, then, in the halakhot of statehood, which are entirely virgin soil, we have no clear halakhic precedent. Yet these issues touch the very foundations of Judaism; who will teach us this knowledge?

The years go by, and along with the turbulence of the ingathering of the exiles, we have experienced the crisis of the latest wars; yet we still have not dealt properly, as Jews, with the basic questions that emerged in the wake of the founding of the State of Israel. From a historical perspective, seven decades are the blink of an eye, and yet as individuals we have only the years of our lives with which to confront the challenges of the age – an age of historically unprecedented transformation and upheaval – and to respond meaningfully and productively.

We may justifiably lament the absence of explicit divine guidance at this fateful historical moment, though it behooves us to recall that even when Israel had prophets, they were not always heeded. Our Sages commented on this: "The removal of a signet ring [by Ahasuerus, so he could give it to Haman] was more powerful than forty-eight prophets and seven prophetesses who prophesied for Israel, for they collectively did not return [Israel] to a better path, whereas the removal of the ring caused them to return to the better path."[3] Nevertheless, we are not exempt from the duty to reach decisions and act on them. Man operates under difficult conditions – his vision is limited, his understanding is constrained, and his spiritual, scientific, and physical resources are insufficient for him to control his fate. As faithful Jews, we are committed to the idea of personal responsibility; we know that human choice must be an act of faith since we will never know whether we made the correct choice. The only certainties are that we cannot evade the duty to choose our path and that God above will orchestrate things so that His will is ultimately done.

Fleeing from confrontation with the demands of confusing historical realities is a repudiation of faith and a denial of God's mastery of the universe, as the prophet Isaiah said:

> Listen, you who are deaf; you blind ones, look up and see! Who is as blind as My servant, as deaf as the messenger I send? Who is as blind as the chosen one, as blind as the servant of the Lord? Seeing many things, he gives no heed; with ears open, he hears nothing.... You are My witnesses – declares the Lord – My servant, whom I have chosen, so that you may know and have faith in Me, and understand that I am He.... (Is. 42:18–20; 43:10)

The Return to Zion

On the one hand, we must look with open eyes at the events that divine providence brings to pass. On the other hand, we dare not fall prey to the temptation to see more than we have been shown and to hear more than has been said. The profound difficulties that beset such an approach are perhaps best described in the context of the experience of our forebears during the Babylonian Exile and the Return to Zion:

---

3. Megilla 14a.

> R. Yehoshua b. Levi said: Why were they called Men of the Great Assembly? Because they restored the crown to its former glory. Moses came along and said: "God, the great (*gadol*), mighty (*gibor*), and awesome (*nora*)" (Deut. 10:17). Along came Jeremiah and said: Gentiles are reveling in His sanctuary – where is His awesomeness? So he did not say "awesome."[4] Daniel came along and said: Gentiles are enslaving His sons – where is His might? So he did not say "mighty."[5] [The Men of the Great Assembly] came along and said: On the contrary! Therein is His might, for He suppresses His inclination in showing patience to the wicked; and therein is His awesomeness, for if not for His awesomeness, how could one nation survive among the nations?
>
> But how could our rabbis (Jeremiah and Daniel) do this and abolish what Moses instituted? R. Elazar said: Since they knew that the Holy One, blessed be He, is truthful, they would not speak falsely about Him.[6]

R. Yehoshua b. Levi is concerned with a very basic question concerning man's stance before God and faith in Him in times when darkness prevails and God's providence is hidden from man. He expresses this question using the descriptions of God in our prayers.

The problem of describing God did not first emerge during the fierce confrontation between religion and philosophy in the Middle Ages. It has always been discussed. The question lies at the heart of religious existence. Thus it is told:

> A certain person went down [to the ark, to lead the prayers] in the presence of R. Ḥanina. He recited: God, the great, mighty, and awesome, the glorious, strong, and powerful. [R. Ḥanina] said to him: Have you exhausted the praises of your Lord? Regarding these [first] three, had Moses not written them in the Torah, and had the Men of the Great Assembly not come along and instituted

4. Based on Jeremiah 32:18.
5. Based on Daniel 9:4.
6. Yoma 69b.

> them, we would not recite them. Yet you say all this? It can be compared to a man who has millions of golden dinars, yet they laud him for having a thousand silver dinars. Is it not an insult?[7]

How can the infinite Divine be encompassed with words? How can the transcendent be imprisoned in concepts? How can the ineffable be described? Yet faith itself is impossible without words that can echo the Infinite and unless the awareness that God is Father and King generates a conception of providence that points beyond, to the unknowable and ineffable. Indeed, no attributes can be ascribed to Him who is beyond all apprehension; yet if He wishes to choose man and bring him close to Him, it can only be within the realm of human experience, only by manifesting Himself through human qualities.

What is faith if not the secure knowledge that the Divine can touch man, and that man can stretch his hand back to God?

If God takes an active interest in the world, then man, too, can shape history and imbue it with a goal and a purpose. But if one believes that man is powerless and history is meaningless, then he mocks and blasphemes the very God he claims to believe in.

For this reason, Jeremiah and Daniel could not utter Moses' formula of praise. With the Temple lying in ruins, despite being built with love and despite the feelings of awe and majesty that it stirred within the people over the centuries, and when the people that God chose to bear His name were downtrodden and enslaved by enemies who gloated about defeating the God of Israel, He chose to hide His face. Where then were His might and His awesomeness?

Then the Men of the Great Assembly came along. Though the survivors of the destruction were pitifully few, and they and their descendants were reduced to abject spiritual poverty, the Men of the Great Assembly began to nourish the hope for salvation. As recorded in Scripture, the Return to Zion was a disappointment at first.[8] Only a

---

7. Megilla 25a.
8. See Ezra 2:64 – "The entire community was 42,360" – and 9:1–2:

> The people of Israel, the priests, and the Levites have not separated themselves from the people of the lands, taking up the abominations of the Canaanites,

minority of the Jews of Babylonia returned. Culturally, religiously, and socially, they were a miserable and impoverished group, to the point that the Sages said: "[The lineage of the residents of] the Land of Israel is muddled in comparison with Babylonia."[9]

The area assigned to them for settlement was a small enclave surrounding the ruins of Jerusalem. They were beset by enemies and subject to the arbitrary whims of their Persian overlords. Internally, they were hopelessly divided by social and religious strife. Many of them had married non-Jewish women and sired non-Jewish children. Even when they managed to realize their greatest aspiration and inaugurate the Temple, after years of struggle and sacrifice, the old men among them wept in disappointment and frustration, for it was but a shadow of the glory that they still remembered from their youth.[10]

The Men of the Great Assembly beheld all of this. They saw that the Divine Presence did not abide in the rebuilt Temple. There was no Holy Ark and no Tablets of the Law in its empty inner sanctum. The high priest did not bear the Urim and Tummim and had not been anointed with the special anointing oil.[11] Of course, no one even dared to mention the promised messianic king. The words of the prophet were unambiguous: "Behold, a man whose name is *Tzemaḥ* (Sprout), and he will sprout up from his place" (Zech. 6:12) – in the future, but not now. Engraved on the gate of the Temple Mount was the insignia of the city of Shushan – a permanent reminder of the authority of the Persian king, on whose precarious mercy the fragile security of the restored Jewish Commonwealth depended.[12]

Yet, most important of all was the very fact of Jewish survival. "All the nations gathered to destroy them, yet some of them survived, for if

---

Hittites, Perizzites, Jebusites, Ammonites, Moabites, Egyptians, and Amorites. They have taken their daughters in marriage for themselves and their sons, mingling the holy seed with the people of the land. The chiefs and officials were the first to commit this sacrilege.

9. Kiddushin 69b.
10. Ezra 3:12.
11. Yoma 21b; Keritot 5b.
12. Menaḥot 98a.

not for awesomeness of the Holy One, blessed be He, how could one nation survive among the nations?"[13]

This inexplicable fact flies in the face of every law of history and gave the Men of the Great Assembly the courage to restore the Divine Crown to its former greatness. Moreover, the very fact of the restoration of a semi-autonomous Jewish polity, however limited its dimensions, is a real manifestation of God's might.

In our generation more than any other in Jewish history, Jeremiah and Daniel would have recognized their own generation. We have witnessed days that were "neither day nor night," when it seemed to every rational observer that Jewish history had almost reached its end. How perilously near to victory was Hitler, may his name be blotted out! How closely did the threat of the "Final Solution" hang over us! Even our bloody annals of slaughter and martyrdom have no parallel to the horrors of the Nazi era, during which ten times "the number of those who went forth from Egypt" were cruelly annihilated. While a million Jewish children perished, could Jeremiah or Daniel pronounce the words "mighty" and "awesome"?

Man is incapable of understanding: "Why do You hide Your face, ignoring our affliction and distress?" (Ps. 44:25). There can be no restitution in this world for all those who were murdered in the Holocaust. A man of faith must also be a man of truth, and so he does not mock the unseen God with false descriptions. The resurrection of Israel does not compensate for the horrors of the Nazi era, and certainly not for the prolonged agony of the exile. The Jewish State can shield us from the terrible threats faced during exile, but it does not herald the end of Jew-hatred, the symbol of humanity unredeemed.

Yet one who beheld the ingathering of the lingering exiles, experienced the first hesitant steps of national rebuilding, and felt the burst of new hope flowing through dry bones[14] can say: "Therein is His might! Therein is His awesomeness!"

---

13. Rashi, Yoma 69b, s.v. *ve'elu hen nora'otav*.
14. See Ezekiel 37:1–4.

The Establishment of the State and the Messianic Idea

Is the State of Israel the long-awaited fulfillment of the prophecies? Surely, only a prophet can tell. Can the footsteps of the Messiah be heard upon the hills? Who among us can presume to recognize the signs!?

Some rely on a dictum from the Talmud – "R. Abba said: There is no more obvious sign of the End of Days than that which is stated: 'But you, O mountains of Israel, send out your branches and yield your fruit to My people Israel' (Ezek. 36:8)"[15] – to see the present age as the End of Days. R. Abba teaches that there can be no redemption unless Israel returns to its land and the mountains of Israel yield their fruit. Yet there is no man who can say that the Messiah's arrival is imminent; if someone makes that claim, he is either deluding himself or attempting to delude us. Who can say what will happen? We have no prophet, and no one knows whether the State of Israel is what the prophets foresaw.

The process of Israel's return to Zion requires us to understand that we must conduct ourselves in a manner that is worthy of a people that has returned to its land and become master of its own fate. We have been fortunate to see the return of the Jewish people to its land and the flourishing of the Land of Israel. We must show our gratitude to God for this and understand the gravity of our responsibility in light of these epochal changes. Yet we must make sure not to interpret the Sages' words superficially, and we certainly must not use slogans like "obvious sign of the End of Days" as a factor in our decision to do something or refrain from doing something. The view that we are presently undergoing a surefire, unstoppable process of redemption is an unparalleled delusion based on nothing. It can, God forbid, cause people to think they can do all kinds of things without the need for prudence or discretion because, after all, this is "obviously the End of Days."

Maimonides set us on the proper course when he wrote, in his description of the establishment of Hanukka:

> In the days of the Second Temple, when Greece ruled, they imposed decrees on Israel.... Israel was therefore in a dire predicament and suffered great persecution, until the God of our

---

15. Sanhedrin 98a.

> fathers took pity on them and saved them from their clutches. The sons of the high priests of the Hasmonean family prevailed and slew them, saving Israel from their hands. They enthroned a king from among the priests, and the kingship was restored to Israel for more than two hundred years, until the destruction of the Second Temple.
>
> When Israel prevailed over their enemies and destroyed them, it was the twenty-fifth day of Kislev. They entered the Sanctuary but could not find but one cruse of pure oil, containing enough to light for only one day. From it they kindled the ritual lamps for eight days, until they crushed olives and produced pure oil. Because of this, the Sages of that generation ordained that these eight days, beginning with the night of the twenty-fifth of Kislev, shall be days of joy and praise on which lamps are kindled.... These days are called Hanukka.[16]

According to Maimonides, the institution of Hanukka as a festival of praise, rejoicing, and lighting candles was ordained by "the Sages of that generation," but it was not ordained immediately after the victory or even that same year.[17] This invites the question: After the Hasmoneans entered the Sanctuary, repaired the breaches made by the Greeks, and kindled the Menora with the cruse of oil, how is it that the Sages of the generation did not ordain a festival to commemorate this great salvation that very year?

The Hasmonean victory and the salvation of Israel came after three years of war. Wars, by their very nature, include victories and defeats. It was impossible to know whether the victory and salvation would be short-lived or whether they were lasting and the war was really over. And how should a lasting salvation, which warrants thanksgiving and rejoicing, be defined? Is an enduring victory only one that lasts forever, or even a victory that lasts for only a certain amount of time? It seems that even in the times of the Hasmoneans, there were those who did not know how to define the victory they had won. The Temple still

16. *Hilkhot Megilla VeHanukka* 3:1–3.
17. See Shabbat 21b.

stood, though it was necessary to repair its breaches, and the priests performed the Temple service as before. Yet prophecy and the Davidic line had been discontinued and would not return. So was the Hasmonean victory worthy of being called "the first flowering of our redemption"?

Apparently, at the time of the events, there was hope that the victory would lead to the restoration of the Davidic monarchy and the return of prophecy. However, when we consider those events, we know that this process remained incomplete. The Second Temple was eventually destroyed. It seems this is why Maimonides mentions that destruction in the ruling cited above.

Let us consider the profound meaning of the institution of "days of joy and praise," based on "saving Israel from their hands… and the kingship was restored to Israel." The Sages ordained the festival to commemorate the Hasmonean victory and the restoration of the Israelite monarchy. Why does Maimonides note that praise and rejoicing were instituted by "the Sages of that generation" instead of using the language of the *baraita*: "A different year (*leshana aḥeret*), they ordained these days as holidays with praise and thanksgiving"?[18]

The Sages certainly did not institute the festival that same year; they could not know that victory was complete and that the war had ended. Yet it seems that according to Maimonides, the *baraita* does not mean to say that it was ordained the next year, but "a different year" ("*leshana aḥeret*" as opposed to "*leshana habaa*"). Maimonides therefore writes: "The Sages of that generation." The Sages who witnessed the salvation and the restoration of the monarchy – albeit not the Davidic dynasty – understood that these days must be proclaimed as days of joy and praise. They instituted the mitzva of publicizing the miracle even though it did not result in the complete and final redemption.

Maimonides emphasizes that the deliverance of Hanukka was one for which we must show gratitude, as the Hasmonean victory was not short-lived. But it was not the victory that heralded the arrival of the Messiah. The Hasmonean victory was a great salvation, and therefore the Sages ordained that it be commemorated for all times, even after the destruction of the Second Temple, by lighting candles, reciting Hallel,

18. Shabbat 21b.

and refraining from fasting and eulogizing. The very fact that "the kingship was restored to Israel for more than two hundred years" is ample reason to institute a mitzva for all time – even though the Davidic line was not restored, and even though it was governed by a priesthood that was frequently corrupt.

This teaches us that God's salvation of the Jewish people is not measured with the yardstick of the End of Days. We certainly anticipate the arrival of the Messiah and of an everlasting salvation. The Talmud tells us that all of the prophets prophesied about the Messianic Era.[19] But there can be a salvation that has nothing to do with the Messianic Era, which we must acknowledge and for which we must thank God, as when He rescued us from enemies that beset us and reestablished the Jewish kingdom. So too, the deliverance of our people in recent generations and the return of the Jewish people to Zion constitute a great salvation, worthy of ordaining the recitation of Hallel. We should state unequivocally that this was God's salvation, even if we cannot yet say with confidence that this is the long-awaited final redemption.

Ordaining the recitation of Hallel for this salvation and acknowledging the significance of our independence will lead the nation to recognize its strength and understand that the establishment of the State of Israel is a historic challenge to renew national life in its homeland according to the light of the Torah. We must recognize that our return to the Land of Israel is an unprecedented salvation, for which we are obligated to express our gratitude.

But are we confident about how this process will play out? The pretentious usurpation of the prophet's role, based on fanciful interpretations and simplistic and superficial understandings of midrashim or "signs from heaven," can, God forbid, result in terrible tragedy. If we do not know how to preserve what we have been given, is God nevertheless "obligated" toward us? There is a great danger in the pretension to know that the footsteps of the Messiah can be heard; it can lead to irresponsible conclusions and policy decisions, with potentially disastrous consequences.

---

19. Berakhot 34b.

It is recounted in the Yerushalmi:

> When R. Akiva would see Bar Kokhba, he would say: "This is the King Messiah!" R. Yoḥanan b. Torta said to him: "Akiva, grass will be growing from your cheeks, and the son of David will still not have arrived."[20]

Maimonides writes that R. Akiva was Bar Kokhba's arms-bearer, explaining:

> Do not think that the King Messiah must perform signs and wonders, bring new things into the world, resurrect the dead, or the like, as fools say. This is not the case, for R. Akiva was a great sage, one of the Sages of the Mishna, and he would serve as the arms-bearer of King Bar Kozba [i.e., Bar Kokhba]. He would say of him that he is the King Messiah until he was killed in his iniquities. Once he was killed, it was known that he was not [the Messiah]. The Sages never asked him for a sign or wonder.[21]

It is interesting that Jewish sources say very little about Bar Kokhba and his revolt; it seems that the Sages did not want to foster the penchant for a new rebellion. However, we learn from other sources that Bar Kokhba initially succeeded in his great battles against Rome, until ultimately the Roman Empire had to bring legions and personnel from as far away as Britain in order to defeat Bar Kokhba. This teaches us how strong he was. From this perspective, we can understand why R. Akiva said of him: "This is the King Messiah."

However, R. Akiva did not pretend to be a prophet. He held the opinion that Bar Kokhba was the Messiah because he viewed Bar Kokhba's triumphs as being no less impressive than the triumphs of the Hasmoneans during the Second Temple era, and perhaps as even more impressive. Ultimately, however, the revolt became a debacle, and then a terrible destruction. Sources indicate that the fall of Bar Kokhba

20. Y. Taanit 4:5.
21. *Hilkhot Melakhim* 11:3.

was more ruinous and catastrophic than even the destruction of the Second Temple.

Even when we have facts, we must interpret them cautiously. The pretentiousness of giving unequivocal interpretations of history is liable to backfire or lead to irresponsible decisions that are not based on reality.

Yet it is difficult for some believing Jews to refrain from trying to hasten the End of Days. Through the centuries, we have suffered from various false messiahs, who arose at times when people lacked the strength to endure, and distress caused people to abandon reason and common sense. The same happened when we returned to our land and the hopes that we had harbored for generations were realized before our eyes. The heart grew excited, and we wondered: How is it that we have not yet reached the final destination, the complete redemption? And so some wish to hasten the end.

On the other hand, there are some who are inclined toward the opposite extreme. Even among the first religious Zionists, there were those who viewed the Zionist project as nothing more than the creation of an asylum for a persecuted nation. They were afraid to articulate the vague sense and notion that God had redeemed them, lest they meet the same fate as the Ephraimites who hastened the end.[22]

We very much want the ancient yearning for a complete redemption to be realized before our eyes. Though the Sages cautioned, "Blasted be the bones of those who calculate the end,"[23] during times of distress and destruction, many great Jewish leaders tried to take comfort and strengthen flagging spirits with messianic imaginings. They latched onto all sorts of supposed omens, and as a result, the concepts of redemption, the World to Come, and the resurrection of the dead were all jumbled together, despite the clear statement of the talmudic sage Shmuel: "There is no difference between the present world and the Messianic Era except for the subjugation of kingdoms."[24]

---

22. Exodus Rabba 20:11.
23. Sanhedrin 97b.
24. Shabbat 151b; Berakhot 34b; Pesaḥim 68a; Sanhedrin 99a. However, the version in Shabbat 63a and Sanhedrin 91b is: "...except for the subjugation of *exiles*."

Maimonides follows the view of Shmuel,[25] explaining that before the Messianic Era, "a prophet will arise to set Israel straight and prepare their hearts…to bring peace to the world."[26] Prophets do not fulfill their tasks in a supernatural manner, but rather, "they inform [Israel] of God's ways and bring them back through repentance."[27] Yet this task of preparing the heart and setting Israel straight has barely begun. Even according to those who think that the Messiah will perform miracles and wonders, free choice will certainly not be taken away from us before his arrival, and as long as our hearts of stone have not been removed, how can we enter his presence?

Maimonides taught us this as well:

> If a king arises from the Davidic line who meditates upon the Torah and occupies himself with mitzvot like his father David, according to the Written Torah and the Oral Torah, who compels Israel to follow it and support it, and who fights God's wars – it is presumed that he is the King Messiah. If he successfully does these things, triumphs over the surrounding nations, rebuilds the Temple in its place, and gathers in the Jewish exiles – he is certainly the Messiah. If he does not succeed in all of this or is killed, then it is clear that he is not the one promised by the Torah. Rather, he is like all of the complete and worthy Davidic kings who died, and God only raised him up to test the masses, as it says: "Some of the wise will stumble so that they may be refined, purified, and cleansed before the time of the end, for the appointed time is yet to come" (Dan. 11:35).[28]

Maimonides teaches that God's test will be twofold: On the one hand – "Do not think that the laws of nature will be abrogated or that any innovation will be introduced into creation in the Messianic Era.

25. *Hilkhot Melakhim* 12:1; see also Letter on Resurrection, *Iggerot HaRambam*, pp. 359–60; *Moreh Nevukhim* III:11.
26. *Hilkhot Melakhim* 12:2.
27. *Hilkhot Teshuva* 6:5.
28. *Hilkhot Melakhim* 11:4.

Rather, the world will continue normally."[29] That is, we must recognize that we are commanded to do everything in our power and marshal all of our ingenuity to ensure Israel's sovereignty on its soil, even when we cannot be certain how things will develop and there are no guarantees that our efforts will succeed. Additionally, these efforts are undertaken with humility, understanding that it is not our power alone that brings success. On the other hand, even when we succeed, we must not think that since God helped us get this far, it is an incontrovertible sign that the present redemption is unstoppable, that we have nothing to fear, and that we, unlike generations past, are immune to the charms of false messiahs. We must remain aware that we have the power to choose, and therefore we are responsible for our own fate.

The Spiritual Value of Israel's Independence

The establishment of the State of Israel, the ingathering of the exiles, the prosperity of the Jewish state, and the triumph of the IDF over powerful enemies are manifestations of God's might and awesomeness, which enable us to face new challenges every day.

There is one simple and basic fact that is there for the whole world to see. It is so simple and so obvious that millions upon millions of people all over the globe see it and acknowledge: The State of Israel exists, and it bears God's name through its very existence and very name. It has restored God's crown to its former glory!

In the light of this basic truth, all other questions take on a different meaning. In fact, it is only because of this truth that all other questions have any meaning at all, for one who sits alone in silence can ask no questions and give no answers. The questions are, of course, manifold and difficult. But there is nothing wrong with admitting that we do not know all the answers.

Yet it is imperative to recognize the basic truth that the religious significance of the State of Israel is not limited to its being the instrument for the attainment of religious ends or even to its being a stage in the process of redemption, even as we pray that it indeed will be so.

29. Ibid. 12:1.

In the case of an individual, though we acknowledge his role as one who fulfills the mitzvot and as a link in the chain of history that leads to the redemption, he has a higher metaphysical significance, for he was created in God's image. This is what defines him even if he does not live up to his role. Even if he falls into the abyss of iniquity, beyond repair or rehabilitation, to the point that the death penalty must be meted out to him, he must be shown dignity out of respect for the Divine image within him.[30]

Likewise, in the case of the Jewish people collectively, Jewish independence has spiritual value beyond its instrumental character. The people of Israel entered into a covenant at Sinai: "Keep My covenant... and you will be unto Me a kingdom of priests and a holy nation" (Ex. 19:5–6). The covenant is binding not only upon us, but also upon God, who has chosen Israel to be His people and has sworn Himself to be our God. Though it defies our understanding, all of our accumulated historical experience demonstrates how the fate of the Jewish people and the fate of God's honor are intertwined: "I scattered them among the nations... and wherever they went among the nations they profaned My holy name in that people said of them: 'These are God's people, who have left His land'" (Ezek. 36:19–20). It is the covenant with God that enables us to face all who rise up against us in every generation.

Some tend to view the twentieth and twenty-first centuries as the post-religious era. Indeed, in some ways that is so. Yet it is a gross error to presume that indifference to religion is all that widespread. The Nazis openly proclaimed their war against biblical religion and against the God of Israel. So did the Communists. There is also no doubt that the resurrection of the nation of Israel on its soil poses a theological dilemma to many Christians. As for Islam, the resurgence of fundamentalist zeal often expresses itself in repeated calls for a "*jihad*" against the Jews.

---

30. See Deuteronomy 21:23. It is forbidden to hang the corpse of one who was executed by the courts from a tree, "for the hanging is blasphemy against God," and see Sanhedrin 46b:

> R. Meir says: They have a parable. To what can this be compared? To twin brothers in one city. One is appointed king, and the other became a highwayman. The king commanded for him to be hanged. All who see him say: "The king is hanged." The king issued a command, and they took him down.

The story Israel's rebirth signifies the renewed manifestation of God's majesty, not only for us, but for others as well!

The man of faith is also the man of truth. Not only does he believe, he also bears witness, and his testimony can be trusted to confirm his faith. "You are My witnesses, says the Lord, and I am God" (Is. 43:12).[31] The Sages explain: "When you are My witnesses, then I am God, but when you are not My witnesses, I am, as it were, not God."[32] This is the great paradox of faith! God's revelation only becomes revealed if we are aware of it and bear witness to it. God is our Redeemer only if we hear His promise as a commandment that must be fulfilled: "He says to Jerusalem, 'Let it be inhabited,' and to the cities of Judah 'Let them be built'" (Is. 44:26).

It is true that some of the first Zionist thinkers were motivated by extremely secular considerations. They anticipated that the Jewish nation would assimilate into the family of nations, much as those who rebelled against religion encouraged assimilation on an individual level. Yet the majority never shared these views, and many clearly emphasized the religious significance of Jewish national renewal.

This was the state of affairs before the Holocaust added a terrible, panicked urgency to the Zionist project. It is strange that the devastating results of schism and sectarianism (which stemmed from the dismantling of Jewish life in the wake of the Emancipation) were so widespread that even after one third of our people was destroyed due to the lack of a homeland, "religious" arguments against Zionism remain in vogue. Certainly any given argument against various secular perspectives is not that important. Clearly, anyone who holds the Torah dear hopes to see it guiding all facets of life. Yet the capricious rejection of the basic concept of Zionism – the great and absolute need for Jewish sovereignty – is horrifying and frightening.

It is clear that Zionism has much in common with other national movements. There is also no doubt that its thinkers meant to provide a shelter for the homeless. Nevertheless, above all, it was a historic need

31. Note that this verse is part of a message to the Jews living in exile, who had survived the years of exile, and who were addressed in the Edict of Cyrus.
32. *Sifrei Devarim* 346.

to fulfill the covenant between God and His people. For the believer, there is a religious need and a religious value in having a total societal framework in which the Torah can operate. Zionism offered the only possibility for meeting this need within the framework of modern political conditions. If the Torah sits abandoned in a corner, even if it is cloaked in gold and scarlet, it cannot bear "faithful testimony." For its testimony to be heard, it needs an independent people living in its sovereign state and building its life according to the Torah's values.

We are living in fascinating and dangerous times. Our faith is tested by unexpected and unfamiliar conditions. Our generation has been granted the opportunity to attest to God's existence in the world by applying the Torah's creative power to a new and developing society. Will we be up to the challenge?

The challenges we face are very great indeed. The existence of the state makes possible the fulfillment of the Torah's greatest aims: the ingathering of the exiles, the building and cultivation of the land, and the fashioning of a just society that sanctifies God's name for all peoples to see. We have the responsibility of realizing these aims. To achieve them we will need all the abilities and all the talents of all Jews everywhere, and we hope that, with God's help, the realization of these goals will usher in the Messianic Era.

Chapter 3

The Religious Significance of the State of Israel, Part II

Collaboration with the Secular State

The advent of the modern era was accompanied by flagging commitment to the Torah and by extensive secularization throughout the Jewish world. The restoration of Jewish sovereignty resulted in the establishment of a state that is both Jewish and secular. Can a society be both Jewish and secular? If large swaths of the population refuse to perform basic mitzvot, how can religious Jews collaborate with them to create shared institutions? More fundamentally, can a halakhic community permit itself to be tolerant of non-religious and even anti-religious approaches to Judaism? What is the halakhic status of non-observant Jews?

During the medieval era, most Jews observed the mitzvot more or less faithfully. Even where Torah knowledge was paltry, the authority of halakha was accepted, even if it was occasionally observed in the breach. Now that this situation no longer exists, is there any other option for religious Jews besides withdrawal and consolidation into groups in which every member accepts Torah values?

The great Eastern European halakhists of the nineteenth century rejected this idea out of hand. We can illustrate this with an example. Rabbi Naftali Tzvi Yehuda Berlin ("Netziv") headed the famed Volozhin Yeshiva – the progenitor of nearly all contemporary yeshivot – for more than half a century. As the premier rabbi of all Diaspora communities, he responded to someone who sought "to take precaution against this generation by completely dissociating from non-observant Jews, much as our patriarch Abraham dissociated from Lot." Netziv's response is unequivocal:

> This suggestion is as harsh as swords through the body of the nation and its survival... and also causes, due to baseless hatred, much bloodshed.... They will persecute one another with a stamp of approval.[1]

In a detailed, reasoned historical analysis of early Judaism, Netziv emphasizes the principle that God's Torah can induce people to obey its words through the power of persuasion, and that only through a process of moral illumination can man's mission be advanced:

> From all this we see that we, the upholders of the religion,[2] are obliged to strengthen our engagement with the Torah. The rabbi and communal leaders must make sure that the teachers are accomplished Torah scholars.... [A father who] drives his son away from secular studies against his will... causes him to rebel and follow a perverse path to attain secular learning.... Rather, the chosen teacher will supervise, ensuring that they do not deviate from the path of the Torah, and he [the student] will succeed in both [Torah and secular studies].

The Torah was not addressed only to a society that is already prepared to attain perfection. It was given to us as an instrument that will bring society to a state of readiness to realize the Torah's values. A free, sovereign Jewish community, even if it is not yet as committed to the Torah as past generations, is the right framework for the Torah to fulfill this vision.

1. *Responsa Meshiv Davar* 1:44.
2. Editor's note: This is a play on words, as Netziv is responding to a claim advanced in the pages of the Orthodox newspaper *Maḥzikei HaDat*, literally, "upholders of religion."

Recognizing that "we are brothers, the sons of one man" (Gen. 42:13) obligates us to demonstrate constant concern for Jewish unity and to take responsibility for all who "call themselves by the name Israel" (Is. 44:5). We must bring close every Jew who identifies as a Jew and view him as a partner in the realization of the historic role of the Jewish people: sanctifying God's name in this world.

The phenomenon of mass disaffection from the mitzvot is not new. It has always existed, yet the prophet was nevertheless commanded to come to Israel's defense. As Maimonides writes:

> In the days of Elijah, all of Israel were wanton idolaters except for seven thousand people ... yet when he rose up to accuse Israel on Mount Horeb ... God responded to him: "Before you accuse Israel, shouldn't you accuse the nations of the world?".... Likewise, during the days of Isaiah, Israel was sinful and continued to transgress.... There were idolaters among them.... Nevertheless, since he said, "I live among a people of unclean lips" (Is. 6:5), he was punished.[3]

Maimonides continues:

> It is not right to despise Shabbat desecrators and drive them away. Rather, bring them close and encourage them to perform mitzvot. [The Sages] have already explained that when a wanton sinner arrives at the synagogue for prayer, we accept him, and we do not treat him with scorn....[4]

Over two hundred years ago, in the Austro-Hungarian Empire, in the wake of the crisis of secularization, there were some who thought that the only way to save the Torah was to renounce responsibility for all of Jewry and withdraw into small communities of the fervently observant, which had the strength to live in isolation from their surroundings. Given the prevailing conditions, this dissociation and isolation can perhaps be

---

3. "Letter Concerning Apostasy," *Iggerot HaRambam*, pp. 35–36.
4. Ibid., p. 59.

justified. However, several generations of sectarian ideological education produced a worldview that was unable to come to grips with the great transformation wrought by the emergence of a sovereign Jewish state.

The miraculous reappearance of the Jewish people on the stage of history, with a territorial state like all other states unaccompanied by the sorts of wonders that are expected to accompany the arrival of the Messiah, charges us with inescapable national duties and poses challenges that Torah Judaism must address.

A decision to withdraw to the margins of Israeli society is a retreat from participation in the Jewish state and hence a denial of the very basis of halakha.[5] It can lead to the third return to Zion becoming devoid of any religious content. Such a step is a rejection of everything the Torah teaches us about the Land of Israel and the Jewish people.

In truth, Israeli society has been undergoing tremendous change in recent decades. There is a mass movement of return to tradition, especially among the youth. Did we cause this? No; it is from God. But we have the great privilege of being God's partners in this great transformation. This should be a source of joy for us, but also a challenge to us to strengthen our love for each and every person.

There is certainly friction and discord between the different segments of society, but the same is true of every society. First and foremost, a society must recognize a basic truth: that it is a single body. Only then can it face the task of finding and creating the conditions for coexistence.

Attitudes Toward the Non-Observant

Nowadays, most people who identify as Jews grew up and were educated without Torah and mitzvot, yet they yearn with all their heart and soul to cleave to their people. Many of them dedicate themselves to building the Land of Israel and risk their lives to defend the Jewish people from its enemies. Over the past two centuries, many authorities have discussed the status of such individuals, especially considering that they publicly desecrate Shabbat, an offence that, in times past, would have

5. See the words of Rabbi Meir of Rothenburg, below, p. 77.

been considered akin to idol worship and grounds for communal dissociation from such an individual.[6]

Halakhists offered different explanations for this ruling, and it is worth quoting Rabbi Aryeh Leib Brody of Lvov:

> The reason we say that a transgressor who desecrates Shabbat is considered a transgressor against the entire Torah is only because public Shabbat desecration was once a clear demonstration of the acceptance of a different faith. The fact that he desecrated Shabbat and observed Sunday as the Sabbath... marked the beginning of his belief in and espousal of a different religion....[7]

That is, the reason for this stringency is to keep away foreign worship.

Furthermore, Maimonides has already taught us to distinguish between a heretic who knowingly rejects the Torah and his children who follow in his footsteps:

> But the children and grandchildren of those misguided individuals, who were led astray by their parents and born and raised on heresy, are akin to a child taken captive among gentiles and raised by gentiles in their religion. It is as though he is under duress, for he was raised in their errors – and so are those who follow the ways of their misguided ancestors. Therefore, it is proper to bring them back toward repentance and draw them near through peaceful means, until they return to the steadfast Torah.[8]

It is not only those who did not get a religious education who should be seen as "captive children." Our generation is not like previous generations. Nowadays, everyone is exposed to the powerful cultural influences of secularist values, which penetrate almost every home. In contrast, the

6. See *Hilkhot Shabbat* 30:15.
7. *Responsa Mitzpeh Aryeh, Oraḥ Ḥayim* 37. I thank my friend Rabbi Eli Reif for bringing this source to my attention.
8. *Hilkhot Mamrim* 3:3. For a broader halakhic discussion of attitudes toward those who do not observe the Torah and mitzvot, see my *Melumdei Milḥama,* "Mutual responsibility in the military," §§4–11.

impact of the religious education provided by parents grows weaker. Hence, there are grounds to view children even of religious families who abandoned observance as "captive children."

However, we must examine this designation of "captive children" from a different perspective. Some view this designation as a form of condescension toward those who do not observe the Torah and mitzvot.

Without a doubt, secular society also includes many people who have good values, from whom it is possible and worthwhile to learn. Many of them contribute their best talents to building the Land of Israel and its society, and to helping the Jewish people and the whole world. We must value and acknowledge their contributions. There are negative manifestations of secular culture, but we must not focus only on those. We must remember that religious society likewise has negative manifestations, and that religious people do not have a monopoly on all that is beautiful, upright, and just.

This is a difficult challenge that faces anyone who truly wants to serve God. For one who observes the Torah and mitzvot, self-righteousness is a real hazard, a dangerous evil inclination, and an immense moral, personal, and social obstacle. It causes society to splinter into groups and subgroups, each claiming superiority over its rivals.

It is important that every individual is happy with his chosen path. One who is not happy with his path will naturally become progressively weaker. On the other hand, when one feels superior to others, he does a disservice to himself and ultimately alienates people. One who studies Torah and believes in God understands man's smallness in comparison to God and does not take credit for himself.

Honest concern for others stems from true humility. Only one who makes efforts to transcend himself and his desires, and tirelessly seeks the truth for its own sake, can appreciate the real value of another and accept the truth from wherever it comes.[9]

A servant of God must understand that if he really wants to cleave to God's ways he must concern himself with the welfare of his fellow and make every effort to assist others, even those completely unlike him, for that is the way of God. He must know that following God's path is not

---

9. *Shemonah Perakim*, Introduction, p. 36.

for boasting, "See how smart I am, how good I am, how virtuous I am!" On the contrary, a servant of God understands that if he can inspire others to honor God, he benefits as well.

Isolationism stems from a feeling that "there is no one besides me." In contrast, openness always makes one aware of the goodness in his fellow. When one truly behaves in accordance with the Torah, even those who are distant from the Torah recognize it, as the Sages said:

> "And you shall love the Lord your God" (Deut. 6:5) – the name of Heaven shall be beloved because of you. If one studies Scripture and Mishna, apprentices under Torah scholars, and is honest in business and speaks pleasantly with people, what do the people say about him? "[Fortunate is so-and-so who studied Torah.] Fortunate is his father, who taught him Torah; fortunate is his teacher, who taught him Torah. Woe unto people who have not studied Torah. So-and-so studied Torah, and look how pleasant are his ways and how refined are his actions! Of him Scripture says: 'And He said to me: You are My servant, Israel, through whom I will be glorified' (Is. 49:3)." But one who studies Scripture and Mishna, apprentices under Torah scholars, and is not honest in business and does not speak pleasantly to people, what do the people say about him? "Woe unto so-and-so who studied Torah. Woe unto his father, who taught him Torah; woe unto his teacher, who taught him Torah. This man studied Torah, and look how corrupt are his deeds and how ugly are his ways. Of him Scripture says: 'Men said of them: These are the people of the Lord, yet they had to leave His land' (Ezek. 36:20)."[10]

This statement offers practical guidance. One who truly conducts himself in consonance with the Torah will not be repulsive to anyone. On the contrary, he becomes like a magnet that attracts people, albeit without taking any credit for himself. Rather, he is grateful to God for the opportunity to benefit others, and even to benefit himself.

---

10. Yoma 86a.

One's attitude toward others is reflected back in others' attitude toward him. As a rule, "As a reflecting pool to the face, so is man's heart to [another] man" (Prov. 27:19). When one relates to others condescendingly and dictates to them what they must and must not do, not only is it inauthentic and unbecoming, but, in practical terms, others will not listen to him. However, if one truly believes that all Jews are like limbs of one body, it will arouse similar feelings among others, and they will share in his desire to be together with them in that one body. One need only open his eyes to see that this is true in the real world.

If our faith is strong, and if we seek to follow the true, authentic path that the Sages of all generations taught us instead of being led astray by our imagination, then we will praise God for the opportunity to participate in the great collaborative project of rebuilding our homeland together with all Jews, regardless of their religious fealty, even as we work doggedly to spread the light of Torah to all, so that it indeed becomes "the faithful witness."[11]

Sharing the Public Burden: The Hesder Yeshivot

Even those among us who recognize the tremendous opportunity to apply the Torah within the Jewish people are deterred by the magnitude of the task. The restored sovereign Jewish polity is not, by nature, prepared to accept the Torah's patronage. Even in ancient times, fashioning a Torah society was a prolonged process that took many centuries. The development of a Torah-oriented community that encompasses the entire Jewish people is now, as always, the end goal that we honestly yearn and strive for, but it cannot be realized in the short term. More importantly, we must build it ourselves. To realize this goal, new duties and roles are incumbent upon us to meet the challenges inherent in such an enterprise. These challenges include participation in the development of the national economy and in contributing to national defense. For hundreds of years, these realms were addressed in Torah literature as a purely theoretical exercise, with no practical conclusions. How will we now address these complex real-world situations?

---

11. See *Hilkhot Tefillin UMezuza VeSefer Torah* 10:11.

There is no doubt that one of the most singular developments in the modern State of Israel is the institution of the Hesder yeshiva, which combines military service and yeshiva study. It is also clear that a similar phenomenon existed during the Second Temple era. R. Akiva's yeshiva was of this type, as the Sages tell us that R. Akiva himself was "the arms-bearer of Ben-Kozva [Bar-Kokhba]."[12] Presumably, R. Akiva's thousands of students followed him into Bar-Kokhba's ranks, though the written record merely gestures in this direction.

In practice, yeshivot did not play a role in the physical protection of Jews for many generations. Nevertheless, it is startling that many people still cannot understand how one can even conceive of the idea of a Hesder yeshiva! The rejoining of the book and the sword has given rise to urgent practical questions as well as weighty spiritual and psychological challenges. On all of these matters, we have only the indirect guidance of the accumulated experience of the generations, because there is no continuous tradition of practical precedent on which to rely.

We are faced with a choice. The first option is to embrace the system that is a direct continuation of the past and has produced innumerable Torah scholars throughout history. The other option is a new system that compels us to accept a heavy responsibility and which, by its very nature, is still very experimental. It is therefore expected that there will be concerns about choosing the second path over the safer, more familiar path. Is it not natural that many would reject an untested and unproven method?

These concerns limit vision and reinforce the isolationist tendencies of those who espouse a sectarian ideology. Some choose a Torah-only approach because Torah is their highest value, as indeed it should be. They believe that they fulfill their duties to their families and to the entire Jewish people by exclusively studying Torah. The Sages said of

12. This is the version found in Maimonides' *Hilkhot Melakhim* 11:3. Similarly, Sanhedrin 93b in MS Herzog. See Mordechai Sabato, *Ketav-Yad Teimani LeMasekhet Sanhedrin (Bavli) UMekomo BeMasoret HaNusaḥ* (PhD diss., Jerusalem, 1996), p. 213: "It was taught: R. Akiva was the arms-bearer of Ben-Kozva." This does not appear in the standard printed versions.

this attitude: "One who says that he has nothing but Torah … does not even have Torah."[13]

There are even those who justify shirking their responsibility to provide for their families and to contribute to the economy, society at large, and national defense by completely denying their obligations. They regard the Torah as the private property of a marginal social group that pays attention only to its own internal affairs, unaware of the needs of others and inattentive to their concerns. For instance, if the drafting of students in isolationist yeshivot would be absolutely necessary for the defense of the country, the logical response of the isolationist approach would be to emigrate from Israel, heaven forfend.

In the times of the Sages, a similar question arose regarding the need to earn a livelihood. The Gemara states:

> Our Rabbis taught: "And you shall gather your grain" (Deut. 11:14). What does this teach? Since it is written, "This book of the Torah shall not depart from your mouth" (Josh. 1:8), I might think that this is to be taken literally. Therefore it says, "And you shall gather your grain" – conduct yourself in the normal way in this respect. This is the view of R. Yishmael. R. Shimon b. Yoḥai says: Is that possible? If a man plows in the plowing season, sows in the sowing season, reaps in the reaping season, threshes in the threshing season, and winnows in the windy season, what will become of the Torah? Rather, when Israel performs the will of the Omnipresent, their work is performed by others, as it says: "And strangers shall stand and feed your flocks" (Is. 61:5). But when Israel does not perform the will of the Omnipresent, they do their work by themselves, as it says: "And you shall gather your grain." Not only that, but they will also do the work of others, as it says: "And you will serve your enemy" (Deut. 28:48). Abaye said: Many have acted in accordance with R. Yishmael, and it was effective for them; [others have followed] R. Shimon b. Yoḥai, and it was not effective for them.[14]

---

13. Yevamot 109b.
14. Berakhot 35b.

Moreover, Maimonides wrote:

> One should always exert himself and endure pain rather than becoming dependent on others and casting himself on the public. The Sages admonished us thus when they said: "Make your Shabbat a weekday, but do not become dependent on others." Even one who was wise and respectable but became poor should work in a trade, even a disgusting trade, and not become dependent on others. It is better to strip the hides of carcasses in the street than to say to the people, "I am a scholar, I am important, I am a priest, so support me." This is what the Sages instructed us. Among the greatest Sages were woodchoppers, transporters of beams, carriers of water to gardens, blacksmiths, and charcoal burners; they did not ask from the public, nor did they accept from them when they gave.[15]

The Sages were adamant that Torah study, which is man's duty toward his Creator, be combined with earning a livelihood, and most obviously this would extend to defense against enemies, and that only such integration would be successful. Regarding the notion that the Torah can endure on its own, the Sages said: "One who engages only in Torah is akin to one who has no God."[16]

Ingathering of the Exiles: Conversion

Another example of the need for public responsibility and a broad-minded Torah approach is the ingathering of the exiles and the challenges it poses to us with respect to encouraging immigration and absorbing immigrants. On the one hand, this challenge makes firm demands on Diaspora Jews:

> Listen to me, O Jacob, O Israel, whom I have called.... Leave Babylon! Flee Chaldea! Declare this with a loud voice; make it heard; bring it to the ends of the earth! (Is. 48:12, 20)

15. *Hilkhot Matnot Aniyim* 10:18.
16. Avoda Zara 17b.

These words were stated regarding the generation of the return to Zion, under Zerubavel.[17] Can people throughout the Diaspora be inspired to listen to these words and fulfill them? On the other hand, the challenge applies to Jews of the Land of Israel as well, who must absorb these immigrants.

The absorption of immigrants in our day has brought up the question of conversion. Who would have thought, fifty years ago, that the Soviet Union, the intransigent superpower, would collapse, enabling its Jews to liberate themselves from that corrupt Communist "paradise"? This miracle happened before our eyes, bringing a wave of new immigrants who have already contributed greatly to strengthening the state. But at the same time, this wave also brought to Israel the results of the mass assimilation of Soviet Jewry. Among these immigrants are thousands of intermarried couples in which even the Jewish spouse often knows next to nothing about Jewish faith, let alone the practical laws of observing Shabbat and keeping kosher. This scenario is similar to the Exodus of our forefathers from Egypt: they had fled from slavery to freedom, but until they received the Torah on Mount Sinai, they had no identity and did not know their destiny.

But the Torah was given only once, at Sinai, and it is now *our* duty to bring all of these new immigrants who came under the protection of the revitalized nation of Israel into the Sinaitic covenant through conversion to Judaism.

This stands in complete contrast to the tradition of Diaspora communities in recent centuries. They had good reason to fear the proliferation of conversions for the sake of marriage, since, by and large, it was the Jewish spouse who turned away from Judaism and not the gentile spouse who came closer to Judaism. In the Diaspora, this was mainly a process of assimilation into the wider non-Jewish world. The identity of Diaspora Jewish communities is always at risk of being absorbed into

17. Compare to Yoma 9b: "Resh Lakish … said to him … as it is written: 'If she is a wall, we will build a silver battlement upon her; if she is a door, we will fashion a cedar panel upon her' (Song. 8:9): Had you made yourselves as a wall and all come to the Land of Israel in the days of Ezra, you would have been akin to silver, which is never subject to decay. Now that you came to the Land of Israel as doors, you are akin to doors, which are subject to decay."

society at large, and the individuals who convert for marriage generally exert centrifugal force on the community.

There may be a precedent from ancient times for the wave of Russian immigration. The mishna mentions a phenomenon that occurred when Ezra returned to Zion: "Ten pedigrees immigrated from Babylon: Priests, Levites, Israelites, *ḥalalim* (children of a priest and a woman forbidden to a priest), converts, and emancipated slaves...."[18] It stands to reason that the immigrants included a significant number of converts and emancipated slaves, who are also, in essence, converts. It is true that this refers to people who converted before immigrating with Ezra, but later some of the immigrants married local gentile women (Ezra 9:1–2; 10:2–3). These were the "Ashdodite, Ammonite, and Moabite women. Many of their sons spoke the Ashdodite language and did not know how to speak the Judean language" (Neh. 13:23–24). Ezra instructed them: "Separate... from the foreign women" (Ezra 10:11), and it says: "They gave their word to expel their wives" (ibid. 19). The fact that the sons spoke the Ashdodite language demonstrates that these women remained gentiles and did not wish to truly convert. However, it is likely that other women indeed converted, and they were certainly not cast away.

We must still address a major difference between the circumstances that prevailed during Ezra's return to Zion and those that prevail today. Today's massive wave brought us hundreds of thousands of immigrants who chose, of their own free will, to join the Jewish people. Not only have they acquired the Hebrew language, but their children study in Jewish schools, and some even send their children to religious schools. On the one hand, these are people who have no presumption of Jewishness and who are not halakhically recognized as Jews, but on the other hand, they have chosen to become part of the Jewish people and are full partners in the State of Israel. They serve in the military and integrate into Israeli society. As a result, Israel has a large population of those who believe, on the one hand, that they are part of society and the state, but who, on the other hand, remain foreigners within the Jewish society they wish to join.

---

18. Mishna Kiddushin 4:1.

It is therefore clear that we must act in order to bring them under the wings of the Divine Presence and to introduce them to Torah and mitzvot. The situation in Israel is completely different from the situation in the Diaspora. There, the children of intermarriage turn away from Judaism, by and large; they "speak the Ashdodite language." In Israel, however, intermarried families speak the holy tongue and in large measure serve in the IDF, defending the Jewish people from its enemies.

The question of converting adults is complicated, but the process of converting children is far simpler.[19] Virtually all of these immigrants circumcise their sons, even if actual conversion is not on offer. The halakha is clear that with parental consent, the children may be converted solely by means of circumcision (for boys) and immersion; it is not required for children[20] to accept the yoke of the mitzvot.[21]

The conversion of minors is based on the talmudic principle that one may accept a benefit on behalf of another, even without their knowledge.[22] In the case of conversion, the rabbinical court is authorized to undertake action on behalf of the minor. However, some have asked whether it is indeed a "benefit" to become a non-observant Jew instead of remaining a gentile. Clearly, the conversion itself is a great benefit, for it brings the convert beneath the wings of the Divine Presence, and even if he performs one mitzva properly, he will earn a place in the next world. On the other hand, there is no guarantee that the minor convert will be educated in the spirit of the Torah and mitzvot; after all, when he grows up he will presumably continue the lifestyle to which he became accustomed in his parents' home or in the homes of his gentile relatives. If he does not receive a Torah education, then in addition to the mitzvot he may perform, he is also likely to perform numerous transgressions, both minor and severe, including those punishable by death or *karet*.

19. For a halakhic discussion, see my *Responsa Si'aḥ Naḥum* (Maaleh Adumim, 2008), §§68–69.
20. We do not see anywhere that the conversion of children depends on the conversion of the mother or that the family must observe the mitzvot.
21. However, when these children come of age and become bar or bat mitzva, they will have the option to object and thus reject the conversion.
22. Ketubbot 11a.

Yet none of this means that there is no "benefit" here. On the contrary, what is to the minor's detriment is also his remedy: we have seen that Maimonides said of a "captive child" that "it is as though he is under duress"[23] and he is therefore exempt from all punishment. Thus, the conversion of the minor, bringing him under the wings of the Divine Presence, is a great benefit, without any possibility of it being a disadvantage.

As noted, we must distinguish between the Land of Israel and Diaspora communities. Outside of Israel, children are raised among gentiles, and there is concern that they will be attracted to their lifestyle. In Israel, the concern is to the contrary: if we do not convert such people, then there will be a large population of non-Jews who are integrated in Israeli society and viewed as an integral part of it. They will gradually be assimilated among the Jewish population, leading to an increase in intermarriage. Who can predict how this will end?

Moreover, what will happen to those who have no choice but to remain gentiles? They may not marry Jews, and in Israel they will not be able to marry gentiles who belong to another religious community. It is akin to the half-slave/half-emancipated man described by the Sages: "He may not marry a slave woman, and he may not marry a free woman."[24] There is no greater social ticking time bomb than this!

We must see this as a religious, social, and national challenge. In order for this process to succeed, Israeli society must view it as a national and social mission. If possible, we must convert minors at a very young age, even before they begin elementary school. In addition, we must create the appropriate frameworks for these children: Jewish enrichment programs in schools and summer camps that will give these children a Jewish education and a connection to Torah and the Jewish faith. Religious youth groups must also extend a hand and become partners in meeting the challenge of bringing these children closer, just as religious youth groups in the Diaspora open their doors to the entire Jewish population and understand that they must create frameworks that are tailored to the needs of the broader community. It goes without saying

---

23. *Hilkhot Mamrim* 3:3; see above, p. 31, note 8.
24. Ḥagiga 2b.

that we should try to persuade the parents to become closer to Judaism as well. However, as stated, by no means should this or anything else be considered a precondition to the conversion of the children.

The challenge we face is this: Do we have the desire and the ability to create an education system for these children that will attract them and their parents to join God's community? We must understand that converting minors will benefit all of Israeli society and is a matter of the highest priority. The sooner we meet this challenge, the better.

On a related note, it is worthwhile to address something else: Must all conversions be subject to a single, central halakhic authority, or can we establish autonomous rabbinical courts? There clearly should not be any law or regulation that dictates that all conversion must be subject to a single, central halakhic authority. Such a centralized authority has never existed in Jewish history, and it would undermine all efforts to convert people to Judaism. If all conversions are subject to a single halakhic authority, then it is likely to slam the door in the face of converts. On the contrary, throughout history, every rabbinical court had license to perform conversions, even in the time of the Sanhedrin. In the time of Hillel and Shammai, we find that Shammai rejected several conversion candidates that Hillel accepted.[25] Clearly there is room for differences in approach toward conversion among rabbinical courts. In fact, diversity of rabbinical courts enables and facilitates the acceptance of converts.

Municipal rabbis should therefore be permitted to perform conversions, as was done throughout history, and likewise they should be allowed to pick the members of their court. Furthermore, municipal rabbis are closer to and more familiar with their constituents than judges in centralized rabbinical courts. They are also in a position to make contact with local institutions and facilitate cooperation between schools, youth groups, and members of local communities who can encourage, guide, and support the process of converting children.

Conversion nowadays is a religious, social, and national challenge of the first rank. We must not avoid or postpone confronting it. We must dedicate ourselves to the cause of converting minors and establish

25. Shabbat 31a.

rabbinical courts for conversion in every city. In this way, we will merit the fulfillment of the verses, "And they will bring all your brothers from all the nations" (Is. 66:20), "And I will rejoice in Jerusalem and take delight in My people" (ibid. 65:19).

Summary

For the first time in thousands of years, during which we prayed and yearned to return to Zion, God has granted us the privilege of returning to our land, where we are now faced with formidable tasks.

With regard to the state, we must cultivate an understanding that real faith demands that we marshal all of our intellectual, emotional, spiritual, and physical resources to build and secure the people and the land. Failure to remain on guard, underestimation of our enemies, inattentiveness to the great obstacles we face – be they economic, social, or military – are not just displays of ignorance and foolishness, but constitute a betrayal of our sacred duties. God's royal crown has been given to us for safekeeping, and we must not delegate that task to others – not even to God Himself!

We have witnessed extraordinary historical processes. The visions of the prophets, filled with amazing wonders that many considered to be embellishments and hyperbole gushing forth from poetic souls, have become cold, hard facts: "In a favorable time I have responded to you, and on the day of salvation I have helped you; I will preserve you and give you as a covenant to the people, to restore the land and bequeath its desolate estates; to say to the prisoners, 'Come out,' to those in darkness, 'Show yourselves'" (Is. 49:8–9). Those who were imprisoned in the Soviet Union and severed from the rest of their people in Ethiopia now walk freely on the streets of Israel as though it was always just so. Who even considered the possibility of such growth in the population of this tiny country? And yet we are experiencing the fulfillment of the verse: "They will neither hunger nor thirst, and neither heat nor sun will beat down on them" (ibid. 10), while a large part of the land yet remains wilderness, waiting to be resettled.

The character of Israeli society in future generations is being determined today. We must imbue it with Torah – not with blind faith that is disconnected from reality, but with resolute, unwavering trust in the God of Israel, who opens our eyes to see His might and bear witness to it.

Chapter 4

The Torah of the Public Sphere: A Preface to the Halakha of the State

Individual, Community, and Society

> "I am that I am" (Ex. 3:14).... R. Yoḥanan said: "I am that I am" to individuals. But as for the masses, against their will, against their desires, even though they break their teeth, I rule over them, as it says: "'As I live,' declares the Lord God, 'with a strong hand, an outstretched arm, and an outpouring of wrath, I will rule over you'" (Ezek. 20:33).[1]

The difference between individuals and collectives is a fundamental one. The mitzvot can be divided into three classes: those that primarily address individuals, communities, or society.

1. **Individuals**: Mitzvot that address the individual include most mitzvot that we must perform on a regular basis, such as "Love

1. Exodus Rabba 3:6.

your fellow as yourself" (Lev. 19:18), giving charity, tefillin, mezuza, and even Shabbat.

2. **Communities**: A community, a *tzibur*, can accomplish much more than any individual or even a group of individuals working together. A group combines the small contributions of each individual member, whereas a community has institutions that subsume the individual. Such institutions are not merely the extension of the individual, but are able to function in ways that go well beyond the capacity of a simple partnership or collaboration.

   Some mitzvot are exclusively communal, and the individual draws his ability to perform them from being part of the community. He does not have the power or ability to fulfill such mitzvot on his own. The appointment of judges is in this category. The community is a decisive component of rabbinic mitzvot as well. Communal prayer is not merely a group of individuals praying together. On the contrary, the *sheliaḥ tzibur*, the community's representative and proxy, can discharge the obligation of individuals as well.[2]

   There is no Torah reading and no recitation of *Kedusha* (and according to one view in the mishna, no *Musaf* prayer)[3] except in a communal setting. Numerous mitzvot require the presence of a rabbinical court: the mitzva to circumcise a child who has no father or whose father refuses to fulfill his obligation, for instance.[4] Even the very obligation to establish a rabbinical court is a communal obligation. The community, in its primary sense, includes all residents of a particular locale. Even if an individual is temporarily absent, he is still part of that community.[5]

---

2. Rosh HaShana 34b.
3. Berakhot 30a; Rashi there, s.v. *ein*: "It was not instituted except in a communal setting."
4. *Hilkhot Mila* 1:1–2.
5. See Rosh HaShana 35a regarding the fulfillment of prayer obligations on behalf of "the people in the fields." R. Gamliel rules that they fulfill their obligation with the prayers of the *sheliaḥ tzibur*. The law is not in accordance with him except on Rosh HaShana and Yom Kippur.

3. **Society**: There is a different type of "community" with special laws. Maimonides calls this community a "*kahal*" and applies it only to the Jews living in the Land of Israel: "No one is called a *kahal* except those who live in the Land of Israel."[6] There are two levels of *kahal*. When the entire Jewish people lives in its land, each tribe is called a *kahal*, and one who has no patrimonial estate is not considered part of a *kahal*.[7] However, there is an even higher level of *kahal*: the totality of Jewish society in the Land of Israel.

The status of the *kahal* differs from that of any other community. For example, the mitzva to establish regional and municipal rabbinical courts is practiced only in the Land of Israel, not outside it: "Outside of the Land of Israel...you do not seat [a court] in every city."[8] It seems to me that the reason for this distinction is that this mitzva is an obligation of the *kahal*. The same is true of the Great Sanhedrin, the supreme rabbinical court: when there are sages who have obtained the original form of *semikha* [ordination], "a supreme rabbinical court is appointed first.... The greatest scholar among them is seated at the head, over them."[9] This all seems to be an obligation of the *kahal*.

Likewise, the mitzva to appoint a king is derived from the authority of the *kahal*, and the king symbolizes this authority. Maimonides describes this beautifully: "His heart is the heart of the entire *kahal* of Israel."[10] It is worth noting that the term "*kahal*" appears in each of the first three chapters of *Hilkhot Melakhim*, which is where Maimonides defines the concept of Jewish kingship.[11]

The power of the *kahal* is so great that all of the Jewish holidays depend on it. If not for the *kahal*, they would all be annulled! This is how Maimonides explains the *sine qua non* of the applicability of the calendar:

---

6. *Hilkhot Shegagot* 13:2.
7. Horayot 6b.
8. Makkot 7a. See also *Hilkhot Sanhedrin* 1:2 and *Kesef Mishneh* there.
9. *Hilkhot Sanhedrin* 1:3.
10. *Hilkhot Melakhim* 3:6.
11. Ibid. 1:4; 2:6; 3:6.

> If we were to suppose, for instance, that the residents of the Land of Israel would disappear from the land – far be it from God to do such a thing, for He already promised that the remnants of the nation would never be completely erased or uprooted… – then our calculation would not help at all, in any way.[12]

Hence, the calendar depends on the *kahal* and the festivals depend on the *kahal*, even during the exile. Being that the *kahal* is independent and sovereign in its homeland, and it has a Sanhedrin and a king of its own appointment, it has the power not only to sanctify time by determining when the months and festivals begin, but also to sanctify "every spot on which your foot treads" (Josh. 1:3), even if it is not in the Land of Israel. Furthermore, it is possible that an explicit mitzva from the Torah can be uprooted, as it were, by the *kahal*. In this regard, Maimonides offers a novel insight about the Torah's prohibition on returning to Egypt: "It seems to me that if a king of Israel conquers Egypt with the consent of the high court, it is permitted; the Torah only forbade individuals from returning there."[13]

Just as it is the mission of each and every Jew to fulfill the commandments of his Creator, i.e., the mitzvot that apply to him as an individual, so too it is the mission of every Jewish community, wherever it may be, to realize God's will in those spheres where only a community and its institutions can do so. Similarly, it is the mission of the *kahal*, Jewish society in the Land of Israel, to realize God's will in spheres where individuals, even large groups of individuals, and even communities, cannot function.

There is no doubt that historical circumstances, social and cultural conditions, and the like have a great deal of influence over the degree to which the Torah's vision can be realized – that is, the degree to which the individual and collective can fulfill their missions. Yet even a cursory survey of Jewish history will show that circumstances produced different, sometimes even opposite, effects on individuals, communities, and the *kahal*.

12. *Sefer HaMitzvot*, positive commandment 153.
13. *Hilkhot Melakhim* 5:8.

The Torah as a Communal Way of Life in the Diaspora

Every individual, by nature, depends on others to satisfy his basic needs, and to help him develop and actualize his talents.[14] Maimonides discusses at length the need for social structures that are shaped and guided by divine law. He characterizes divine law as being concerned with the welfare of society as well as the welfare of the souls of individuals[15] and explains that the goal of the whole Torah is the improvement of the soul and of society.[16] Clearly, it is not sufficient for a religion to claim that it promotes the perfection of society and illuminates the soul by teaching the truth. Its lessons and the real-world effectiveness of its laws must be examined and tested both philosophically and historically.

Maimonides marshals much explicit evidence from the past in order to demonstrate the power, effectiveness, and virtuousness of the Torah as a primary influence on the Jewish people,[17] to the extent that our very existence as a nation is secure thanks only to the Torah: "This, to my mind, is likewise an indication of the eternity of the Law because of which we have a special name."[18]

Moreover, Maimonides' words are predicated on the implicit assumption that, at least with respect to the perfection of society, the positive impact of the Torah is easily observable, despite the harsh reality of the exile that was decreed upon us, as a result of which large portions of the Torah could not be implemented. If the Torah had such a significant influence during the exile, when it could only be fulfilled partially, then certainly when it is realized fully, within a society governed by the Torah, its impact will be even greater.

---

14. *Moreh Nevukhim* I:72, 184–194.
15. Ibid. II:40.
16. Ibid. III:27.
17. Even though this and similar claims are brought by Maimonides and other Jewish thinkers in defense of the Jewish faith, which was a minority faith in comparison to other faiths, this obviously does not derogate from the truth of the claim in itself.
18. *Moreh Nevukhim* II:29, p. 342. Compare to *Moses Maimonides' Epistle to Yemen*, trans. Boaz Cohen, ed. Abraham S. Halkin (New York: American Academy for Jewish Research, 1952), p. vii: "Israel's indestructibility is the result of a Divine pact betokened by the perpetuation of the Torah in our midst...."

The Torah deals extensively with society and government. Social matters are the subject and content of most mitzvot of the Torah.[19] It is evident that the Written Torah was sparing with details about political structure and administration; it is hard to imagine that the precise form of political administration that was suitable for an agrarian economy four thousand years ago would remain the right prescription for all times. Rather, the Torah offers certain principles that are interpreted more broadly in the Oral Torah, in accordance with the needs and conditions of every era.

During certain eras, the vast majority of Jews observed the mitzvot, as those responsible for bearing the covenant. Although there was no Jewish sovereignty for almost two thousand years, most Jewish communities enjoyed a measure of autonomy before the era of Emancipation. The unified, organized community was maintained within the framework of the *kehilla*. While it is true that looming external threats to the individual and community alike contributed to communal solidarity, for the most part the vitality of the *kehilla* was drawn from internal sources.

Even though Jewish communities were scattered all across the globe, among nations with vastly different forms of government, and despite their exposure to unbridled persecution and terrible pressures, most Jewish communities managed their internal affairs in similar ways.

All communities abided by the same basic halakhic framework, from which they derived the principles of their basic organizational structure. Therefore, when the authorities did not intervene, almost all of them displayed the same organizational methods and maintained the same legal system. The great distance between communities was bridged by a common loyalty to the Torah, which unified them.

It is interesting that at certain times and in certain places, Jewish self-government was expanded to include a power that nowadays is reserved by the state exclusively: armed defense. Thus, for example, in *Hilkhot Melakhim*, Maimonides explained the laws of warfare that

19. *Moreh Nevukhim* III:35, p. 538: "It is known that all the commandments are divided into two groups: transgressions between man and his fellow man and transgressions between man and God ... even though in reality they sometimes may affect relations between man and his fellow man."

apply only when there is Jewish sovereignty. Nevertheless, he wrote in *Hilkhot Shabbat*:

> Gentiles who besieged Jewish towns... if they have murderous intent... they are confronted with weapons... and it is a mitzva for every Jew who is able to come to go out and help their besieged brothers and rescue them from the gentiles on Shabbat. It is forbidden for them to tarry until after Shabbat. After they rescue their brothers, they may return to their places, together with their weapons, on Shabbat.[20]

This paragraph was codified in *Shulḥan Arukh*[21] about four hundred years later, even though its author restricted his work to laws that apply in time of exile.

These rulings were not just theoretical. There are documented instances of Jews who armed themselves to protect their communities. For example, even before Maimonides' time, in 1099, the Crusaders under the command of Godfrey of Bouillon breached Jerusalem and concentrated their forces against the Jews who had defended their quarter. A year later, Jewish soldiers fought to protect Haifa, which had a majority-Jewish population at that time.[22] In Poland, we find a Jewish defense force operating during the Khmelnytsky Uprising of 1648,[23] and several years later, in 1664, young Jews organized themselves to defend the Jewish quarter of Lemberg (Lviv).[24] For the most part, of course, even when Jews had autonomy, it was limited and did not include bearing arms. In any case, armed Jewish defense in the Diaspora was unlikely to succeed and was generally completely hopeless.

20. *Hilkhot Shabbat* 2:23.
21. *Oraḥ Ḥayim* 329:6.
22. See *Encyclopedia Hebraica* 6:454.
23. See *A History of the Jewish People*, ed. Haim Hillel Ben-Sasson (Cambridge: Harvard University Press, 1976), p. 657; Joel Raba, "The Decrees of 5408–5409: The Events and Their Significance," in I. Bartal and I. Gutman, *Kiyyum VeShever: Yehudei Polin LeDoroteihem* (Jerusalem: Merkaz Zalman Shazar, 1997), vol. 1, pp. 170–86.
24. S. M. Dubnow, *History of the Jews in Russia and Poland* (Philadelphia: The Jewish Publication Society of America, 1916), vol. 1, p. 161.

However, there were other areas in which Jewish self-government was substantial. This allowed unique Jewish institutions to develop and Jewish culture to flourish. Jewish communities in different lands, even in rival empires, corresponded with one another. The authority of the Torah was accepted by the entire Diaspora, and therefore rabbinic responsa were requested and sent across the world. Even the greatest upheavals could not sever the connection between the Jews of different lands.

The *kehilla* crystallized because of the exceptional confluence of certain unique conditions. Once a Jew chose to adhere to Judaism, it was inconceivable – and in fact, all but impossible – to dissociate from the Jewish community. It was possible to leave the *kehilla*, but only by converting to another religion. Each *kehilla* included all the Jews within its geographic reach. In general, community members wanted to belong to the community, though this affiliation was often born of necessity, as the social, economic, and legal needs of community members (beyond purely "religious" needs) were met by communal institutions. Jewish autonomy was a complete and comprehensive entity.

Jewish communities were isolated pockets of a unique sociopolitical structure all across the medieval world. Even as Jews lived amidst other societies and under the rule of tyrants, they often obtained a large degree of autonomy, and their communal structure was based on democratic principles, as halakha demands.[25] Additionally, it is worth noting that the phenomenon of illiteracy was all but absent from Jewish society,[26] at least from its male members, and the Jewish public acknowledged Torah learners as members of the upper class, who in turn reinforced the strength and democratic basis of the community. There was a strong sense of shared identity and common destiny with all Jews, even those in small and remote locales. Social responsibility was the hallmark of every Jewish settlement, and communal authority was exercised mainly to strengthen the most economically disadvantaged members of the community. There was a clear sense of belonging to the Jewish people, which encompassed all communities throughout the Diaspora.

---

25. See below, "The Structure of the State According to the Torah," parts I and II.
26. This stood in contrast to gentile society, where literacy was rare.

Affiliation with the community was usually chosen freely, even though it entailed significant responsibility. Despite the limited resources and severely limited powers of the *kehilla*, it managed to bind its members to an eternal people, and thus communities developed a sense of mutual responsibility for other communities around the world, irrespective of international borders and prevailing regimes. Even when Jews were expelled from their homes and countries, if they managed to escape with their lives, they could find communities that would accept them with open arms, offer them protection, and promote their welfare to an extent that was not seen among other nations, even the most enlightened among them, including in the modern era.

In every locale and under every regime, Jews took care of the needs of their brethren. Whenever there was a temporary lull in repression by despotic rulers, the Jews managed to create economic conditions for members of their community that were better than those of the lower classes of the general population (and the peasant class generally constituted the majority of the population). Maimonides attests: "We have never seen or heard of a Jewish community that has no charity fund."[27] The principle that "all of Israel are guarantors for one another"[28] became an inviolable law everywhere Jews settled. A "Jewish state" transcended every earthly border. Its constitution was the Torah, and its citizens, despite differences of language and political residency, had equal rights. This people had no king and no kingdom, nothing but memories and yearnings for an ancient, shared homeland, yet remained a single unified people. Over the centuries, we learned how to sustain a nation that is aware of its special identity even when disconnected from its land.

These were the visible results of the practical application of the Torah even under the severely limited conditions of the exile. It was obvious to all that the Jewish people's incomparable ability to survive and rejuvenate stemmed directly from there. The outstanding spiritual and scholarly attainments of so many major Jewish personalities grew

27. *Hilkhot Matnot Aniyim* 9:3.
28. Shevuot 39a; Maimonides, *Hilkhot Shevuot* 11:16.

out of an environment rich with Torah and fertile with wisdom, which developed in spite of the harsh conditions imposed on it.

A basic premise of independent communal life was the creative balance, fostered by halakha, between freedom and authority. Jewish society was fundamentally voluntary, meaning that each individual was free to choose whether or not to join the community. This feature is most surprising when compared to other autonomous communities. Clearly, social pressures and various forms of social sanction did their part to keep individuals within the communal framework, but ultimately, any Jew who was willing to worship the Cross or praise the Prophet would be rewarded by those in power. The temptations were so great that there were some who could not withstand them; they chose to abandon Judaism. Yet most chose to identify with Jewish society and participate in it. Most chose Judaism willingly, thereby freely accepting the rules and discipline of the *kehilla*, whose power to enforce was limited and whose punishments were almost all moral and predicated on widespread consent. The fact that so many chose to cling to Judaism attests to the character of the organized Jewish community and to the legal system that created it, and that it, in turn, perpetuated.

Thus, the most prominent features of most Jewish communities, wherever they may be, are a faithful testament to the divine origins of the Torah, as Maimonides states.[29] No other system of law, not even those on which empires and superpowers were founded, could govern society so perfectly and realize the goal of refining society – not to mention the failure of these legal systems to accomplish the second goal that Maimonides mentions, namely, spiritual cultivation and improvement of the individual.

Emancipation and the Breakdown of the Community

The process of Emancipation – the granting of equal rights to Jews – began with the French Revolution in 1789 and slowly spread to other states in Western Europe. The Emancipation effected major changes in Jewish society. Numerous restrictions that had long been

29. See above, chapters 2 and 3.

imposed on the Jews were removed, but the price that Jewish society paid for this freedom was heavy indeed.

A full treatment of the social and historical processes relating to the Emancipation that affected Jewish society lies beyond the scope of this work. We will therefore comment briefly on several specific points that have ramifications for the present discussion.

The modern state assumed most of the power that had belonged to the church, and therefore it could not accept the continued self-government of Jewish groups. Jews, as individuals, could enjoy all individual rights, but Judaism as a communal and social way of life was no longer acceptable. Freedom of religion was granted universally, but the scope of religion was confined to the realm of individual conscience and public worship. Even with regard to the family, the most basic social and biological unit, halakha could no longer be the determinative legal framework. The Jewish laws of marriage, marriage contracts, financial maintenance of the household, divorce, etc. were rendered moot from the perspective of the state. Under the best of circumstances, the Jewish marriage ceremony was recognized as a valid marriage procedure by the state, but the legal and civil ramifications of this practice were whatever the state determined. Halakha became all but meaningless.

As a result of Emancipation and the major historical changes that accompanied the development of the modern nation-state, the Jewish enclaves in which the Torah was given expression crumbled quickly. Loyalty to traditional faith could now only find expression in the realms of individual worship and acts of kindness, and these realms had become increasingly narrow and limited.

Religious devotion was channeled toward insularity and sectarianism, while the general framework of a well-regulated Jewish way of life – for all Jews – weakened steadily. Age-old communities were rent apart, with each group relating to its competitors with suspicion. These groups often could not overcome their mutual antipathy, even when they faced a common threat, and thus many Jews became alienated from their roots. Throughout that period, generations grew up knowing little, if anything, about their Jewish heritage and its relevance to the world they inhabited.

The Torah as a National Public Way of Life

The voluntary nature of the community made it into a unique social unit and gave it the ability to survive and endure until recent generations, when the development of the modern nation-state in Europe led to the breakdown of the *kehilla*. When it lost its autonomy and its jurisdiction was restricted to the ceremonial aspects of religion, it lost its ability to unify, leading to a process of disintegration, assimilation, and flight from Judaism.

For Judaism to thrive, it is necessary to maintain its national way of life. The success of the Torah depends on the presence of frameworks for Jewish communal and national life. In the absence of even a semblance of Jewish independence, the Torah loses the space in which it can operate and consequently its most significant feature: a way of life that provides the conditions that can sustain and promote spiritual growth. Where the Torah is completely excluded from matters of state, the path toward fulfillment of man's divine mission is blocked.

The divine nature of the Torah is called into question when there is no such space in which it can operate. It cannot be a "faithful testament," for how can one ascertain its truth? Negation of the Torah's earthly manifestation is a corruption and falsification of Judaism. Therefore, the creation of a new format for the preservation of the national character of the Jewish people is both a need and a vital Torah value.

This is the background for the emergence of Zionism. The new nationalism sought to reestablish and restore national life and to deepen the national dimension of the Jewish people precisely when the forces of dispersal and schism worked to destroy the fabric of Jewish life. The return of the Jewish people to its land and the establishment of the Jewish state create a new opportunity to apply the Torah to every aspect of life – the individual, the social, and the national – so that it can fulfill its role as a "faithful testament."[30]

---

30. See *Hilkhot Tefillin UMezuza VeSefer Torah* 10:11: "The Torah scroll... is the faithful testament to everyone in the world, as it states: 'And it will be there as a testament for you' (Deut. 31:26)."

Chapter 5

The Structure of the State According to the Torah, Part I: Principles

The Purpose of the Torah: Perfecting the Soul and Perfecting Society

Maimonides taught:

> The Law as a whole aims at two things: the welfare of the soul and the welfare of the body.... Know that between these two aims, one is indubitably greater in nobility, namely, the welfare of the soul... while the second aim – I mean the welfare of the body – is prior in nature and time. The latter aim consists in the governance of the city and the well-being of the states of all its people according to their capacity. This second aim is the more certain one, and it is the one regarding which every effort has been made precisely to expound it and all its particulars. For the first aim can only be achieved after achieving the second one.... This cannot be achieved in any way by one isolated individual. For an individual can only attain all this through a political association, it being already known that man is political by nature....

> The true Law then, which as we have already made clear is unique – namely, the Law of Moses our Master – has come to bring us both perfections, I mean the welfare of the states of people in their relations with one another through the abolition of reciprocal wrongdoing and through the acquisition of a noble and excellent character.... I mean also the soundness of the beliefs and the giving of correct opinions through which ultimate perfection is achieved.[1]

This basic distinction between perfection of the soul and perfection of the body can be discerned within the Torah itself. We find that the Sinaitic covenant was made twice. The first time was after the miraculous Exodus from Egypt and the splitting of the sea. Moses read the "Book of the Covenant" to the people, and they replied: "*Naaseh venishma*," "We will do and we will heed" (*Parashat Mishpatim*, Ex. 24:7). The second time was after the people of Israel had breached the covenant by making the Golden Calf. Moses prayed for the covenant to be renewed, and the Holy One, blessed be He, responded in the affirmative (*Parashat Ki Tissa*, Ex. 34).

Parashat Mishpatim begins with the verse: "These are the rules that you shall set before them" (Ex. 21:1). In a series of short, precise statements, the Torah sets out a synopsis of criminal and civil law, from the penalties for murder, assault, and theft to the regulation of relations between master and slave, lender and borrower, and the finder of a lost object and its owner. In the last ten verses (Ex. 23:10–19) of the dense sequence of mitzvot listed in chapters 21 through 23 of Exodus, there is a brief survey of what we would nowadays call "religious law" or "religion": exclusive belief in one God, Shabbat, the three pilgrimage festivals, the Sabbatical year, and forbidden foods.

In his Torah commentary, Ibn Ezra comments that this last segment of "ritual" mitzvot is repeated almost verbatim when the covenant is renewed,[2] explaining that these mitzvot were repeated because they constitute the "terms" for maintaining the covenant between God and

1. *Moreh Nevukhim* III:27, pp. 510–11.
2. Exodus 34:17–26; Ibn Ezra on 34:26.

His people. They enable every Jew to have a special bond with the Almighty, which gives vitality to the soul and sustenance to the spirit.

Most mitzvot in *Parashat Mishpatim* are addressed to the governing authorities. This section ends, according to Ibn Ezra, with the admonition, "You shall not oppress a stranger" (Ex. 23:9), which prohibits giving preferential treatment to a Jew in his quarrel with a resident alien.

Thus, the Torah's legal system comprises two parts. The first, which is in the purview of the governing authorities, addresses social matters; the second pertains to every Jew.

This division between two realms, the civil and the spiritual, has important halakhic ramifications. Leaders are tasked with the enforcement of interpersonal laws. Within this realm, they have a great deal of both legislative and administrative power. They are limited only by the basic requirement that their actions not undermine the principles of honesty and justice presented in the Torah. A Jewish government that dares to violate these would lose its right to govern; on the other hand, a worthy government that functions justly enjoys the Torah's approval.

This is an expression of the clear distinction between the two forms of perfection toward which the Torah strives and between the various ways of attaining those perfections. The first, "the welfare of the body…the governance of the city and the well-being of the states of all its people according to their capacity," depends on the proper functioning of the state. It can be achieved only by means of "political association," that is, of an organized social structure. The second, higher form of perfection, that of the soul, is a very personal matter that each person can attain on his own, by means of general spiritual growth.

The Authority of the King

According to the Torah, there are two parallel sources of legislative and judicial authority. One authority is that of the king, who represents the entire nation and its independence. "His heart is the heart of the entire congregation of Israel";[3] "A king over whom no man in Israel has authority and above whom in his dominion is only the Lord his God."[4]

3. *Hilkhot Melakhim* 3:6.
4. *Hilkhot Shegagot* 15:6.

His power is the "power of dominion,"[5] and this authority is conferred upon the king's appointees as well.

The second authority is that of the Sanhedrin and the courts subject to it. Their virtue is the "power of Torah scholarship."[6] "The high court in the Temple is called the Great Sanhedrin.... The wisest of all of them is appointed their head, and he is the leader of the assembly. The Sages call him the president (*nasi*) in all instances, and he takes the place of our teacher Moses."[7]

It is clear that over the years, circumstances wrought changes in how the two authorities operated. Some believe that when the monarchy was abolished, its power was transferred to the Sanhedrin.[8] Likewise, both powers – the power of dominion and the power of Torah scholarship – were combined in Moses.[9]

But even after the loss of its independence, a remnant of Israel's monarchy remained. This is how Maimonides describes the status of the exilarch ("*reish galuta*"):

> The dominion of the exilarch over all Israel is like the dominion of a king who rules by his might. God therefore refers to him as a "rod"; the [Sages] said: "'The rod shall not depart from Judah' (Gen. 49:10) – this refers to the exilarchs in Babylonia, who

5. *Sefer HaMitzvot*, negative commandment 316.
6. Ibid.
7. *Hilkhot Sanhedrin* 1:3.
8. *Derashot HaRan*, Feldman edition (Jerusalem: Makhon Shalem, 1977), Discourse 11, p. 192: "When there is no king in Israel, the judge combines both powers – the power of the judge and the power of the king."
9. *Midrash Tanḥuma*, Buber edition, *Koraḥ* §6: "Moses was king and Aaron his brother high priest." Regarding Deuteronomy 33:5 ("And there was a king in Yeshurun"), Ibn Ezra comments: "This refers to Moses, from whose mouth the leaders of the nation heard the Torah explicitly." To similar effect is the commentary of Rav Saadia Gaon on the same verse. Similarly, Maimonides writes in his *Commentary on the Mishna* (Shevuot 2:2): "You have already learned that Moses was a king and is counted among the kings, in addition to being a prophet. About him it says: 'And there was a king in Yeshurun.'" This is also implied in *Hilkhot Melakhim* 2:6, where Moses is cited to illustrate the king's duty to be humble.

> subjugate Israel with a rod,"[10] that is, against their will, by compulsion. You see that we pay no attention to his wisdom, only to his pedigree and to his having been appointed with the consent of the people of his locale alone.[11]

Some *Rishonim*[12] considered the question of how these two sources of power differ. What was the king's jurisdiction, and what was the Sanhedrin's? This is not the place to address the scope of the power of each authority and the relationship between them. We will merely note that there was some degree of overlap between the two authorities with respect to enacting precautionary measures ("*migdar milta*").[13] The present discussion will focus on defining the parameters of the judicial authority of the ruling power – the monarchy.

The basic function of the governing power is to ensure the security of the entire population, without exception. The first test faced by King Saul, the first king of Israel, was to prove that he was willing to accept responsibility for every part of the nation, including those who lived far from the center, in Yavesh-Gilad, where they were exposed to the intimidation of King Nahash of Ammon.[14] The meaning of this test is clear: Even though Samuel anointed Saul as king, and even though there had been a great assembly of the entire nation at which a constitution was written ("Samuel expounded to the people the rules of the monarchy and recorded them in a document" [I Sam. 10:25]), and even though the people welcomed the new king with shouts of "Long live the king!" (ibid. 24), his rule remained weak. In today's parlance, his crown was not recognized as being completely legitimate. It was only after Saul passed the test in Yavesh-Gilad that Samuel declared: "Come, let us go to Gilgal and there inaugurate the monarchy" (ibid. 11:14). A king who protects the rights of all his subjects is worthy of the throne

10. Sanhedrin 5a.
11. *Commentary on the Mishna*, Bekhorot 4:4.
12. *Derashot HaRan*, Discourse 11; Abarbanel's commentary on Deuteronomy, at the beginning of *Parashat Shofetim*.
13. On "*migdar milta*," see below, p. 121, n. 16, and the chapter titled "The Authority of Rabbinical Courts and the Torah View of Punishment."
14. I Samuel chapter 11.

and must be obeyed. A king who evades his duty to protect the nation, or even a small part of it, loses his right to reign.

An equally important governmental function is to establish justice, for only through justice can the population be protected from lawbreakers in its ranks.

These two functions are essentially one. Government is the means of ensuring survival against both internal conflict and external threats. As Maimonides states concisely: "A king is appointed in the first place only to do justice and make war, as Scripture says, 'And our king will judge us and will go before us and fight our wars' (ibid. 8:20)."[15]

The role of "judge" is listed first because executing justice is the first obligation of the king. It is for this reason that the people requested a king and even accepted the onerous obligations that having a king entail, as specified by Samuel.

Nahmanides refers to the domestic aspect of the king's role as "the customs and ways of civilized society."[16] Rabbeinu Nissim writes:

> Men need judges to judge between them, for in their absence, men would eat each other alive and humanity would become corrupt. And every nation requires some form of political order… and Israel needs this just as the other nations do. But if lawbreakers were not punished… the structure of society would break down completely, for, in the absence of the fear of punishment, the number of murderers would dramatically increase. Therefore, for the well-being of society, the Holy One, blessed be He, mandated the appointment of a king…. The king can punish without prior admonition as he deems fit for the good of the kingdom. We find, then, that the appointment of a king serves a common purpose for Israel and for the other peoples, who require a societal structure.[17]

---

15. *Hilkhot Melakhim* 4:10.
16. Commentary on Exodus 15:25 (Chavel trans.).
17. *Derashot HaRan*, Discourse 11 (Silverstein trans, CreateSpace Independent Publishing Platform, 2014).

Earlier we cited Ibn Ezra's observation in his commentary on the Torah: "From 'these are the rules' (Ex. 21:1) to 'six years' (Ex. 23:10), the Torah sets forth civil statutes, and the high priest[18] and the judge, who is the king, are required to study and know them."[19] It is clear that he regarded judgment – the laws that apply to interpersonal relations and the proper functioning of society – as the centerpiece of the king's judicial function.

Similarly, Rabbi Avraham, the son of Maimonides, defines "affairs of the kingdom" on the basis of Psalms 101:5. "'He who slanders his friend in secret I will destroy'.... This describes [King David's] course when he returns from seclusion to deal with affairs of the kingdom.... His involvement is in accordance with the will of God.... He punishes the wicked perpetrators of evil and sowers of strife."[20] The psalm in its entirety speaks of interpersonal transgressions and can be seen as expounding its opening verse: "Of kindness and justice I sing" – "Of the mercy and justice that I do for Israel... as Scripture says: 'And David did justice and righteousness for all his people' (II Sam. 8:15)."[21] Ibn Ezra explicitly relates the verse in Psalms to the king's special powers to wipe out evildoers: "'I will destroy' – in accordance with the laws of the monarchy."[22]

The *Rishonim* likewise explained Psalm 72, David's prayer for his son Solomon, as describing the activities of the king. There, too, the detailed description is limited to interpersonal matters, on which political order and social stability depend:

> For Solomon: O God! Give Your judgments to the king and Your righteousness to the king's son. Let him judge Your people with

18. In his view, it seems, the high priest also plays a role in government. However, this does not appear to be the view of Maimonides, as nowhere does he include governmental functions among the duties of the priesthood.
19. Commentary on 34:26.
20. *HaMaspik LeOvdei Hashem* (A Comprehensive Guide for Servants of God), pp. 176–77 in the (Hebrew) Dori edition (Jerusalem: Keren Hotzaat Sifrei Rabbanei Bavel, 1972).
21. Radak on Psalms 101:1. By citing II Samuel 8:15, he relates to Sanhedrin 6b, which is quoted at the beginning of the chapter titled "The Authority of Rabbinical Courts and the Torah View of Punishment."
22. Commentary on Psalms 101:5.

> righteousness and Your poor with justice. Let the mountains bear peace to the people and the hills, justice. Let him judge the poor of the nation, save the children of the indigent, and crush the oppressor.... He will deliver the needy who cry out, the poor who have no helper. He will have pity on the poor and the indigent, and he will save the lives of the indigent. From oppression and violence he will save their lives, and their blood will be precious in his eyes.

In a midrash, the Sages already noted that this psalm speaks of the king's special authority to judge and punish in a manner differing from Torah law:

> David said, "Master of the Universe, give Your judgments to the king's son. Just as You judge without witnesses and without admonition, so shall Solomon judge without witnesses and without admonition." The Holy One, blessed be He, replied to him, "So shall he do".... And that was the case of the two harlots, as it says: "Then came two harlots" (I Kings 3:16). When they saw this, they exclaimed: "Fortunate are you, O land, whose king is a free man."[23]

The king's judicial authority is limited to interpersonal matters and to ensuring the proper functioning of a just society. This authority is rooted in the consent of the governed and in God's choice of the king through His prophet. Scripture makes this explicit: "All the elders of Israel gathered around" (I Sam. 8:4). The Sages explained: "R. Eliezer said: The elders of that generation made a proper request, as Scripture says, 'Give us a king to judge us' (ibid. 8:6)."[24] After the prophet Samuel told them what having a king entails and attempted to intimidate and admonish them by describing its onerous burden, "the nation refused to heed Samuel and said, 'No! A king shall be over us... and our king shall judge us' (ibid. 8:19–20)." After the king was chosen in the presence of the entire nation, "the entire nation shouted out, 'Long live the

---

23. *Midrash Tehillim* (Buber), 72:2.
24. Sanhedrin 20b.

king!'" (ibid. 10:24). Samuel again lectured them on the consequences of appointing a king: "Samuel expounded to the people the rules of the monarchy and recorded them in a document" (ibid. 10:25).

The inauguration of David is described similarly: "All the tribes of Israel came to David at Hebron... and David made a covenant with them at Hebron before the Lord, and they anointed David king over Israel" (II Sam. 5:1–3). The covenant between the king and the nation included the rules governing the monarchy, and the population even made demands and set conditions, as set forth in connection with King Rehoboam: "All Israel came to crown him king.... They spoke to Rehoboam, saying...'If you now ease the harsh service imposed by your father and the heavy yoke he placed on us, we will serve you'" (I Kings 12:1–4). And when he declined to heed them, they refused to accept his kingship: "All Israel saw that the king had not heeded them, and they answered him, saying, 'We have no portion in David, nor any share in the son of Yishai; to your tents, O Israel'" (ibid. 16).[25]

Other verses may be cited to demonstrate that the authority of the king of Israel is based both on the mitzvot of the Torah and the instructions of the prophets and on the consent of the nation.

25. See also Rabbi Zvi Hirsch Chajes, *Torat HaNevi'im,* ch. 7 ("The Status of a Jewish King"; in *Kol Sifrei Maharatz Chajes* [Jerusalem: Divrei Chachamim, 1958], p. 46):

> For all the rules of the monarchy are simply a matter of the relationship between the king and the nation, and these arrangements were satisfactory to both sides, the people having been willing to give up their riches and property for the common good.... And it was not only their riches and property that they gave up for the glory of the king and for the benefits that would result from his rule. They also committed with their very lives, for the king was authorized to kill any man who defied the order of the king, and the entire nation consented to this when they established the monarchy.

See his lengthy treatment with respect to this agreement. Rabbi Chajes brings a proof from Y. Sanhedrin (2:6): "'You shall place a king over yourselves' – it does not say 'I shall place,' but 'You shall place.' You place him above you."

However, there are several limitations on the judicial authority of the king:

1. Equality of all before the law.

A major principle of halakha is that the law of the domain is the law ("*dina demalkhuta dina*").[26] This principle applies to any regime, whether Jewish or not. However, Maimonides formulated a guiding principle: "The general rule is that any law legislated by the king for all, not for just one person, does not constitute theft. But if he takes from one man only, against a law that is known to all, he has perpetrated injustice against him, and this constitutes theft."[27]

2. The king is subject to the law.

In the ancient world, and not infrequently even in contemporary times, kings or rulers struck fear into the hearts of their people and took from them whatever they wanted. They "have been so haughty and have said: 'I am a god; I sit enthroned like a god'" (Ezek. 28:2). In contrast, a king of Israel is not only responsible for the law, he is also subject to it, for the law is God's, and it was not created by the word of the king. "Behold, a king shall reign in righteousness, and ministers shall govern with justice" (Is. 32:1). This principle was so strongly emphasized that the Sages applied it to the supreme King of kings, God Himself, even though His deeds cannot be compared to the actions of mortal kings. The Sages quote a Greek dictum describing the standard protocol among gentile kings: "The law was not written for the king." They respond: "But the Holy One, blessed be He, is not like that. Rather, He issues a decree and is the first to uphold it.... 'They shall observe My observances.... I am the Lord' (Lev. 22:9). I am the first to observe the commandments of the Torah."[28]

---

26. Bava Kamma 113a; *Mishneh Torah, Hilkhot Gezeila VaAveida* 5:11; *Shulḥan Arukh, Ḥoshen Mishpat* 369:8.
27. *Hilkhot Gezeila VaAveida* 5:14. See the next note, where it is demonstrated that this rule applies whether the king is Jewish or not.
28. Y. Rosh HaShana 1:3. See also *HeArukh HaShalem*, s.v. *Agraphos*, n. 3.

When the Sages wanted to denigrate a king who seized power unlawfully, they expressed it by saying: "[The king] is not judged,"[29] meaning that he is immune to the law.

It is worth noting the contemporary implications of this principle. Throughout Jewish history, the privilege that the members of our Knesset have arrogated to themselves – legal immunity – was unthinkable.[30] This is precisely what certain kings were criticized for! Unfortunately, we have not seen any opposition to this from the religious parties.

3. *One does not obey a king in annulling a mitzva.*

The decree of a king is indeed binding on his people. However:

> One who contravenes the king's decree because he was occupied by mitzvot, even by an easy mitzva, is exempt. Between the words of the Master [=God] and the words of the slave [=the king], the words of the Master take precedence. It goes without saying that if the king decreed the annulment of a mitzva, he is not obeyed.[31]

Since the king's legislative and judicial function is to improve the world, he has no part to play in all those areas of the Torah that involve relations between man and God. In contrast, the Sanhedrin, which has the power to adjudicate and instruct with respect to the entire Torah, also has the power to suspend part of the Torah when needed and under certain conditions.[32] Just as it has the authority to erect safeguards for the mitzvot, so too it has the authority to institute enactments that preclude fulfillment of a mitzva.[33] Not so the king. He does not have the

---

29. Mishna in Sanhedrin 18a; see the Gemara on 19a.
30. There are grounds for limited immunity so as to enable proper functioning of the Knesset, but not for sweeping immunity. Thus, for example, there are no grounds for immunity from traffic violations, which are not connected to the work of a Knesset member in any substantive way, or from crimes that harm another person or his good name – insulting a private citizen, for example. Thus far, this issue has not been properly regulated.
31. *Hilkhot Melakhim* 3:9. See also *Sefer HaMitzvot*, positive commandment 173.
32. Yevamot 89b–90b.
33. See Pesaḥim 92a.

authority to annul even a minor mitzva, or even to institute that people passively refrain from fulfilling a mitzva. His authority is limited to governing society.

Still, we find in the Talmud that King David issued instruction in other areas of halakha:

> Thus said David before the Holy One, blessed be He: "Master of the Universe, am I not pious? For all the kings of the east and the west sit in cliques, in their glory, but my hands are sullied with blood, amniotic fluid, and placenta, so as to render a woman pure for her husband! Moreover, I consult with Mephibosheth my teacher on everything I do, saying to him, 'Mephibosheth my teacher, did I adjudicate correctly? Did I find guilty correctly? Did I exonerate correctly? Did I correctly render this pure? Did I correctly render this impure?' And I was not ashamed." R. Yehoshua b. R. Idi said: "What is the Scriptural basis? 'I will speak of Your decrees before kings, and will not be ashamed' (Ps. 119:46)."[34]

Clearly, this passage is intended to highlight the differences between King David and other kings. Because he is wise and a servant of God, he involves himself in matters devoid of the trappings of royalty. Like any Torah scholar he adjudicates and issues rulings on ritual matters and interpersonal matters alike. He engages in this activity not because he is a king, but because of his piety.[35]

---

34. Berakhot 4a.
35. See Shabbat 14b: "When King Solomon instituted *eiruvin*." Yet when Maimonides codifies this law, he uses the following precise formulation: "This matter was instituted by Solomon and his court" (*Hilkhot Eiruvin* 1:2). See also Avoda Zara 36b – "David's court decreed," codified by Maimonides as: "David and his court decreed" (*Hilkhot Issurei Bia* 22:3). Through his careful wording, Maimonides conveys that David and Solomon did not issue these decrees by royal fiat, for in such matters, the king *qua* king has no authority. Rather, since the courts issued the enactments, and David and Solomon were sages who sat on those courts, the enactments were attributed to them. Accordingly, even though the Talmud mentions only Solomon, Maimonides adds "his court," because it could not have been any other way. As for David, the Talmud mentions only the court, but since it is explicitly stated in

The piety and modesty of King David and some other members of the Davidic dynasty allowed for them to be counted among the Torah sages. This stands in contrast to the kings of the Northern Kingdom of Israel, as Maimonides writes:

> The kings of the Davidic dynasty, though not seated in the Sanhedrin, may judge the people and may be judged if there is a case against them. However, the kings of [the Northern Kingdom of] Israel do not judge and are not judged, lest it lead to untoward consequences, for they do not submit to the words of the Torah.[36]

Maimonides explains this more extensively in *Hilkhot Melakhim* (3:7): "Because their hearts are unrefined, it will lead to untoward consequences and weaken the law."

In addition to these three limitations, there is one more basic feature of the king's judgment.

4. Special judicial procedures

As mentioned, Maimonides rules that "kings of [the Northern Kingdom of] Israel do not judge and are not judged." What is the meaning of this assertion? Isn't exercising justice to improve the social order one of the king's principal roles? The meaning is that they do not judge in the same way as the Sages. They are not bound by the same rules of judicial proceedings, and they are not authorized to rule on matters of ritual or religious law. Their jurisdiction is limited to those areas that pertain to the social order. Therefore, judges appointed on the king's authority may rule only on areas under governmental responsibility, that is, the social order.

Judicial proceedings before a king, or before judges appointed by the king, were completely different from judicial proceedings before the Sanhedrin:

Mishna Avot 4:4 that David was "the head of the seventy elders," we see that he, too, was among them.

36. *Hilkhot Sanhedrin* 2:5.

> If one commits murder without any direct evidence or without having been admonished, even if there is but a single witness, or if one accidentally kills his enemy – the king has the authority to put such a person to death, thereby improving the world in accordance with the needs of the time... in order to intimidate and deter the wicked of the world.[37]

License to kill "murderers and the like"[38] was granted to all kings of Israel, not just those of the Davidic line. Maimonides informs us of this with his wonderfully precise wording: "If a king of Israel wished to kill them under the laws of the monarchy and to improve the world"[39] – even a king of Israel, not only a king of the House of David.

Apparently, when a king was appointed, the scope of his powers was defined – this is the content of the covenant the people forged with the king, as described in Scripture (II Sam. 5:1–3) and explained above. This seems to have been the norm in later periods as well, and even among kings of the Northern Kingdom, where the halakhot related to the state were limited as much as possible, given the needs of the time.

The Legitimacy of the Judicial Authority of the Monarchy

There is a basic principle that must be addressed. The source and legitimacy of the king's judicial and legislative authority are based on "*migdar milta*," the need to take the measures necessary to ensure the welfare of society. Such measures are limited in scope, in accordance with society's changing needs. Let us briefly outline[40] the basic conditions for exercising authority to ensure the welfare of society, to which the king's judicial power is subject:

---

37. *Hilkhot Melakhim* 3:10.
38. *Hilkhot Rotze'aḥ UShmirat HaNefesh* 2:4.
39. Ibid.
40. For a fuller treatment of the basic characteristics and features of "*migdar milta*," see below, in the chapter titled "The Authority of Rabbinical Courts and the Torah View of Punishment."

1. Consent of the governed

The king's authority is rooted in the consent of the people as well as in having been chosen by God's prophet. This is stated succinctly by one of the *Rishonim*: "To the extent that the people accord their king glory, to that extent will they have kingship – to the point that if they should desire to divest him of all of his glory, they would be divested of all of their kingship."[41] To this we can add that we derive the primacy of compromise (which is based on the principle of consent) over pure justice from David, about whom it is said: "David did justice and righteousness for all his people" (II Sam. 8:15). The Sages say about this: "But if there is justice there is not righteousness, and if there is righteousness there is no justice! Rather, what type of justice also incorporates righteousness? Compromise."[42]

2. Obvious benefit

A king selected by the nation, given its confidence, and placed on the throne of justice must act in a manner that makes his justice apparent to all and must not discriminate, in any of his enactments, between different strata of society. Otherwise, his rulings lack all validity.

3. Temporary measures

The Sages stressed that a king's rulings are considered temporary measures ("*horaat shaa*") that do not determine halakha for all time:

> How do I interpret "Kohelet sought to find matters of virtue" (Eccl. 12:10)? Kohelet wanted to pronounce judgment based on intuition – without witnesses and without admonition. A heavenly voice issued forth and said to him: "And that which He

41. *Derashot HaRan*, Discourse 11 (Silverstein trans., CreateSpace Independent Publishing Platform, 2014).
42. Sanhedrin 6b. On the unique virtues of compromise, see below, in the chapter titled "The Authority of Rabbinical Courts and the Torah View of Punishment."

> wrote is upright and true" (Eccl. 12:10) – "by the mouth of two witnesses…" (Deut. 17:6)[43]

Maimonides likewise ruled:

> If one commits murder without any direct evidence or without having been admonished, even if there is but a single witness… the king has the authority to put such a person to death, thereby improving the world in accordance with the needs of the time.[44]

Maimonides cites an extreme example of a temporary measure catered to the needs of the time. It is not only the king's judgments that are valid as temporary measures; his legislation likewise draws its validity from being *horaat shaa*.[45]

Thus, the three features of exercising authority to ensure the welfare of society apply both to the very position of king as well as to the justice system that operates under his influence and power.

---

43. Rosh HaShana 21b. The Sages' criticism is not directed at the king's authority to issue temporary rulings or adjudicate special cases, but at Solomon's desire to judge based on his own intuition as a judicial method that would completely uproot the Torah's system of justice and as a judicial method that is not based on the rule of law.
44. *Hilkhot Melakhim* 3:10.
45. It is necessary to explain the difference between the *horaat shaa* of a rabbinical court and the rulings of a king. A rabbinical court has the authority to issue rulings and mete out punishment as a temporary measure, but it must be made explicit that the measure is *ad hoc* and temporary (see *Hilkhot Mamrim* 2:4). The king, however, has the authority to legislate and adjudicate for the sake of the welfare of society even beyond the present and well into the future, as long as it is in accordance with the needs of the time. Note that Maimonides distinguishes between them: with regard to the king, he uses the terminology "law of the monarchy" and "to improve the world." See *Hilkhot Rotze'aḥ UShmirat HaNefesh* 2:4: "If a king of Israel wished to kill them under the laws of the monarchy and to improve the world… and likewise if a rabbinical court saw fit to kill them as a temporary measure, if the hour demanded it…" See also *Hilkhot Sanhedrin* 18:7: "It was a temporary measure or the law of the monarchy." And *Hilkhot Melakhim* 3:10: "The king has the authority to put such a person to death, thereby improving the world in accordance with the needs of the time."

In a later chapter, we will explain that the Sanhedrin and the Sages strove mightily to avoid coercion and punishment.[46] However, for the welfare of the state and society, it was sometimes necessary to activate a justice system that draws its authority from public consent, by means of which it is possible to deter criminal behavior and advance the common good. This system is identified with the law of the monarchy more than with the law of the Sanhedrin and Torah leadership. In any case, this justice system cannot be activated without public acceptance of and consent to all forms of judicial and legislative activity.

But there is a fundamental difference between a rabbinical court that metes out extrajudicial penalties and corporal punishment and a monarchy that does the same. Although both act for the betterment of society, and both require public consent, the Torah authority has license and power in all matters of Torah law, whereas the monarchy only judges matters pertaining to the social order. Not even the consent of the governed can grant the king license to issue rulings pertaining to the mitzvot between man and God. The law of the monarchy is only for the purpose of repairing the world, and the king has no power outside of that realm. Even within this realm, he should refrain from coercion to the degree possible: "Truth, judgment, and peace shall you adjudicate at your gates" (Zech. 8:16) – judgment that comes with peace.

Communal Government

The need to protect the social order has of course endured, even as the monarchy was abolished and the Sanhedrin discontinued. Thus, once these institutions were no longer in place, the power of local communal government, under the elected leadership of the "seven selectmen,"[47] grew stronger. The term "selectmen" – "*tuvei ha'ir*" in Hebrew – refers

46. See below, the chapter titled "The Authority of Rabbinical Courts and the Torah View of Punishment," pp. 115 ff.
47. Megilla 26a. See also Y. Megilla 3:2: "Seven members of the city represent the entire city." Likewise, see Josephus Flavius, *Antiquities of the Jews*, trans. W. Whiston, Book IV, 8:14: "Let there be seven men to judge in every city, and these such as have been before most zealous in the exercise of virtue and righteousness." On the seven selectmen, see *Responsa Rashba* 3:394.

to people in charge of the public welfare, not necessarily judges who specialize in adjudication and rendering halakhic decisions.

> The seven *tuvei ha'ir* mentioned frequently are not the seven most outstanding men in wisdom, wealth, or prestige. Rather, they are seven men selected by the community to govern local affairs.[48]

Just as the Babylonian exilarch possessed a remnant of the authority of the monarchs,[49] so too, in every city and province, the *tuvei ha'ir* performed part of the king's function of maintaining social order, to the extent that they could. In general, their power also depended on relations with the regional rulers. Halakhic authorities viewed the *tuvei ha'ir* as the heirs of the monarchs, not of the Sanhedrin. They were voted into office by the residents, and they had authority to take measures necessary to ensure public welfare.[50] In a case of disagreement among them, they would follow the majority.[51]

Let us consider a fundamental distinction between the authority of the *tuvei ha'ir* and the authority of rabbinical courts: With respect to exceptional powers, judges on contemporary rabbinical courts should not be viewed as heirs to the authority of the Sanhedrin, because *semikha*, the chain of ordination that extends back to Moses, has been discontinued. Rather, their authority stems, at most, from the fact that "we act as their proxies," that is, that rabbis after the age of ordination operate as the representatives of the duly ordained Sages of yore by adjudicating routine cases of monetary law.[52] However, the *tuvei ha'ir,* who govern the community, are the heirs to royal authority, and they have power to do *anything* that the times require – as long as they have been properly appointed by the community.[53]

---

48. *Responsa Rashba* 1:617.
49. See above, at n. 10.
50. *Shulḥan Arukh, Ḥoshen Mishpat* §2 and Rema 37:22.
51. See *Responsa Rashba* 5:285 and Rema on *Ḥoshen Mishpat* 18:1, as well as the commentaries ad loc.
52. Bava Kamma 84b.
53. See *Tur, Ḥoshen Mishpat* §2, *Shulḥan Arukh, Ḥoshen Mishpat* 2:1, and *Me'irat Einayim* ad loc. 9.

Beit Yosef cites a responsum of Nahmanides:

> But if one transgresses the laws of the province, it is necessary to do what the times require, for if you did not say that, they would not be permitted to impose fines or act in matters that are not usual, where we do not act as [the ancient rabbis'] proxies, such as robbery and battery; similarly, there would be need for prior admonition, yet [the Sages] said, "We administer corporal punishment and penalties...[54] not to transgress the words of the Torah but to create a fence around them."[55]

It should be noted that, through the course of history, the boundary between the rabbinical court and the *tuvei ha'ir* was sometimes blurry, and occasionally the same institution exercised both functions.[56]

The power of the majority to elect officers and authorize them to administrate all communal affairs is anchored in the positive mitzva to follow the majority – a mitzva that remains valid even today, when we have no Sanhedrin and no court of rabbis who were given the original *semikha*.[57]

Because this all relates to measures that improve society, it is evident that even contemporary officials take the place of the monarchy,

54. See below, the chapter titled "The Authority of Rabbinical Courts and the Torah View of Punishment," pp. 121–22, n. 16.
55. *Beit Yosef, Ḥoshen Mishpat* 2. This is a responsum of Rashba, but printers mistakenly attributed a collection of his responsa to Nahmanides (printed as *Responsa Rashba HaMeyuḥasot LeRamban* §279). Rabbi Yosef Karo himself noted this in the introduction to *Beit Yosef*, but wrote that he nevertheless cites these responsa as responsa of Nahmanides so that the reader can find them quickly. See also *Responsa Rashba* 4:311.
56. See the commentary of Rabbi Avraham, the son of Maimonides, to Exodus 11:22 (*Perush al Bereshit UShemot LeRabbi Avraham ben HaRambam*), ed. E. Weisenberg (London: S. D. Sassoon, 1959), p. 300. He explains that the "officers of the thousands" appointed by Moses were given both of these tasks.
57. See Maimonides, *Sefer HaMitzvot*, at the end of his enumeration of positive mitzvot, where he lists sixty positive mitzvot "that are necessarily obligatory for every person, at all times, in all places, and under all conditions," including mitzva §175, the mitzva to follow the majority.

and they also have powers that were ascribed to the Sanhedrin, such as allowing the government to declare war.

However, with respect to more serious matters, like capital cases, "they are admonished to act only with the consent of the town elders, so that they act only in cases of great need, and with deliberation."[58] In consultation with the other city elders and leaders, the seven selectmen have broad powers.

As mentioned, the Gemara states that communal governance was assigned to "the seven selectmen."[59] Maimonides was asked whether the number must be precisely seven, and he responded that it does not, and that the number seven is merely representative: "It merely represents a large number... and the selectmen of the town – scholars, men of Torah, men of good deeds – to teach us that it is fitting that guidance issue from those who act upon it themselves."[60] These comments demonstrate the desirability of appointing leadership or a council that is as representative as possible,[61] because this council is in lieu of the monarchy. It is not like a rabbinical court with a fixed number of judges. However, if the community members wish, they may designate a single leader; as long as they have accepted him, they must obey him.[62]

It certainly is proper and desirable that the leaders be "scholars, men of Torah, men of good deeds," though even with respect to descendants of King David, Maimonides wrote that "we do not consider his

58. *Beit Yosef, Ḥoshen Mishpat* 2, in the name of *Responsa Rashba*.
59. Megilla 26a.
60. *Responsa Rambam* §271.
61. See Rema, *Ḥoshen Mishpat* 2: "The *tuvei ha'ir* do not have power in these cases; they can only force the community with respect to what... they accepted upon them unanimously. However, they have no authority to change anything that will bring profit to some and loss to others, or to confiscate money without unanimous consent. In all cases they follow the city's customs, certainly if they accepted them upon themselves for everything. This is what seems correct to me." See below, the chapter titled "The Authority of Rabbinical Courts and the Torah View of Punishment," pp. 126–27.
62. *Responsa Rambam* §270.

wisdom, only his pedigree and whether his appointment was with the consent of the local citizens."[63]

The criterion for choosing selectmen is their suitability to the administrative tasks incumbent upon them, whether internal or external. One who has the requisite skills is worthy of being appointed; if he has other virtues, so much the better.

Space does not permit us to discuss all of the detailed laws of municipal administration, as expressed in halakhic codes and responsa. We will content ourselves with a responsum of Maharam of Rothenburg,[64] codified by Rema in *Shulḥan Arukh*:

> [With regard to] all public needs concerning which they cannot achieve consent, they should convene all taxpaying homeowners and agree that each of them will express his opinion for the sake of heaven. Then they follow the majority. If a minority refuses, the majority can compel them, even by means of gentile courts, and spend money on this [need], and they will have to pay their share. One who refuses to express his opinion in accordance with the injunction, his opinion is not considered, and we follow the majority of those who express their opinion.[65]

This ruling codifies a very important principle that appears time and again in the responsa of the *Rishonim*: Even a majority is not decisive unless each and every person is given the right to participate in the decision-making process. Only then is it permitted to discount the voices of abstainers. However, if the minority is not given the right to express its positions, the validity of the majority decision is negated.[66] Nevertheless,

63. *Commentary on the Mishna*, Bekhorot 4:4. Above, n. 48, we cited *Responsa Rashba* 1:617. Due to the difference between an administrative function and Torah-based judgment and instruction, sometimes one who is fit for one role is not fit for the other, and vice versa, even though both are called "judges," as Rabbi Avraham, the son of Maimonides, explained in his commentary cited above in n. 56.
64. Cited in *Teshuvot Maimoniyot* to *Hilkhot Shekhenim* 6:27.
65. *Shulḥan Arukh, Ḥoshen Mishpat* 163:1
66. See, for instance, *Responsa Rashba* 5:126. A relatively recent expression of this principle appears in *Responsa Ḥatam Sofer, Ḥoshen Mishpat* 116.

it remains clear that in order to administrate public affairs, it is necessary to follow the majority, as Rosh writes:

> If the community agreed on something, an individual cannot protest; regarding this, the Torah said: "Incline after the majority." Otherwise, there is no way to improve society, for when will the entire community agree unanimously?[67]

Throughout history, even in undeveloped countries, Jewish communities managed their internal affairs in compliance with the laws codified in *Shulḥan Arukh*. Of course, minority groups of one sort or another occasionally emerged and tried to circumvent or abolish halakha, making it necessary to reemphasize the position of the halakha. Nevertheless, the fact remains that, in general, after turning to a well-known rabbi who was acceptable to the entire community, they would accept the halakha and act accordingly. Thus, even in the absence of sovereignty and state power, there was a system of control in that occasionally the ruling of a well-known rabbi helped ensure that the basic rights of all citizens were protected.[68]

As is well known, most large communities throughout history had two types of leadership. The community appointed a rabbi and judges who were greatly learned in Torah and possessed the "power of Torah scholarship." In addition, they appointed a local leader and a community council – the *tuvei ha'ir* – to oversee matters that required attention. They even had the power to appoint the rabbi and other religious functionaries, subject to the assent of the rest of the community.[69] Occasionally, the two forms of leadership were combined, but more often they were separate, just as the Sanhedrin and monarchy had been. The "*tuvei ha'ir*" generally dealt with ensuring the welfare of society within the limits imposed in the Diaspora, thereby continuing, on a small scale, the role of the king.

---

67. *Responsa Rosh* 6:7.
68. See, for example, *Responsa Rashba* 5:136, which was sent "to the community of Majorca" regarding taxation, and ibid. 179, "to Valencia."
69. See *Responsa Tzemaḥ Tzedek HaKadmon* §2.

Nevertheless, it must again be emphasized that the king's authority is limited to the realm of ensuring the welfare of society, and even within that realm, he must strive to avoid compulsion to the degree possible. Yet he has no jurisdiction over mitzvot between man and God – and the same applies to any regime that continues the role of the king.

Is There a Preferred Type of Government?

Do the Torah and halakha dictate a specific type of government?

At first glance, the answer to this question is affirmative, as the Torah explicitly states: "You shall place a king over yourselves" (Deut. 17:15). Although the Sages disagreed about whether this verse grants permission or dictates an obligation, Maimonides rules in accordance with the opinion that it is a mitzva, enumerating it as a positive commandment: "The commandment wherein we are commanded to appoint a Jewish king over us."[70] Several positive and negative mitzvot pertain to the appointment of the king,[71] and Maimonides devotes an entire section of *Mishneh Torah* to *Hilkhot Melakhim UMilḥemoteihem*, "The Laws of Kings and Their Wars."

The first mitzva that Maimonides lists in the heading of *Hilkhot Melakhim* is: "To appoint a king over Israel." However, Maimonides adds an explanation: "A king is not installed initially except by word of a court of seventy-one elders and a prophet."[72] He later adds a fundamental limitation:

> Once David was anointed, the royal crown was his, and the monarchy belongs to him and his deserving male progeny forever, as it is said: "Your throne will be established forever" (II Sam. 7:16). It only belongs to the deserving....[73]

70. *Sefer HaMitzvot*, positive commandment 173.
71. See negative commandments 362–65.
72. *Hilkhot Melakhim* 1:3.
73. Ibid. 7.

It is thus clear that, *ab initio*, it is unthinkable that a king would be appointed as long as we have no prophet, and as long as we do not know which families are descendants of David and Solomon.[74]

However, it is interesting that Maimonides writes about the possibility that the monarchy will be restored even before the advent of the *mashiaḥ*, and that such a king may come from different stock.[75] It would not be desirable to appoint such a king, and the Sages made several enactments to lower the stature of these kings "because they are arrogant, and the result will be injustice and harm to religion."[76] This halakha is not just history, as Maimonides does not generally record temporary enactments whose time has passed and which will never again be applicable.[77] The fact that Maimonides lists enactments that the Sages made with respect to non-Davidic Jewish kings demonstrates that it is possible that, in time, such kings will arise on their own among the Jews, in which case these enactments will apply to them.

In any case, it is clear that such a king should not be appointed *ab initio*, though if he takes power, it is necessary to reconcile with the resulting situation. This is, in fact, how the Sages dealt with the Hasmonean kings. Nahmanides' comments on the Hasmonean dynasty are well known:

---

74. See *Commentary on the Mishna*, Introduction to the Tenth Chapter of Sanhedrin (*Perek Ḥelek*), p. 145: "For there is no Jewish king except from David, and specifically from the progeny of Solomon"; likewise in *Epistle to Yemen* (ed. Cohen and trans. Halkin), p. xv.
75. *Hilkhot Melakhim* 1:9.
76. *Hilkhot Melakhim* 3:7; see also *Hilkhot Sanhedrin* 2:5 and *Hilkhot Edut* 11:9, where Maimonides likewise writes the laws pertaining to Israelite (non-Davidic) kings, "lest they lead to injustice."
77. The Talmud (Yoma 5b) wonders about the need to clarify laws that are no longer practicable: "Whatever happened, happened!" See a similar case in Ḥagiga 6b, where it is asked: "What is the practical ramification?" Rabbeinu Ḥananel explains: "What practical ramification is there for us? Whatever happened, happened!" (see *Tosafot* there, s.v. *mai*). Likewise, it is asked (Ketubbot 3a): "Before the enactments of Ezra, whatever happened, happened!" In light of all this, it is unthinkable that Maimonides would bother to cite the Sages' enactments against non-Davidic kings, in multiple instances, unless there is some practical ramification.

> This was also the reason for the punishment of the Hasmoneans, who reigned during the Second Temple. They were saints of the highest order, without whom the Torah and mitzvot would have been forgotten in Israel. Yet they suffered terrible punishment. The four sons of the pious elder Hasmonean, who reigned one after another, despite their might and success, were slain by their enemies. Then the ultimate punishment came.... They were all exterminated because of this sin...that the king was not of the progeny of Judah or the dynasty of David.[78]

While no king, not even a non-Davidic king, should be appointed *ab initio* except by a prophet[79] and a court of seventy-one, this does not mean that the return of prophecy is a *sine qua non* of the restoration of the monarchy. After all, there was no prophet during the Hasmonean era. It is thus evident that if the Sanhedrin appoints a king, or if a king rises with the support of the Sanhedrin and the people, he has monarchical status and has all of the powers of a Jewish king – including the power to put murderers and traitors to death. However, the assent of the Sanhedrin remains a necessary condition for the appointment of a king.[80]

Ralbag writes:

> This informs us that the anointment of a king should be at the [Gihon] spring, by a high priest, a prophet, or the Sanhedrin, for it is likely to be said of those whom they choose that they are the chosen of God.[81]

78. Commentary on Genesis 49:10.
79. See *Hilkhot Melakhim* 1:8.
80. *Hilkhot Sanhedrin* 5:1. However, see *Commentary on the Mishna*, Keritot 1:1: "If there was a conflict and a quarrel over which scion of David to appoint, whether A or B, and afterward there was unanimous agreement about one of them, or if he was followed by the majority, or if the Sanhedrin or a prophet or a high priest appointed him." However, it seems that Maimonides means that even when the Sanhedrin appoints a king, it might be with or without the express agreement of the people.
81. Commentary on I Kings 2, eighth *to'elet*.

He explained the reason for this:

> The king shall be appointed by the high court, for it is they who are inclusive of all Israel.[82]

However, without the consent of the Sanhedrin, the king's authority is not complete, and he consequently should not be viewed as a king, rather as a prince (*nasi*), a leader, or the like, and he does not have license to put people to death.[83]

Maimonides' position here is consistent with his view that it is possible to renew the original *semikha* and convene a Sanhedrin even today: "It seems to me that if all the sages in the Land of Israel agree to appoint judges and ordain them, they will be considered to have *semikha*, with the authority to impose punitive fines and to grant *semikha* to others."[84] Since a court of seventy-one can be reinstituted, it is also possible to appoint a king. Accordingly, Maimonides specifies the halakhot pertaining to such a king.[85] As a practical matter, however, we are very far from the reinstitution of the Sanhedrin.

Given that the restoration of a monarchical regime is neither practical nor desirable nowadays, we can ask: Does halakha recommend a different form of government?

This would be akin to someone saying that he is building himself the halakhic kitchen. Is there such a thing? There are clear rules governing what is permissible to eat and what is forbidden, based on the rulings of rabbis throughout history, but even so, halakha does not

82. Commentary on Deuteronomy 17:15.

83. My friend Rabbi Eli Reif notes that some *Rishonim* maintain that the power to judge capital cases is not exclusive to the monarchy, but also applies to any governmental authority that the public accepts and empowers to do so. See Meiri on Bava Kama 84b; *Responsa Rashba* 2:292; *Responsa Rivash* §251; *Responsa Maharik* §189; *Responsa Maharam Lublin* §138.

84. *Hilkhot Sanhedrin* 4:11. See my explanation in *Yad Peshuta* on Maimonides' introduction to *Mishneh Torah*, p. 34, s.v. *kol Yisrael*.

85. However, since the appointment of a king depends on the Sanhedrin, which also has the authority to deliberate and expound the Torah using the thirteen hermeneutic principles, as explained in *Hilkhot Mamrim*, it can also produce new rules that apply to the king.

dictate preference for any specific kitchen. Certainly there are halakhic concepts and principles that must be implemented in every kitchen, but halakha does not determine which recipes to use. No kosher kitchen will have pork or a mixture of milk and meat, but a kosher kitchen can be vegetarian, Chinese, Indian, dairy, meat, or even both as long as there is adequate separation. These would all be kitchens that conform to halakha, but there is no such thing as the halakhic kitchen.

The same applies to forms of government and governance. When it comes to the desired governmental structure – presidential or collegial, a unicameral or bicameral legislature, based on the British, French, or American model, or any other form of government – the Torah tells us nothing. The public may decide to elect a president for a ten-year term or a two-year term, a parliament with 20, 50, 120, or any other number of members, and empower them to govern the state.[86]

In any event, a leadership should be designated to address the needs of the state. It has already been explained that the appointment can be of a single head or *nasi*, and all who have accepted his authority are required to obey him. It is preferable, however, to establish a leadership council comprising several representatives. Rabbi Yitzḥak Abarbanel explained the matter at greater length; it is worthwhile to cite a summary of his remarks in praise of an assembly chosen for a fixed term:

> Reason suggests that the view of the majority should be followed against that of an individual, and that it is more likely that an individual person will sin ... than that many will sin when they come together as a group. For if one strays from the path, the others will correct him. And if their leadership is only temporary and they are destined to give an accounting of it after some time, the fear of man will be upon them.[87]

86. *Responsa Rambam* §271: "Know that when the Sages speak of 'seven selectmen' (Megilla 26a) – the number seven is not specific; it merely represents a large number...." See also ibid. §270 and above, p. 76, at n. 59.
87. Commentary on Deuteronomy 17:14.

Let us consider the fact that even though our sources include a general description of the institutions of the monarchy and the Sanhedrin, they contain almost no description of executive institutions. It is neither possible nor advisable to provide hard-and-fast guidance for all generations regarding the structuring of these public institutions. Public institutions must be adapted to the public of every time and place; they depend on the social, cultural, and temporal developments, and so there can be no fixed or permanent rules.[88] Each era must develop institutions that are suited to the public and accepted by them. If not, the results will likely be very problematic, whether because the institutions are not suited to their era or because they are not accepted by the public.

However, there are halakhic principles that obligate every Torah-based regime. Just as a kitchen that violates the laws of *kashrut* goes against the Torah, so too, a regime that deviates from what the Torah permits is invalid according to halakha.

Earlier,[89] we cited the principles and limitations of a Jewish monarchy. These principles apply to any regime that undertakes the functions of the monarchy. In addition, we must consider the halakhic basis for the Israeli system of government – the principle of partnership – and its manifold implications.

Citizenship as Partnership

For many centuries, halakhic jurisprudence was based on the idea that, with respect to anything pertaining to the structure of the community, the members of the community are akin to partners,[90] and all basic rights and obligations of all members of the community are equal.

This halakhic principle appears in the mishna (Bava Batra 1:5). In the midst of a discussion of the laws of partnerships, there is an abrupt shift, and the legal concept of partnership is broadened to include residents of a city: "They compel him to build the city a wall, gates, and bolt." In his commentary, Maimonides explains: "'They compel him' means that each and every person can compel his fellow in this regard."

88. See *Haamek Davar* on Deuteronomy 13:4.

89. See this chapter, section "The Authority of the King," p. 59.

90. *Responsa Maharam Schick, Ḥoshen Mishpat* 19.

This transition is so smooth and simple that the notion of a partnership among residents of a city seems to have been well known and self-evident. The Talmud develops the mishna's terse statement, and the basic principle that emerges from its discussion is that a city, like a legal entity, is conceived of as a partnership of its residents; they share the obligation to maintain the proper functioning of the city, and they share the privileges and benefits that the city provides. Who is counted as a city resident? The answer appears in that same mishna: "How long must he be in the city to be considered one of the townspeople? Twelve months, and if he bought a residence there, he is considered one of the townspeople immediately." It is clear that this amount of time is an example and can change, and that there can also be other considerations for determining who counts as one of the townspeople.

What is the source of this idea of partnership? Does it remain valid for an entire state, or only a single city? Does the principle apply at all times and under every regime, even when there is a king?

There are several entire sections of the halakhic corpus that are developed from allusions latent in a single word or even a single letter of the Torah. In spite of this, the Torah describes at great length how "all the soil of Egypt belonged to Pharaoh.... The land was Pharaoh's" (Gen. 47:20). This state of affairs was not peculiar to ancient Egypt; it remains in effect, in various incarnations, among all nations, to this very day. Sometimes the king himself is considered owner of all the land, in which case the residents are all his serfs and subjects: "I have on this day acquired you and your land for Pharaoh" (ibid. 23). Sometimes the kingdom is the owner of all its lands but grants certain rights to residents. However, even in today's most progressive states, this idea of national land ownership remains in force, with numerous legal ramifications.[91]

Do not think, however, that the Torah included this passage to teach us about gentile legal systems. The meaning of this passage

91. In British law, for example, the sovereign has the right to dispossess owners of any land, since, by law, the kingdom itself is primary owner of the land; this right is called "eminent domain." It is true that, over time, various limitations have been applied to this law, but in principle it remains in effect to this day.

becomes clear only when contrasted with the law that the Torah prescribes for Israel:

> You shall proclaim release throughout the land for all its inhabitants. It shall be a Jubilee for you: each of you shall return to his estate.... The land must not be sold beyond reclaim.... If your kinsman is in straits and has to sell part of his holding, his nearest redeemer shall come.... If he lacks sufficient means to recover it...in the Jubilee year it shall be released, and he shall return to his holding. (Lev. 25:10–28)

Lest one say that the king has a different status and, unlike the average buyer, can buy land forever – this is not the case! This was the precise reason that King Ahab of Israel was condemned. He wanted to acquire the vineyard of Naboth of Jezreel, but the latter said to the king: "Heaven forfend that I give the legacy of my ancestors to you" (I Kings 21:3).

Even during that morally inferior era, the social restraints and Torah-based limitations on monarchical authority were so strong that even the wicked King Ahab could not carry out his scheme to dispossess Naboth of his estate. Following the advice of his wife, Queen Jezebel, Ahab abominably arranged for false charges to be brought against Naboth, who was condemned to death in a show trial. The monarchy could then confiscate his vineyard. It was against this that the prophet Elijah thundered: "Thus said the Lord: Have you murdered and also inherited?" (I Kings 21:19).

The prophet emphasizes that in the future as well, "the prince shall not take property away from any of the people and rob them of their estates. Only out of his own estate shall he endow his sons, in order that My people may not be dispossessed of their estates" (Ezek. 46:18).

There are circumstances under which a king is permitted to take extraordinary measures: "He may encroach to build a road, and none may protest. The king's road has no fixed size; it all depends on what he needs. He does not divert roads because of this one's vineyard or that one's field; rather, he goes straight ahead to wage his military campaign."[92]

---

92. *Hilkhot Melakhim* 5:3.

It is clear from the conclusion – "to wage his military campaign" – that this law applies only in emergency situations, when the king is waging war or there is an urgent collective need. It also applies nowadays to any political leadership that has the same function as the king.

Medieval halakhists were well aware that the Jews settled in gentile territories at the favor of kings and did not have civil rights. They therefore distinguished between gentile kings and Jewish kings:

> Because the land is [the king's] and he can say to them: If you do not obey my commands, I will expel you from the land. But Jewish kings may not, because all of Israel are partners in the Land of Israel.[93]

In those days, Jews received permission to settle in gentile lands under specific conditions, and these conditions were binding on them. The difference between full citizenship and a mere residency permit is that a citizen is a partner in society, and his rights as a partner cannot be taken away from him.

The Land of Israel is the heritage of the entire nation. Every Jew is a partner in the Land of Israel, and this partnership cannot be revoked or abrogated. Every Jew has personal rights to the land, which cannot be taken from him or his descendants, forever. This concept became so entrenched that even when we were in exile, disconnected from our land, the *Geonim* ruled that every Jew has the actual legal right to four cubits of land in the Land of Israel; on this basis they ordained, for example, that a person can give money to an authorized agent by dint of ("*agav*") that land.[94]

It is worth noting that it also follows from this principle that even today, the authorities do not have power to forbid or prevent upstanding Jews from immigrating to the Land of Israel on account of health-related, social, or economic reasons. Such a law or directive is automatically null and void.

93. Ran on Nedarim 28a, s.v. *bemokhes ha'omed me'elav.*

94. *Hilkhot Shluḥin VeShutafin* 3:7; see also Nahmanides on Bava Batra 44b, s.v. *vetu.*

Thus, in contrast to the Egyptian practice, the powers and privileges of a Jewish king do not stem from his ownership of the land, as it is not his; rather, the king's rule is anchored in a covenant between him and the people, as we explained above, and as the prophet said:

> All the elders of Israel came to the king at Hebron, and King David made a pact with them in Hebron before the Lord. And they anointed David king over Israel. (II Sam. 5:3)

It thus emerges that even when Israel had a king, and even a king from the Davidic dynasty, the regime was based on the principle of the partnership of all citizens. Consequently, the laws of partnerships are valid as laws of the state. Though this is not the place to elaborate, a brief survey of *Hilkhot Melakhim* is sufficient to demonstrate this contention.[95]

The great innovation of the aforementioned mishna in Bava Batra is that even when there is no basis for treating the land as jointly owned, all the residents of a city are nevertheless considered partners, even outside of the Land of Israel, where the land does not belong to them.[96] By virtue of the very fact that they live there, they are each granted the status of a partner.

Furthermore, the same applies to the entire Jewish people. The mishna teaches: "What are 'objects that belong to those who ascended from Babylon'? For example, the Temple Mount, the Temple courtyards, and wells along the highway."[97] In his commentary on the mishna, Maimonides writes: "The notion of 'objects that belong to those who ascended from Babylon' refers to objects that are jointly owned by all

---

95. Compare to *Hilkhot Melakhim* 4:6: "[The king] confiscates fields, olives, and vineyards for his servants when they stage a war and spread out over these places, if they have nothing to eat but these; and they must pay their value." It is specifically at a time of war that the king has the right to repossess property, since the entire country is in danger. However, this right is only temporary, and he must remunerate the owner of the repossessed property even for property taken during war, as explained in *Hilkhot Melakhim* 4:5–7.
96. See, for example, *Responsa Rashba* 3:428.
97. Mishna Nedarim 5:4.

who make pilgrimages.... They are built with public funds, so everyone has ownership of them."

Having the status of a partner means that all other partners are responsible to him, and he, of course, is responsible to them. It follows that the majority cannot expel some of the residents without taking care of them, or in a manner that deprives them of their rights. On the other hand, an individual citizen or even a group of citizens who live in a city cannot dissociate from the partnership that the city comprises. Rather, they must share the burden with their peers. This principle was tested numerous times during the medieval era, when wealthy individuals managed to reach separate agreements with the authorities and did not wish to share in the tax paid by the rest of the Jews to the regime.

Maharam of Rothenburg was asked about such cases, and he marshaled several proofs from the Talmud in ruling:

> One who wishes to dwell among them can be compelled with regard to charity, even if he had never joined them before. Likewise, he can be compelled to share in the tax burden.[98]

His words in the following responsum are particularly fascinating:

> It is proper to be strict with regard to these matters even without proof from the Talmud, for if anyone can simply dissociate from another, it would often lead to a terrible breakdown. Must we explain the reasons for the separatists?[99]

This logic is so fundamental to the halakhic worldview that there is no need to marshal evidence for it. It is akin to that which the Talmud declares: "Why do I need a prooftext? It stands to reason!"[100]

---

98. *Responsa Maharam MiRothenburg* 3:10 (Cremona ed.).
99. Ibid. §222, cited in *Teshuvot Maimoniyot, Sefer Kinyan* (The Book of Acquisition) 29 and in *Shiltei Giborim* at the beginning of Bava Batra. The last line is a quote from Pesaḥim 70b.
100. Ketubbot 22a.

The principle of partnership, which limits the king's power, has an important ramification for the present era. There are still dangerous situations in which the monarchy or government is authorized to place lives at risk. Didn't our patriarch Jacob say: "If Esau comes and attacks one camp, the remaining camp will escape" (Gen. 32:9)? Sometimes, one part must be risked in order to save the rest. This, however, only applies when there is an immediate, existential threat and there is no recourse other than saving some while knowing that others will fall in battle. Such a strategy is permitted only when the dangers are clear to everyone and when the government is trusted completely, and everyone agrees with the government that this is the only correct path. And even in such a case, when there is certain danger and it is permitted to act in this way, it is necessary to carefully consider the damage that such a desperate move would entail. The benefits must outweigh the costs.

On the other hand, under circumstances that, in the assessment of experts, entail future risks, the considerations become more complicated. In any event, when there is no consensus of expert opinion regarding specific measures – some believe that the measures will alleviate the risk, while others believe that, on the contrary, they will heighten the risk – there must be broad support among the people for any step that is directed against a part of the population.

Likewise, even though the government technically has license to give up parts of the land and even to evacuate citizens from their homes, this does not apply when the measure will not lead to any benefit,[101] and if the potential benefit is a matter of dispute among experts, the broad agreement of the people is required before such a step can be undertaken. Therefore, in addition to security considerations, basic conditions for the evacuation of any settlement is both the agreement of the Knesset and a referendum. Barring that, uprooting innocent citizens from their homes is not permitted – not by the Torah, and not by basic morality.

There are several basic principles that Western democracies have adopted, which are embodied in the idea of partnership, and which the extreme left wing of Israeli politics has chosen to deny. It is a crooked

101. Space does not permit us to give this issue a full treatment; the present discussion merely outlines the basic principles.

line indeed that leads from the "holy cannon" that Jews pointed at fellow Jews during the early days of the state,[102] to use of the IDF to uproot settlements in Israel.

In every progressive state with a free and democratic regime, it is unthinkable for the government to use its military against its own citizens except in the most extreme cases. The use of the military against civilians is the most obvious indicator of a tyrannical regime. Democracies glory in the fact that the state and its military are there to protect all of their citizens.

We must not ignore the fact that an attack on the principle of partnership, with the goal of expanding governmental powers and enabling it to act capriciously against part of the nation, undermines the foundation of our freedom.

However, we must also remember that there is another side. According to the partnership principle, even when the government errs, as long as it is clear that its intentions and actions are not clearly immoral and illegal, then even when citizens protest, it is forbidden for them to protest violently. They certainly may not attack IDF soldiers, who are their brothers, and they certainly must not act against other innocent civilians who are not participating in the operation, even if it will serve as a deterrent. Harming soldiers is a severe transgression, since anyone who raises his hand to strike another is considered wicked. The same is true of harming the innocent. Such actions endanger our very existence as a nation, just as the sectarian zealots of the last days of the Second Temple caused its destruction. The consequences of such actions cannot be foreseen.

Democratic Government and the Establishment of the State of Israel

The legacy of two thousand years of self-government (even though it was not complete independence) is deeply embedded in Jewish culture. It would have been reasonable to suppose that, with the renewal of Jewish sovereignty, that legacy would have an influence. In fact, the

102. Editor's note: The term Ben-Gurion used referring to the weapon used to sink the *Altalena*.

signs of its influence are discernible in the development of Israeli society since its independence.

Since World War II, more than a hundred states have won independence. Nearly all of them began with democratic institutions, based on the institutions of the outgoing colonial regime. Israel is exceptional in that it built its democratic institutions on its own; Britain, the colonial power that ruled the Land of Israel before the establishment of the state, did not set up democratic institutions before it left, both because it was forced to leave and because it saw no reason to bother organizing a constitution for a Jewish state that it expected to be stillborn.

During the first decades of the State of Israel, the prophecies of pretentious experts about the rapid demise of Israeli democracy were common. Such predictions can still be heard today. In fact, from the perspective of a sociologist examining the realities of this country, this conclusion can appear quite logical. From the time of its birth, Israel has faced wars on all fronts. While the battles raged, hundreds of thousands of penniless immigrants inundated the young state, many coming from Arab countries whose systems of government were still feudal and autocratic. Some even still practiced slavery. How could democracy survive and even flourish under such harsh conditions?

According to the prevailing view, the idea of democracy originated in Greece. However, we cannot ignore the fact that Greek democracy was limited to a narrow stratum of the public. The free citizens constituted a minority that lived and flourished through the labor of slaves. Thus, for example, Aristotle defines the relationship between master and slave as follows: "He who is by nature not his own but another's man, is by nature a slave; and he may be said to be another's man who, being a slave, is also a possession. And a possession may be defined as an instrument of action, separable from the possessor.... It is clear, then, that some men are by nature free, and others slaves, and that for these latter slavery is both expedient and right."[103]

It is not necessary to explain how far Athenian doctrine is from the Torah, which emphasizes time and again that we were slaves in

---

103. Aristotle, *Politics* I:4–5 (Everson trans.), pp. 15–16.

Egypt and that our entire purpose is to be servants of God, not slaves to human beings.[104]

Maimonides describes the Israelite king that all must honor:

> Just as Scripture accords [the king] great honor and requires all to honor him, so it commands him to have a low and humble heart.... He shall be gracious and merciful to great and small alike; he shall conduct affairs according to their desires and benefit; he shall show compassion for the honor of even the smallest of them.... It also states: "If you will be a servant of this people today" (I Kings 12:7). He shall always act with excessive humility. We have no one greater than our teacher Moses, who said, "What are we?" (Ex. 16:8), and he suffered their burden, troubles, complaints, and anger, as a nursing father bears an infant.[105]

Even the king was expected to see himself as the servant of the people; certainly, then, other public officials must see themselves thus. Although the biblical model of government was monarchical, it derived its power from the covenant between king and people, so that individual rights were anchored in Torah law and halakhic tradition, as we have explained.

Democracy is delicate. It requires hundreds of years of sensitive cultivation and maturation. In lands where democratic values and principles are anchored in every level of culture, democracy is stable and secure. However, in nations where the democratic idea is a foreign implant, it withers and dies. In Israel, democracy is strong and vibrant. Preserving democracy in a nation that is renewing itself and whose population keeps multiplying as it absorbs more and more immigrants from undeveloped countries is a phenomenal achievement that must be explained. The explanation can be found in our history and our halakhic traditions of political administration.

The word "democracy" does not appear at all in halakhic literature until the modern era. But is it conceivable that a nation that returns

104. Regarding the Torah's attitudes toward slavery, see *Pathways to Their Hearts*, ch. 2, section "Slavery," p. 39.

105. *Hilkhot Melakhim* 2:6.

to its land with ancient traditions about self-government under foreign rule, and which treats each citizen as a partner in the community, would want anything less? There are some who try to create an impression that democracy and Judaism are incompatible. That is not the case! Their idea of democracy is that each person does whatever he wants – and this truly has nothing to do with Judaism.

The preferred democracy is the one that is derived from the Torah, the prophets, and the halakha as it has been applied throughout the generations. It empowers every element of the public to influence, as full partners in society, the actions of the government. It provides a structure that enables just, responsible, efficient, and effective government. The age-old tradition of communal governance in the exile, where community members had the status of partners, laid the groundwork for the acceptance and stability of the democracy that has been established in the State of Israel.

Chapter 6

The Structure of the State According to the Torah, Part II: Practical Applications

Proportional Representation and Direct Elections

The architects of the new State of Israel were primarily European Jews who were several generations removed from real experience with Jewish self-government. Some of them had even rebelled against tradition for various reasons. Even many Jews who remained Torah observant, especially those from Western lands, did not view the halakhot that pertain to state and governance as being of practical relevance under present conditions, but as halakhot reserved for the Messianic Era, which are studied without the intention of contemporary observance.

As a result, the modes of government in the nascent Jewish state were based on non-Jewish models, which were more familiar to its founders. Thus, we found ourselves chained to the proportional representation system, which has all but paralyzed the government. In contrast, over the course of many generations, most Jewish communities held direct, personal elections. This form of election expresses the trust that voters and their elected representatives have in one another, and in the view of halakha, this relationship of trust is necessary. Additionally, experience demonstrates that there are few successful democracies that use the proportional representation system. Nevertheless, the proportional representation system has become a fixed feature of our state.

The Sages found Scriptural support for the requirement of a direct connection between the public and its elected officials. When Moses set up an administrative apparatus to govern the Israelites, he acted, or so it seems, on the advice of Jethro, who recommended: "You shall also seek out from among all the people capable men.... Set these over them as leaders of thousands, leaders of hundreds, leaders of fifties, and leaders of tens" (Ex. 18:21). This is a clear, hierarchical, top-down plan, in which Moses was to personally appoint all of the officers.

However, the Torah informs us that things played out differently in practice. Moses turned to the people and said: "Get for you men who are wise, discerning, and familiar to your tribes, and I will appoint them as your heads" (Deut. 1:13). The Midrash explains:

> "Get" ("*havu*") – the word "*havu*" means nothing other than counsel.... "Familiar to your tribes" – they should be known to you. If he wraps himself in his tallit and comes to sit before me, I do not know which tribe he is from, but you know him, because you grew up among them. Therefore, it states: "Familiar to your tribes" – they should be known to you. R. Shimon b. Gamliel says: There is no panel that is seated before people about which they do not complain, saying, "Why is so-and-so seated? Why not so-and-so?" Therefore, it states: "Familiar to your tribes" – they should be known to you.[1]

Appointments do not require only public consent, but also, and primarily, the public's election of people they know. This will ensure that elected officials have a sense of responsibility toward those who elected them. Leadership must be allowed to develop among the people, and local leaders who prove themselves capable are those worthy of making the leap to the national arena. Additionally, only the smallest regions are

1. *Sifrei Devarim* 13. On the requirement of public assent, see above, pp. 73–79.

politically and socially monolithic, while larger regions are more diverse. Therefore, if Knesset members were elected as regional representatives, it would not pay for them to adopt extreme positions. Representatives would have to know how to meet the needs of most of their constituency, which usually contains a diversity of opinions and needs. In this way, elected officials would get used to considering the needs of the entire nation.

However, if all appointments, local and federal alike, are made by parties, there is no chance for real leadership to emerge. The reason is simple: under such conditions, party operators and activists mainly address the sector of the public that is identified with that party, whether out of ideology or because of the benefits it brings them, and the rest of the public is of no interest to them.

The words of R. Shimon b. Gamliel are an apt description of the present situation, wherein no one can explain why one individual was included in a party's Knesset faction while another was left out, whether a particular politician has the right qualifications to serve, and whether he has the relevant experience. In many cases, the public is not familiar with the members of the Knesset, only with the heads of the parties.

This guideline – "They should be known to you" – was implemented throughout history in the election of communal officials. Slowly but surely, we are beginning to recognize the damage that stems from the proportional representation system.

Although the direct elections model was suitable for relatively small communities, an attempt to implement it at the level of an entire state will create problems. For the most part, ordinary people do not know the candidates, and experience shows that candidates in a direct election require a great deal of campaign funding. By its very nature, this invites corruption and excludes everyone but the extremely wealthy or extremely well-connected from running for office. Some states divide their territory into relatively small regions, each of which elects a small number of representatives (often only one). However, in populous countries, even this solution does not eliminate the problem.

We must therefore think deeply to find a method that strikes the proper balance. In any event, as long as at least part of the Knesset is not chosen by direct election, the stability of the government will be tenuous. Instead of learning from the cumulative experience of centuries of communal life, we were deceived by the shiny exterior of a system that is not espoused by most true democracies and which is the legacy primarily of states that merely pay lip service to democratic principles.

It seems to me that if those who embrace the Torah were to speak up about this matter and bring the Torah's message to the public, they would find an attentive audience, even among those who were not previously attuned to the words of the Torah.

Central Government and Local Government

The concept of partnership, which does not necessarily depend on land ownership,[2] was not only the foundation of Jewish communal structure in the Diaspora, but also provided a basis and precedent for including non-Jews in those partnerships, albeit with restrictions. We learn in a *baraita*:

> A city that has gentiles and Jews appoints a gentile tax-collector and a Jewish tax-collector; they collect from the gentiles and from the Jews; they provide the needs of gentile paupers and Jewish paupers; they attend to sick gentiles and sick Jews; they bury the gentile dead and the Jewish dead.[3]

This states explicitly – and apparently this was practiced in mixed cities in the times of the Sages – that both Jewish and non-Jewish representatives are elected to the city administration, and they address the common needs of all the townspeople. By the same token, non-Jews may be included in governing a state.[4] In the case of officials elected by an entirely Jewish community, their authority extends to the construction of a synagogue and the like. However, in a mixed community, the partnership is limited to matters of social welfare.

2. See above, p. 88.
3. Y. Gittin 5:9.
4. On the status of non-Jewish residents and citizens of a Jewish state, see below, in the chapter "A Jewish and Democratic Society," p. 139.

Nevertheless, it is clear that a partnership at one level does not preclude the possibility of a more limited partnership at a different level. Thus, for example, even though all the residents of a city are partners with respect to municipal matters, craftsmen of a particular type may create a partnership with respect to their specific concerns.[5] The presence of one partnership does not prevent the existence of another partnership, whether it is broader or narrower. One person can be part of several partnerships at the same time.

Likewise, in a mixed city, some needs are limited to a particular segment of the public, and so there must be a balance between the responsibility of that segment of the public to undertake the funding of its own needs and the responsibility that devolves upon the municipal partnership.

The distribution of authority from the central government to local or regional bodies is very desirable, but if there is no delegation of responsibility alongside authority, then the authority is not real, and the result is merely the imposition of additional layers of stifling bureaucracy on the public.

It is of great importance that the elected leaders of a partnership at one level have no right or authority to intervene in the matters of partnerships on other levels. Rather, at each level of partnership, all of the partners at that level elect leaders and officers. To the extent that smaller groups regulate their own affairs, feelings of partnership and involvement are strengthened, and society itself becomes healthier. The concentration of power at the highest levels, far from the average citizen, causes alienation and disengagement.

The Sages had great esteem for what we call "team spirit" today – awareness of and pride in being part of a collective. These feelings are cultivated when every member of a group knows and identifies with every other member. The greater the share of each partner in the

5. Cf. *Shulḥan Arukh, Ḥoshen Mishpat* 231:28: "Craftsmen may inaugurate regulations with respect to their craft, agree among themselves that one will not work on the day of his fellow, etc.... Rema: Craftsmen may only establish regulations if there is agreement. However, [if only] two or three of them [agree to the regulation], it is ineffective [and is not binding on the others]."

administration of the group, the greater the solidarity of the group; conversely, the more the conduct of the group is directed by distant central authorities, the weaker each individual's sense of involvement becomes.

Surprisingly, this approach finds expression even with respect to mitzvot between man and God, for which it is possible to arrive at a single, unequivocal ruling that obligates everyone. The Talmud recounts:

> Our Rabbis taught: In the locale of R. Eliezer, they would chop down trees to make charcoal to forge iron [implements with which to circumcise] on Shabbat.... R. Yitzḥak said: There was one city in the Land of Israel that followed R. Eliezer, and they would die in their proper time. Moreover, on one occasion the evil kingdom decreed against circumcision, but they did not impose the decree on that city![6]

As long as the people of that locale identified with the Torah of their venerated rabbi, even though he was in dispute with the vast majority of Jewish Sages, those Sages saw no reason to divert them from their path and forcibly bring them into line with all other Jewish communities. On the contrary, the Sages heaped praise on them for their adherence to local tradition, even viewing it as the reason that they were spared from persecution.

It is in this context that various local customs and prayer rites developed, and as long as they do not cause damage broadly, all customs are acceptable: "Each river on its course."[7]

The Scope of the Knesset's Authority

It was clear from the very start that it would be impossible for the state to bridge major divides about basic questions among the people by means of a constitution. The matter of drafting a constitution was wisely brushed aside. If a longstanding democracy like the United Kingdom could manage without a constitution, why couldn't Israel? Nevertheless, the political ideology of those who shape public opinion exerts influence,

---

6. Shabbat 130a.
7. Ḥullin 18b.

consciously or unconsciously, over the governing of the state, especially given the absence of a constitution.

With the establishment of the state, the sharp differences of opinion within religious circles – specifically, between Zionists and opponents of Zionism – were temporarily quieted. It seems that the anti-Zionist religious leadership allowed itself to move on at the outset of independence, both because of its sense of guilt for opposing the *aliya* [immigration to Israel] of Eastern European Jews prior to the Holocaust and because of the desire to believe that the Gates of Mercy, which had been closed while six million Jews perished, were again opening.

However, both anti-Zionist and Zionist religious Jews, along with a significant segment of so-called secularists, pinned illusory messianic hopes on the Jewish state.[8] After two thousand years of powerlessness, the idea of independence carried a messianic charge. It always bothered religious Jews that the lion's share of the Zionist project was realized by secular Jews, a challenge that was intensified when it became clear that the positions of power in the fledgling state were held by Jews who had abandoned religion. Messianic thinking cultivated the belief that the state would magically return the Jewish people to its Torah, despite Maimonides' assertion, proven by historical experience, that only "the welfare of the body" is in the purview of the political order, while "the welfare of the soul" is a personal matter that cannot be realized as the goal of a partnership.[9] Almost everyone ignored the halakhic principles and historical experience which emphasize that these two realms, though overlapping, are separate, and that government pertains only to its own realm.

In the first elections after the Declaration of Independence, all segments of the religious community – Zionist and anti-Zionist alike – banded together in the hopes that their parliamentary power would help them advance "religious legislation," as though it was clear to all of them that when it came to moral and social issues there was no need and no place for the promotion of Torah values. Two centuries of

8. On the dangers of messianic ideology, see above, in the chapter titled "The Religious Significance of the State of Israel, Part I," pp. 16 ff.
9. See above, p. 59.

emancipation had imbued both observant and non-observant Jews with the idea that religion is limited to matters of ritual and worship. This was a twofold problem: on the one hand, it created a sense that religion can be expressed only in the realm of worship and has no political or social message, but on the other hand, it gave the impression that the state can influence the degree to which its citizens uphold ritual observance. It is also possible that there was a prevailing naïve belief that on matters of morality and interpersonal obligations, there was no real difference between religious and secular Jews, since Jewish moral values were ostensibly accepted by all. Therefore, no religious legislation purported to advance the Torah's social and economic views on justice and equality. Rather, it was primarily directed toward the ritual and ceremonial aspects of halakha, by means of which its proponents aimed to influence the Jewish character of the state.

This also seems to have reawakened some old disputes. The *ḥaredi* parties gave up on the state and its institutions and worked to isolate their constituents from the rest of the population, as they had done under foreign rule. Thus, their primary focus was to obtain benefits and address the specific needs of their constituents while forgoing involvement in the secular aspects of statecraft. Religious Zionism, on the other hand, continued its efforts to sanctify the state. Even among secularists, many accepted the view that the state must involve itself in all realms and that its authority is unlimited – extending even to matters between man and God.

This hidden assumption, that the Knesset has the authority to take a position on religious matters, is what sparked disagreement, time and again, over the question, "Who is a Jew?" Though it would have been fitting for halakhists to protest vehemently that any fundamentally halakhic issue lies beyond the authority of the Knesset, it seems that, aside from pragmatic considerations, it was utopian thinking that caused the failure of both religious Zionists and religious anti-Zionists to imagine a Jewish lawmaking body that does not combine the authorities of both the monarchy and the Sanhedrin. This was despite the experience of Jewish communal life, in which the two forms of leadership, rabbinic and lay, almost always exercised authority in separate (albeit sometimes overlapping) realms, and despite explicit discussions in halakhic literature of the practical and halakhic reasons for the separation of religious authority from the communal administrative authorities.

As we have explained,[10] townspeople are defined as partners already in the mishna. The idea of partnership is the basis of halakha's social and political doctrine, as it does not necessarily pertain to the residents of a single city, but also to any group of people who join together to meet their common needs. Thus, the laws of partnerships can be applied to various professional guilds with limited areas of activity, to a community, a city, and even to an entire modern state.

It is self-evident that as the population grows and the differences in lifestyle among citizens become wider and deeper, the common denominator shrinks and the scope of common needs that can be met collectively becomes increasingly narrower.

With respect to the provision of religious needs, it seems that some issues are outside the authority of the general partnership, and therefore require the creation of sub-partnerships of citizens of the same religion to provide their needs, similar to today's religious councils, with the exception that the council members should be elected by the synagogue-going public. If there is general agreement, then the overarching partnership – that is, the state – may fully or partially fund the operations of the sub-partnerships that address the needs of society's subgroups. However, if there is no such agreement, the funding for religious needs might not be within the purview of the state's authority.

The laws of partnerships are binding not only with respect to the promotion of goals shared by the entire public; they also protect the vital special interests of minorities from being harmed by the majority or by another minority.

In a partnership, no partner or group of partners has the right to impinge upon the rights of another partner. With regard to matters that apply jointly to the entire public, majority opinion prevails, on condition that the minority was given the opportunity to express itself and attempt to persuade others. However, with regard to a minority's vital needs, the majority has no authority to prevent it from pursuing its own interests, or, needless to say, to impose obligations on it that run counter

10. See above, p. 85.

to its beliefs. The supreme leadership is tasked with keeping minorities from harming one another, and nothing more.

The idea of partnership also implies the balancing principle of restricting government authority to the specific powers granted to it. The Torah grants the government the authority to address the public's specifically material needs – defense, economic policy, social welfare, and the like, which, by their very nature, are shared by the entire public – while insisting on the principles of morality and justice. Partnership is, in its essence, a social concept; in the words of the Sages, it is "between man and his fellow." It was created in order to promote the defense and socioeconomic well-being of the entire society.

Since, according to the Torah, the government draws its authority from the consent of all partners, it is self-evident that it does not have the power to legislate against the Torah; if no partner has the right to do so as an individual, then no group of individuals can grant this right to its representatives. In truth, though, the government has no authority to legislate about religious matters at all, even if the legislation complies with the Torah, as this right is reserved for Torah scholars.

Authority over religious matters is not placed in the hands of any partnership. Even in Jewish communities whose members all accepted the values and commandments of the Torah,[11] halakhic decisions were not assigned to elected representatives or even the majority decision of a council of the entire community. The spiritual plane was never included in the jurisdiction of the partnership, and it goes without saying that the partners never even considered creating substitutes for the Torah and mitzvot.

There was always a clear distinction between the authority of the general leadership, which dealt with the material realm, and that of Torah scholars, which dealt with the religious realm, even though, in actuality, their spheres of activity occasionally intersected and even overlapped, since the two realms cannot be completely separated. Rabbis were elected by the public, but their authority stemmed primarily from their Torah. The public election simply affirmed that the community accepted their authority. On the other hand, with respect to the

11. See above, pp. 78–79.

community leaders, it was precisely their election by the community that gave them power and authority – authority that was recognized by the Torah and halakha.

The general picture that emerges is of a vast partnership that includes the entire public and is governed by an umbrella administration, under which there are all sorts of smaller partnerships, composed of subgroups, which operate in more limited spheres.

The scope of the state's executive power is determined by the greatest common denominator of the needs of the entire population. Any deviation from these parameters undermines the basis of the partnership. It is also clear that the religious sphere lies completely beyond these dimensions.

A Constitutional Court

Who supervises the government and its various branches to ensure that they do not exceed their authority? Who decides cases of disputed authority between different branches of government? These questions are central to the proper functioning of a state.

The prevalent approach (though some disputed it[12]) was that when such problems arose in Diaspora communities, they were under the rabbis' jurisdiction. It was their job to supervise the actions of the communal leaders and ensure that they did not exceed their authority. Communal enactments required the approval of the community rabbi, who was responsible to oversee the functioning of communal institutions and certify that they operate properly and lawfully.[13]

12. See *Responsa Rivash* §399. *Responsa Ḥatam Sofer, Ḥoshen Mishpat* 117 implies agreement. However, see *Pitḥei Teshuva, Ḥoshen Mishpat* 236:6.
13. See Bava Batra 9a. Maimonides defines the communal role of the rabbi as follows (*Hilkhot Mekhira* 14:11): "…a distinguished sage to order the affairs of the polity and foster prosperity among its inhabitants." See *Ḥoshen Mishpat* 231:28, and see above, p. 77, n. 66.

This is essentially the role of a constitutional court, albeit with one major difference. In the context of the traditional community, the Torah's standards were accepted by all, and the values on which Torah scholars acted were agreed upon by the entire community.

This is not the case in today's State of Israel. Just as the scope of the state's executive authority is limited to shared needs, so, too, the values that guide the body responsible to oversee the government must be shared. Any attempt to deviate from consensual values is immoral and could endanger the public peace. A constitutional court can operate only if it has gained the full trust of the public; otherwise, everything breaks down. If the court itself becomes the representative of one of the subgroups attempting to impose its opinions and values, then the entire regime is in danger of collapsing.

Take, for example, the issue of *kashrut* (kosher certification). Only rabbis are authorized to issue rulings on the laws of *kashrut*, and their authority stems from their knowledge of Torah, not from having been appointed by the government. Any attempt by the Supreme Court to intervene and establish procedures for determining *kashrut* is completely invalid. Only rabbis who are accepted by the community have the authority to determine who can be trusted halakhically and who cannot. A non-rabbinical court that intrudes and interferes in this realm acts in a totally unacceptable manner, and its ruling has no validity.

The same applies to all areas that are subject to the authority of the rabbinical courts. This is true even if the Supreme Court purports to act in accordance with halakhic criteria, and certainly when its verdicts are based on non-halakhic standards.

Although the Supreme Court has a role to play in supervising the proper protocol for governing the relationship between the rabbinical courts and other authorities, such as the secular courts, the proper protocol must itself be accepted by all parties.

We must wake up before it is too late and ascertain the foundations of the social contract on which the State of Israel is based. We must work to create the right tools for oversight, and perhaps there should be a special constitutional body, in which all segments of the population are represented, so that the whole public views it as a faithful guardian of its rights.

Jewish Sovereignty

Over the course of many generations, the Jews developed the characteristics of minority populations. Circumstances compelled our constant vigilance against whichever enemies were lurking. Our relationships with non-Jews were always accompanied by extreme caution and even fear; this was what the survival instinct demanded. Our cultural identity developed within the walls of the ghetto, and in the best case, behind social barriers, which were also impregnable, to a large degree, from the outside in. Because we adapted to our minority status, we were able to endure the exile.

Our suffering as a minority was mitigated somewhat due to our faith in the God of Israel and His covenant with us. We drew our self-assuredness and our will to keep struggling for survival from this faith. Thus the Jew maintained his dignity and restraint, even when he was degraded and humiliated by those surrounding him.

As Jews, whose most notable feature from time immemorial has been the lack of mastery over our own fate, we cannot accept our newfound power as a foregone conclusion. As the eternal victims of violence, aggression, and exploitation, which reached their pinnacle with the "Final Solution," we cannot get used to the use of force, even to impose justice. As individuals and as a people, we are not yet accustomed to thinking and feeling, behaving and reacting, like a nation in control of its land and its fate.

Our lack of natural self-reliance is signified in many ways. Due to our lack of self-confidence in our ability to rule with the power we now have, we are occasionally too quick to relinquish the stature we deserve due to our status as a majority; we behave as though we were still a minority that must fight for justice and beg for mercy.

This can be illustrated with a small but typical example. The Arabs never viewed Jerusalem as a matter of great importance. Moreover, long before the establishment of the State of Israel – almost two hundred years before, in fact – the Jewish community was the largest of the communities in Jerusalem's Old City. During the nineteen years of Arab rule over the Old City (1948–1967), they did nothing there except destroy any vestige of Jewish presence, while the parts of the city under Israeli rule flourished.

With the Israeli victory in the Six Day War, the Temple Mount came under Jewish control. To the surprise of the Muslim Waqf, they were given full administrative control of the Temple Mount,[14] subject to the demand that the rights of all visitors of every religion would be protected – every religion but Judaism, that is.

In fact, Jewish prayer is forbidden by the Waqf. Any Jew – and there have been many already – who is caught with a prayer book or book of Psalms on the Temple Mount can expect to be expelled aggressively from the site by the Waqf's guards. Jews who have the audacity to call out "*Shema Yisrael*" will be met with violence. No wonder the *muezzin* of the Al-Aqsa Mosque on the Temple Mount can broadcast incitement that encourages "believers" to protest and riot.

How did such an intolerable situation come about? How have we allowed it to endure? Our military power has unfortunately made many of us prideful and arrogant, but we still have not acquired the simple, healthy national pride that most free nations feel.

We must also clarify our religious position vis-à-vis the Temple Mount.

As a matter of strict law, there is no prohibition against ascending the Temple Mount, and Maimonides himself wrote that he ascended.[15] However, over time, there were *posekim* who ruled stringently, and others were concerned that encouraging people to ascend the mount would cause Jews to ascend without first undergoing ritual purification. However, we see that in reality it is specifically those Jews who are not concerned about ritual purification who ascend the mount freely. The sweeping religious ban published by rabbis of the past generation in particular resulted in terrible indignity, legitimized the prevention of Jews from ascending the mount, and harmed Jewish sovereignty over it. The window of opportunity opened by the Six Day War is now closed, and today we certainly must act with political caution and wisdom, but we

14. Editor's note: For Rabbi Shlomo Goren's (then the Chief Rabbi of the IDF) description of these events, see Rabbi Shlomo Goren, *With Might and Strength: An Autobiography*, ed. Ari Rath (Jerusalem: Maggid Books, 2016), pp. 346 ff.
15. See Maimonides' note that appears in *Iggerot HaRambam*, pp. 224–25, and see Rabbi Yitzhak Shilat's note on p. 226 ad loc.

must find ways to allow more Jews to ascend the Mount and to allow Jewish prayers there. We trust that God will open another window of opportunity for us.

Indeed, there are halakhic difficulties with permitting mass Jewish ascent of the Temple Mount, due to the requirement of *mora mikdash* (treating the Temple with reverence). However, it is doubtlessly possible to make arrangements for individuals who wish to visit specific areas on the mount. We must educate people about the proper way to visit the mount. On the one hand, Maimonides explains that the laws of ritual purity and impurity were intended, *inter alia,* to foster a sense of "seldom set foot in your neighbor's house" (Prov. 25:17), that is, that we should not enter holy places on a constant basis. Moreover, when we visit the site of God's Temple, we must behave, as Maimonides writes, "with trepidation and awe and fear and trembling, as it is said: 'In God's house we walked, aquiver' (Ps. 55:15)".[16] On the other hand, we must not neglect the holiest of places or refrain from ascending to it. We certainly should not stop ourselves from ascending out of concern that other nations will oppose it.

Deepening our common roots in the past and identification with our common destiny will empower and inspire us, will strengthen the connection of each of us with the rest of the nation, and will reinforce our faith in the justness of our national path through history.

Practical Conclusions

We will briefly suggest the ramifications and conclusions for the present that emerge from our discussion of ruling authorities:[17]

A. The political leadership, which functions like the ancient monarchy and like the selectmen of later periods, must be elected by the people, which grants it limited authority. Clearly, the Knesset and government should be viewed as the ruling authorities, but, in my opinion, due to the requirement of being "publicly

16. *Hilkhot Beit HaBeḥira* 7:5.
17. These conclusions are a summary of both parts of "The Structure of the State According to the Torah."

appointed,"[18] it is necessary for at least some Knesset members to be elected personally; that is, each region's residents directly elect their representatives.

B. There must be a separation between the political authorities – the Knesset and government – and Torah authority. This does not imply American-style separation of church and state, but a separation of the jurisdictions of the two authorities, so that the Torah authority has a constitutionally recognized status. The authority of the Knesset will likewise be limited to specific spheres, as explained below.

C. The Knesset and government must deal only with matters of social welfare, the ordering of affairs among citizens, defense, and diplomacy. The Knesset's authority to legislate is recognized by Torah law as well, but must be done only within the parameters of public consensus. In every sphere, consensus based on dialogue is preferable to legislation and coercion.

D. Centralization of government power and top-down administration is undesirable; the government must deal only with matters of interest to the entire nation, while municipal authorities will address local problems.

E. All matters pertaining to Torah, mitzvot, and halakhic rulings that govern the relationship between man and God are subject to the exclusive jurisdiction of the Torah authority. The Knesset shall have no authority to make laws with respect to such matters.

F. The Knesset has no authority to make laws that replace the commandments of the Torah, except with respect to monetary matters. Even in such cases, the laws must adhere to universally accepted principles of justice. However, the Knesset has the authority to legislate criminal law, just as the king had such authority.

G. It is forbidden for the government to compel a citizen to violate Torah law.

H. It is forbidden for the government to infringe upon the basic civil rights defined by the Torah. Therefore, the government has no authority to issue a command to uproot communities or

18. See above, p. 74 and n. 53, as well as pp. 96–98.

dispossess and expel residents from their homes, whether the residents are Jews or Arabs, unless it serves a clear and present defensive need or a future defensive need about which there is a general public consensus.[19]

I. Coercive power is necessary for maintaining proper social order, but this power is granted to the government only with public consent, and it should be wielded as seldom as possible. If there is a need for far-reaching changes, or for coercive measures, such as the uprooting of settlements, God forbid, or the relinquishing of territory in the Land of Israel, then a referendum must be conducted in order to obtain public consent. The law that the majority is tantamount to the entirety is well established.[20]

The principles listed above are inadequate for precisely determining the system of government, but they indicate a direction and can help shape it and ground it on principles of justice and morality.

19. See above, pp. 89–90.
20. Horayot 3b. See Maimonides' *Hilkhot Mamrim* 2:5 and *Ḥiddushei HaRitva* on Avoda Zara 36a: "There is no difference between all of Israel and most of Israel, for the majority is tantamount to the entirety."

Chapter 7

The Authority of Rabbinical Courts and the Torah View of Punishment

Compromise or Justice?

The Torah's instructions "Justice, justice you shall pursue" (Deut. 16:20) and "You shall remove the evil from your midst" (21:21) are two sides of the same coin.

Maimonides began his *Sefer Shofetim* (Book of Judges) with the laws of courts, calling them "The Laws of the Sanhedrin and the Punishments They May Impose." At the beginning of these laws, he defined in brief the mitzva to appoint magistrates (*shofetim*) and marshals (*shoterim*):

> It is a positive commandment of the Torah to appoint magistrates and marshals in each and every locale.... Magistrates are the judges who are empaneled on the court, before whom litigants come. Marshals are armed with rod and strap. They stand before the judges [to enforce their judgments]; they circulate in markets and stores, correcting standards and measures and striking all those who perpetrate injustice. All their actions are at the direction of the judges. And anyone who is observed to have

> transgressed is brought before the court, where he is condemned in accordance with his guilt.[1]

In *Hilkhot Sanhedrin,* Maimonides enumerates no fewer than thirty mitzvot, apart from the mitzvot listed elsewhere in *Sefer Shofetim.* The issue of law enforcement is a central and weighty one throughout *Mishneh Torah,* which reflects its importance to the Sages.

Nevertheless, there is a tannaitic dispute whether judges must rigorously decide the disputes that come before them according to the letter of the law, or whether it is preferable to pursue compromise:

> R. Eliezer b. R. Yose the Galilean says: It is forbidden to arrange a compromise [in a dispute], and one who arranges a compromise (*botze'a*) is a sinner. And one who praises the one who arranges a compromise is a blasphemer. About him it is said: "The covetous (*habotze'a*) blesses himself, though he despises the Lord" (Ps. 10:3). Rather, let the law pierce through the mountain, as it is said: "For judgment is God's."
>
> R. Yehoshua b. Korḥa says: It is a mitzva to arrange a compromise, as it is said: "Truth, judgment, and peace shall you adjudicate at your gates" (Zech. 8:16). Surely where there is judgment there is no peace, and where there is peace there is no judgment! Rather, what kind of judgment incorporates peace? A compromise. Likewise, it is said about David: "David rendered judgment and charity for all his people" (II Sam. 8:15). Surely where there is judgment there is no charity, and where there is charity there is no judgment! Rather, what kind of judgment incorporates charity? A settlement.[2]

The halakha was decided in accordance with R. Yehoshua b. Korḥa:

> It is a mitzva to say to the litigants at the outset: "Do you want the law, or do you want to compromise?".... Any court that

1. *Hilkhot Sanhedrin* 1:1.
2. Sanhedrin 6b.

> consistently arbitrates compromises is praiseworthy. It is said about it, "Truth, judgment, and peace shall you adjudicate at your gates." What kind of judgment incorporates peace? A settlement. Likewise, it is said about David: "David rendered judgment and charity for all his people." What kind of judgment incorporates charity? A settlement, that is, a compromise. When does this apply? Before a verdict is rendered; even if [the court] has heard both sides and knows which way the law inclines, it is a mitzva to settle. But once a verdict has been rendered, and it has been pronounced, "X, you are liable; Y you are free of liability," it is no longer permitted to arbitrate a compromise. Rather, let justice pierce the mountain.[3]

In the clash between two exalted values – truth and justice on the one hand; peace and charity on the other – which is to be preferred? R. Eliezer b. R. Yose the Galilean views the commandment to render lawful judgment as absolute; let justice pierce the mountain. But in R. Yehoshua b. Korḥa's view, the mitzva of the judges to adjudicate between their brethren is not an end in itself but serves a higher end: restoring peace to disputants. After all, all the ways of the Torah are peace! Arbitrating compromise and settlement between litigants is not enumerated among the Torah's 613 mitzvot, yet doing so rises above and beyond the mitzvot and laws that suggest a verdict one way or the other. Accordingly, if a judge perceives the possibility of reaching a compromise, he must do so, even at the last minute, thereby leaving both litigants pleased[4] and

---

3. *Hilkhot Sanhedrin* 22:4. Likewise, *Tur, Ḥoshen Mishpat* §12 states: "It is a mitzva to initially offer them a compromise," and see *Beit Yosef* ad loc. Maimonides also wrote in the introduction to his *Commentary on the Mishna* (p. 48): "He should follow the path of compromise in most of his cases. If a judge is able to never render verdicts and always reach a compromise between the litigants, it is even better. But if he cannot make a compromise, he should render a verdict."
4. See *Mekhilta DeRabbi Yishmael, Yitro, Mesekhta DeAmalek* 2 (p. 196 in the Horowitz-Rabin edition): "'I will adjudicate between a man' refers to judgment that does not include compromise; 'and his friend' refers to judgment that includes compromise, wherein [the litigants] depart from one another as friends."

avoiding the need to compel them to accept a ruling. Even though the court has authority to compel, it is preferable for it not to use that power.

Penal Policy

The fact that the overarching goal of law is to improve society, and the principle of a justice that promotes peace, influence the theory of punishment as well.

The punishments that may be imposed by a court are many and varied. The Torah sentences various offenders to fines and corporal punishment, and even decrees capital punishment for a substantial number of offenses. Each of the four types of capital punishment entails a positive commandment: "The command we were given to kill those who transgress certain commandments."[5] However, we also learn in a mishna:

> A Sanhedrin that killed once in seven years is called "destructive." R. Elazar b. Azarya says: Once in seventy years. R. Tarfon and R. Akiva say: "Had we been on the Sanhedrin, no one would ever have been put to death." R. Shimon b. Gamliel says: "They would have caused the proliferation of shedders of blood in Israel."[6]

The Gemara[7] expresses puzzlement that R. Tarfon and R. Akiva sought to prevent capital punishment in all circumstances. To be sure, numerous conditions must be met before the accused can be put to death. For example, there must be two qualified witnesses who testify that they admonished the accused and that he, with a clear mind, acknowledged the admonition, subjecting himself to capital punishment, and committed murder in full view of the witnesses. Preconditions such as these certainly mean that few will be sentenced to death, and it is understandable that capital punishment would become a very rare phenomenon, occurring only once in seven or even once in seventy years (such numbers indicate a long period of time and are not meant literally).

5. *Sefer HaMitzvot*, positive commandments 226–29.
6. Mishna Makkot 1:11.
7. Makkot 7a.

But how can anyone guarantee that no one would ever be executed by the Sanhedrin? R. Yoḥanan and R. Elazar explained what R. Tarfon and R. Akiva meant: based on the power that the Torah grants to judges, it is possible to eliminate capital punishment. The Torah requires that the witnesses be thoroughly cross-examined. There are certain questions that must be asked, but other questions, though they need not be asked, will still disqualify the testimony if, once asked, the witnesses do not know the answers. For example, the judges may ask the witness to a murder: "Did you see whether he killed a *tereifa* or one who was intact?"[8] R. Ashi takes this further, stating: Perhaps the victim had a previous wound in the exact spot where the sword of the killer pierced him. It is highly unlikely that the witnesses had previously examined the victim at exactly that spot, and the information cannot be ascertained through postmortem examination, and therefore the killer would not be put to death.

It is thus clear that beyond all the detailed laws governing the court's operation, and in addition to all of the mitzvot that are incumbent upon the judges in their deliberations, there remains room for "penal policy."

The purpose of punishment is to deter others from committing the same offense in the future. When it is no longer effective as a deterrent, and one commits an offense, then the justice system must gravitate toward the opposite extreme: refraining from the application of the most severe punishment – execution – even to the most wicked offenders. We have two opposing tendencies here. On the one hand, we deter offenders with threats of severe punishment, but on the other hand, we refrain from imposing severe punishment, for if the courts were to put offenders to death frequently, the entire society would deteriorate, God forbid, to the level of murderers.

This is the basis of R. Shimon b. Gamliel's dispute with R. Tarfon and R. Akiva. They maintained that it is preferable to avoid capital punishment entirely, while he was concerned that without the deterrent effect of capital punishment – even if seldom imposed – bloodshed

8. If the victim had been a *tereifa*, a person suffering from certain fatal preconditions, the killer would not be subject to the death penalty.

would proliferate. Accordingly, capital punishment should not be ruled out totally, and its deterrent effect must be taken into account, even though extensive deliberation must be undertaken before putting someone to death, and great care must be taken to avoid hasty executions.

There are two ways to understand the view of R. Tarfon and R. Akiva. They may have believed that humanity had already improved to the point of no longer needing a deterrent, and that all past incidents were exceptional, unlikely to recur. Alternatively, they were convinced that, in their generation, capital punishment no longer served as an effective deterrent, in which case there would be no point to court-ordered bloodshed. Indeed, it might have the opposite of its intended effect: if people came to view these harsh sentences as acts of violence, no different than the excesses of any other cruel regime, not only would the imposition of the death penalty fail to cause them to improve their ways, but they would, God forbid, develop contempt for the Torah and its bearers. Since there is no obligation to impose a death sentence, and it is always possible to circumvent it technically, it is preferable to avoid it entirely.

Rabbeinu Ḥananel adopts the latter interpretation in a similar context. The Gemara states: "Forty years before the destruction of the Temple, the Sanhedrin went into exile and convened in a shop... so they did not judge capital cases. Why? When they saw the proliferation of murderers and that they could not judge them, they said, 'Better that we exile ourselves from place to place so that we do not condemn them...for the place [in the Temple] is determinative [of our power to put offenders to death].'"[9] Rabbeinu Ḥananel comments on this: "For when they saw that people took bloodshed lightly and thus murderers proliferated, they said: 'Let us arise and exile ourselves from this place.'" Capital cases could be tried anywhere only as long as the Sanhedrin convened in the Chamber of Hewn Stone in the Temple. Once the sages of the Sanhedrin ascertained that their sentences no longer deterred murderers, they left the Chamber of Hewn Stone and thus relinquished their authority to judge capital cases.

But this should not be seen as an act of desperation. The Yerushalmi recounts: "It was taught: Forty years before the destruction

9. Avoda Zara 8b.

of the Temple, capital cases were eliminated, and in the days of Shimon b. Shetaḥ [some texts have: Shimon b. Yoḥai], monetary cases were eliminated. R. Shimon b. Yoḥai said: 'Praised be the Merciful One that I am unable to judge!'"[10] Why would R. Shimon b. Yoḥai utter praise and thanksgiving over the fact that the court's authority to adjudicate in accordance with Torah law was abolished? Even if there is good reason to refrain from adjudicating capital cases, in accordance with the view of R. Tarfon and R. Akiva, why refrain from adjudicating monetary cases? The *Rishonim*[11] explained, based on the context in the Yerushalmi, that R. Shimon b. Yoḥai was referring to the preference of compromise over strict justice and giving thanks for the fact that the court no longer had the power to coerce litigants to accept their judgment. As a result, judges had to work out compromises that would be acceptable to both litigants, thus sparing the judges from the guilt associated with misapplication of true Torah law. And even though the letter of Torah law was not carried out, the Torah's greater goal – a peaceful judgment – was attained. What we have here, then, is not the annulment of the mitzva to adjudicate, but the elevation of the judicial process to a higher level.

This was explained nicely by one of the greatest Torah scholars of recent generations, Rabbi Yosef Eliyahu Henkin, in his treatment of the Sages' division of world history into three epochs:[12] the age of chaos, the age of Torah, and the age of the Messiah. The Sages further stated that the Messiah was born on the day that the Temple was destroyed[13] – meaning that the age of the Messiah began already then. How is this to be understood? Rabbi Henkin explains:

> It is the Messiah's task to instill a spirit of understanding and fear of God and to discipline verbally, without a need for corporal punishment (see Is. 11:4). That the Messianic Era began at the

10. Y. Sanhedrin 1:1, and compare to ibid. 7:2. See also *Perisha* on *Tur, Ḥoshen Mishpat* 12:6.
11. *Sefer Mitzvot Gadol* (*Semag*), positive commandment 107; see the explanation of Rabbi R. Stein ad loc. This opinion of *Semag* is cited in *Tur, Ḥoshen Mishpat* §12, and see *Bayit Ḥadash* n. 6 ad loc.
12. Avoda Zara 9a.
13. Y. Berakhot 2:4.

> destruction of the Temple... means that Israel began to accept the rule of the Torah without bow or sword. The abolition of capital punishment that resulted from the Sanhedrin's exile to a shop, and the abolition of monetary penalties that resulted from the abolition of *semikha* (the conferral of juridical authority), may have been brought about by God, may He be blessed, as preparation for the Messianic Era. They were then charged with eliminating the impulse to shed blood, just as the impulse to serve idols has been eliminated from their hearts.[14]

This notion is consistent with Rabbeinu Ḥananel's above-cited explanation, namely, that so many people took bloodshed lightly and were not deterred by the prospect of punishment. The abolition of capital punishment itself diminishes the prevalence of violence within society and has an educational value that influences broad segments of the public. Thus, when they abolished capital punishment, they were making a statement of protest about the severity of shedding blood – even that of a murderer. In the long arc of history, raising the nation's overall moral level can reduce depravity even on society's fringes.

Punishment as a Temporary Necessity

The tendency to avoid strict law enforcement, for all its benefits, is fraught with risk, especially in the interpersonal realm. Weak responses by judges and governing authorities can bring disaster upon society. Isn't the basic obligation of those responsible for justice to protect the poor from their oppressors? How can that be done without any coercive force? Indeed, the prophet laments and admonishes his contemporaries:

> Alas, she has become a harlot, the faithful city that was filled with justice, where righteousness dwelt – but now murderers. Your silver has turned to dross; your wine is mixed with water. Your rulers are rebellious and companions of thieves, every one loves bribes and chases rewards; they do not judge the case of the orphan, and the widow's cause never reaches them. Therefore,

14. Rabbi Y. E. Henkin, "*Ketz HaYamin*," *HaDarom* 10 (1959), p. 6.

> says the Master, the Lord of Hosts, the Mighty One of Israel: "Oh, I will be relieved of My foes; I will wreak vengeance on My enemies!" (Is. 1:21–24)

This problem, of course, exists even when the court possesses and exercises its full authority. The Torah severely limits the imposition of punishment, subjecting it to many preconditions that constrain the judges. A court cannot issue a punitive sentence without witnesses and without the accused having been forewarned. Witnesses and cross-examination are technically required even in cases of monetary law. The laws of evidence are extensive and complex. On a practical level, a process that comports fully with the halakha in all its details has only a slim chance of resulting in the accused being convicted or found liable. There is considerable tension between, on the one hand, the halakha's demand that we fulfill the requirement of "the community shall rescue" (Num. 25:25) the accused, and, on the other hand, the goal "to break the hand of wickedness" (Ps. 10:15). It seems that the latter goal is at a disadvantage. In one of his responsa, Rashba depicts this situation and its ramifications:

> For if you base everything on the laws articulated by the Torah, meting out no punishment but for those that the Torah prescribes, for battery and the like, the world would be destroyed, for everything would require witnesses and forewarning. This is as the Sages said: "Jerusalem was destroyed only because they based all their judgments on the judgments of the Torah."[15] This applies all the more so outside of the Land of Israel, where monetary penalties are not imposed. We would find that reckless people would breach all the world's boundaries, rendering the world desolate.... In each and every place, courts do sometimes render judgments in order to repair the breaches of the generation.... [The Sages] stated that the reason [for these judgments] is not to violate the words of the Torah, but rather to safeguard

15. Bava Metzia 30b.

the Torah....[16] They do so in every generation and every locale

---

16. Yevamot 90b: "R. Elazar b. Yaakov said: I heard that the courts may impose corporal punishment and other penalties not specified by [Torah] law – not to violate the words of the Torah, but to safeguard the Torah." R. Elazar is relating to two different categories: corporal punishment and other penalties.

However, Maimonides does not cite this *baraita* anywhere. He likewise omits the dictum from Ḥullin 110b: "All positive mitzvot whose rewards are specified are in the purview of human courts to enforce." For this reason, Rabbi Isser Zalman Melzer writes in *Even HaEzel* (*Hilkhot Keriat Shema* 2:13, section 6) that Maimonides indeed maintains that the courts do not compel observance of most positive commandments.

However, *Maggid Mishneh* is in disagreement. Maimonides rules with respect to obligatory positive mitzvot (*Hilkhot Issurei Bia* 1:8): "If the court flogged them on account of rebelliousness (*makkot mardut*) to keep them away from transgression, they have the power to do so." *Maggid Mishneh* (ad loc.) cites a *baraita* from Ketubbot 86a–b: "They clearly stated vis-à-vis positive commandments, such as [one who said] 'I will not build a sukka, I will not take a lulav,' that they flog him until his soul departs."

In my humble opinion, Maimonides states his opinion explicitly and with elegant rationale in *Hilkhot Sanhedrin* 24:8: "Likewise, a judge should censure those who ought to be censured, curse, and flog them...to stop them from acting, or because they did not act, as it is said: 'And I censured, cursed, and flogged them' (Neh. 13:25)." Maimonides adds the words "to stop them from acting, or because they did not act" to the talmudic source (Moed Katan 16a), thus including both prevention of the commission of an offense ("to stop them from acting") and coercion to perform a positive mitzva ("because they did not act"). This is akin to *Hilkhot Matnot Aniyim* 7:10: "One who does not want to give charity...is compelled by the court and flogged until he gives what he has been assessed to give." It is clear that this all falls under the category of "repairing a breach" ("*migdar milta*"), for which the court has been granted the authority to "create safeguards and reinforcements as it sees fit" (*Hilkhot Sanhedrin* 24:4).

Regarding positive mitzvot whose reward is specified, Maimonides ruled on one who humiliates his parents (*Hilkhot Mamrim* 5:15): "The court can flog him with *makkot mardut* and penalize him as they see fit." This accords with the view of R. Ḥisda (Ḥullin 110b). In my *Yad Peshuta* to *Hilkhot Issurei Bia* 12:4 and 15:3 I explained that the court does not compel the observance of a positive commandment unless, it its view, it serves some general public utility, not just to make sure that this person fulfills the mitzvot that are incumbent on him individually. Coercion is intended to prevent a rebellion against the Torah and to promote society's welfare.

See Meiri's *Beit HaBeḥira* ad loc., which cites Y. Bava Batra 5:5: "They explained this statement, that it is not in the purview of human courts to enforce, to mean

> when they find that circumstances demand it to discipline fools and immature people who act perversely in their crookedness.[17]

We have here a type of vicious cycle and a seeming paradox. How can the judges' authority to administer punishments to meet the needs of the moment exceed the authority granted them by the Torah to adjudicate in accordance with its written commandments and laws? And what good is it to abolish enforcement of adjudication and punishment in accordance with Torah law only for it to be replaced with enforcement of rulings issued "to repair the breaches of the generation"?

Three distinctions, all stemming from a single principle, can be drawn between laws of the Torah and the court's extralegal authority to administer punishment even beyond Torah law. The application of means beyond Torah law must: (1) be temporary; (2) have obvious utility; and (3) be accepted by the community.

Temporary

Maimonides writes:

> The court is authorized to flog one who is not liable to be flogged and to execute one who is not liable to be put to death – not in order to violate the words of the Torah, but to safeguard the Torah. When the court sees that the people have become unrestrained in some matter, it shall create safeguards and reinforcements as it sees fit; all as temporary measures, not that it should be established as law for all generations.[18]

that they are not penalized for it." However, the courts may still do as they see fit, as Maimonides ruled (cf. *Me'irat Einayim, Ḥoshen Mishpat* 117:2 and *Shakh* 1 ad loc.).

It emerges from all of this that all of the various forms of coercion available to a court that are not specified by the Torah are for the purposes of ensuring the welfare of society.

17. *Responsa Rashba* 3:393, likewise cited in *Beit Yosef, Ḥoshen Mishpat* §2. The view of *Maggid Mishneh* is also evident from Maimonides' *Hilkhot Malveh VeLoveh* 11:8.
18. *Hilkhot Sanhedrin* 24:4, also cited in *Tur, Ḥoshen Mishpat* §2.

Only temporary measures can be accepted as proper responses to exigencies. It is absolutely forbidden to permanently deviate from the laws of the Torah.

Obvious Utility

Maimonides writes: "Not in order to violate the words of the Torah, but to safeguard the Torah." Only if it is evident to all[19] that the court's action promotes justice and curbs wickedness does it effectively safeguard the Torah. But if the broader public forms the impression that the court acted with unjustified or capricious violence, the court will not have safeguarded the Torah; instead, it will have promoted disdain for the entire system of justice and will have encouraged others to violate the Torah's laws.

Communal Acceptance

We must distinguish between the Sanhedrin, which had full authority in matters of Torah law, and all rabbinic courts that followed the abolition of the Sanhedrin. The punitive authority of the Sanhedrin in order to address the concerns of the day, even beyond what is specified in Torah law, is far broader than that of other courts, due to its broad authority to interpret and legislate. *Sifrei* states:

> R. Eliezer said to them: "Didn't Shimon b. Shetaḥ put eighty women to death by hanging in Ashkelon?" They said to him… "It was necessary at that time, to teach others."[20]

19. See Rabbi Zvi Hirsch Chajes, *Torat HaNevi'im,* ch. 5 ("*Horaat Shaa*"; in *Kol Sifrei Maharatz Chajes,* p. 32):

    I saw in *Tosafot,* Yevamot 90b…the gist of their explanation is that certainly when the general benefit that will result from this uprooting [of Torah law] is apparent to all, in that situation, even a sage may uproot…for by means of the severe punishment that they will mete out to evildoers, other people will be cowed and afraid; they will hear and be scared, and they will no longer be lax about prohibition. However, if the great utility is not obvious to all, then even if the sage concludes that this uprooting is necessary, nevertheless, if the utility is not seen clearly, we do not uproot a Torah commandment.

20. *Sifrei Devarim* 221.

However, even the Sanhedrin, whose authority is derived from earlier generations, all the way back to Moses, still needs communal consent to their appointment.

> And the Lord spoke to Moses, saying: "See I have called by name Betzalel..." (Ex. 31:1–2). R. Yitzḥak said: We do not appoint a leader over the public without first consulting the public, as it is stated: "See, the Lord has called by name Betzalel" (ibid. 35:30). The Holy One, blessed be He, said to Moses: Do you consider Betzalel suitable? He replied: Master of the Universe, if You think him suitable, surely I do also! Said [God] to him: All the same, go and tell them. He went and asked Israel: Do you consider Betzalel suitable? They replied: If the Holy One, blessed be He, and you consider him suitable, surely we do![21]

We find that Moses said something similar to Israel, telling them to appoint judges "familiar to your tribes" (Deut. 1:13), about which the Sages commented:

> "Familiar to your tribes" – they should be known to you. If he wraps himself in his tallit and comes to sit before me, I do not know which tribe he is from [and if he is suitable], but you know him, because you grew up among them. Therefore, it states: "Familiar to your tribes" – they should be known to you.[22]

The same idea emerges from the terms and procedures for appointing judges, as Maimonides summarizes:

> The Sages said that the high court would send messengers throughout the Land of Israel. Whoever they found to be wise, afraid of sin, humble... and agreeable to people would be appointed as a judge in his city....[23]

---

21. Berakhot 55a.
22. *Sifrei Devarim* 13.
23. *Hilkhot Sanhedrin* 2:8.

Agreeable to people – that is, the townspeople favor his appointment, and he is acceptable to them.[24]

It is also worth citing the words of Rabbi Yitzḥak Abarbanel:

> Israel was commanded to appoint judges.... It was our teacher Moses who commanded Israel to appoint judges, as it says: "Get for you men who are wise, discerning..." (Deut. 1:13).... When it comes to the appointment of judges, there are kingdoms where this is done directly by the king, for he is the one who commands that in a particular city, A and B shall be judges this year, and so forth for all other cities. Since the king is the head of the judicial system, it is he who controls all of the organs under him – that is, the judges. This is the law and the practice throughout the kingdom of Castille....
>
> There are also lands in which the appointment of judges is given to the people of the land. Each year, they appoint judges and officers whom they deem most fair, and the king has no say. This is the custom in some territories in Spain, in France, and throughout the West.
>
> The master of all prophets explained that it is not proper that the judges of Israel be appointed directly by the king. Rather, the people should appoint them. That is, each tribe shall appoint the appropriate judges in each of their cities. It is said regarding this: "That the Lord your God has given you for your tribes" (Deut. 16:18). That is, the Lord your God has given the appointment of judges over to the tribes, that it is they who should appoint them in their cities, and not the king.[25]

---

24. See also *Hilkhot Sanhedrin* 3:10: "It was the manner of the early Sages to flee from appointments and take pains not to sit in judgment unless they understood that no one was as worthy as them, and that justice would be corrupted if they persisted in their refusal. Even so, they would not sit in judgment unless the people and the elders pressed and urged them." When the public favors them to this extent, there is a likelihood that their rulings will be accepted. However, if a judge tries to impose his opinion on recalcitrant litigants, and he has no broad public support, it will cause quarrels, disputes, and a loss of trust in him.
25. Abarbanel on Deuteronomy 16:18.

In contrast to the Sanhedrin, which had general authority, including the authority to impose punishments necessary for the times, the authority of later courts was more limited. Not only was public consent required for their appointment, but the scope of their authority also required public consent.

Tur states: "Specifically the greatest sage of the generation… appointed judge by the *nasi*, or by the publicly appointed selectmen, but not regular judges."[26]

The source of the law cited in *Tur* is from its author's father, Rosh.[27] It indeed seems from the words of Rosh that the "greatest sage of the generation" can be appointed only by the *nasi*,[28] but historically,[29] public consent was also required for the appointment of judges.[30] However, no specific or fixed procedures were established for obtaining public consent; various methods – a communal assembly or the appointment of representatives, for example – were used, but the requisite principle was that without public consent, there is no authority.

Rema, in his glosses, notes that there are those who disagree and limit the power of selectmen even though they were chosen by the townspeople as their representatives:

> The selectmen only have power to compel the public with respect to longstanding practice or things that are accepted with unanimous consent. However, they are not empowered to change anything that benefits one at the expense of the other or to confiscate funds without unanimous consent. In any event, we follow the

26. *Tur, Ḥoshen Mishpat* §2. See also *Shulḥan Arukh, Ḥoshen Mishpat* 2:1.
27. Bava Kamma 9:5.
28. See *Derisha* to *Tur* ad loc.
29. See *Yam Shel Shlomo*, Bava Kama 9:7 (I thank Rabbi Eli Reif for bringing this source to my attention).
30. Editor's note: For a broad survey of this issue, see Simha Assaf, *Batei Din VeSidreihem Aḥarei Ḥatimat HaTalmud* (Courts and Their Procedures in the Post-Talmudic Era) (Jerusalem: Defus HaPoalim, 1924); on the power of communal consent, see *Responsa Tashbetz* 1:159.

> local custom, certainly if the community accepted the leadership's authority on all matters.[31]

All concur, then, that community representatives and judges have no power or authority unless the community has empowered them. According to one view, even then, these officials may not introduce any innovation, even for the pressing needs of the day. According to this view, new enactments, duties, and levies require unanimous consent; a mere majority will not suffice. Clearly, this requirement is difficult to implement, and certainly in the large social framework of a state, though if the community explicitly consented from the outset to grant broader authority to its appointed officials, their consent would grant the officials broader authority.

There appears to be a difficulty. On the one hand, the authority to do what is necessary for the times is derived from the Torah, which authorizes "the court in each place and at all times to impose corporal punishment...."[32] On the other hand, the power of the judges is effective only if they are accepted by the public – "the public appointed them." If the Torah is the source of the authority, why must the community appoint or recognize them? The Torah commanded the court to enforce its judgments and authorized it to do so! And if they do not have this power according to the Torah, what good is communal acceptance?

To be sure, the public can grant judges power over their possessions, for each person can renounce ownership of his property, and so he can also grant the court the right to confiscate his property. But how can they grant such authority over their persons, empowering the court to impose lashes or imprisonment? A person's body is not his to renounce, and one may not wound oneself,[33] much less permit others to do so!

In fact, the source of the court's authority is the Torah; without authority sourced in the Torah, the court would be powerless to impose

31. *Shulḥan Arukh, Ḥoshen Mishpat* 2:1; see *Sefer Me'irat Einayim* 13 ad loc.
32. *Hilkhot Sanhedrin* 24:5. Cf. *Responsa Rashba* cited above, pp. 120–22. See the broader discussion of this issue in my book *Hadar Itamar* (Jerusalem: Daat Torah, 1972), pp. 171–73.
33. See *Hilkhot Ḥovel UMazik* 5:1.

corporal punishments and other penalties. That was true even when courts comprised those who had received the original *semikha*, tracing back to Moses, and so it is certainly true today, when that *semikha* is gone. However, in the cases under discussion, the practical benefit of the measures imposed by the court must be clear to all. If a judge were, on his own accord, to exercise the power vested in him by the Torah to impose punishments and issue rulings on the basis of novel, unusual criteria that exceed standard Torah law, his actions would be regarded by the community as violent and capricious – even if his intentions were for the sake of Heaven, and even if he sincerely meant only to act for the welfare of society as he perceived it. In such a case, the decision, rather than firmly reestablishing the rule of justice, would merely provoke the populace into asking: Who appointed you as a judge and gave you the authority to act so forcefully? But if the community has elected its officials, recognized their authority, and even specified exactly what powers they have been granted, then even if they impose rulings that are not based on Torah law, the public will treat them with proper respect and understand that they are acting for the common good and meeting the needs of the day. In that way, the benefit of the court's actions will be apparent to all, and society will be protected. It was in such circumstances – and only in such circumstances – that the Torah granted them this authority.

The consent of the community must be expressly granted to specific individuals whose authority they recognize. It is clear that if the entire community, or even a majority of it, or its elected representatives, expressly vote on specific procedures, even if they grant a court authority to forcefully impose them, their utility will be clear to all. In such cases, the Torah, too, affirms such procedures.

It thus turns out that the authority of Torah leadership stems from both the Torah and the community.

Summary

There is constant tension between aspiring to the Torah's social ideal of undisturbed peace and tranquility, and recognizing reality, which sometimes requires us to fight against dangerous acts perpetrated by lawless and unjust individuals. Even if the majority of the people is suffused with a love of truth and peace, exercising power to curb criminal tendencies at the margins of society is unavoidable. The key to resolving this tension is to anchor coercive power in the will of the people. Those whom the majority has appointed are empowered to use coercive measures, and this power does not detract from the principles to which we aspire.

This problem existed even when the Temple stood, the Sanhedrin met in the Chamber of Hewn Stone, and courts constituted by sages with the original *semikha* convened in every district and city. This is actually the main reason for the Sages' instruction to favor compromise over strict application of the law, as we have explained.

In this context, faced with social transformations, there will likely be additional changes whose purpose is to preserve the balance between institutional authority and the authority granted it by the people – for instance, the creation of ways to oversee the operations of the rabbinical courts, similar to what already exists for the general courts, an ombudsman for complaints about judges, or the like. There is definitely room for a body of this sort to oversee the rabbinical courts. Of course, we must carefully consider how to build such bodies and how to limit their authority in order to create the proper balance, in accordance with Torah values.

To be sure, the rifts and divisions within the people make it impossible to establish rabbinical courts for the broader public at this time. However, if the community that is committed to Torah were to establish courts that displayed a thoroughgoing understanding of the major changes that have taken hold in contemporary society – in commerce, industry, international law, etc. – and develop a legal system that could address these major changes, and if they won the acceptance and trust of the public, there is no doubt that the ever-increasing pressure on the secular courts would intensify the movement, which has already begun, toward rabbinical courts. People will flock toward these rabbinical courts specifically because they will prefer compromise to strict application of the law.

We have seen that Torah authority today has no power whatsoever to apply coercive measures without the consent of a public which recognizes its authority and grants it this power, and even then, only in cases where damage is being caused to others, as in cases of family disputes, divorce, child support, etc. In every case, it is best for the rabbinical court to try to limit its application of coercive authority to the degree possible.

Chapter 8

A Jewish and Democratic Society

Introduction

The idea of creating a "new nation"[1] in the Land of Israel has attended Zionism from its very beginning. Jews longing to leave the ghetto were attracted to revolutionary movements and turned their backs on their ancestral faith. Groups committed to revolutionary ideologies joined the Zionist movement, with the hope of applying Marxist doctrine to the entirely new society taking shape; some of these revolutionaries held key positions in the New Yishuv. These trends underwent various iterations through the years and manifested in more or less extreme forms, but the basic core – disassociation from the historical Jewish community and Jewish beliefs – never completely disappeared.

The stream that led the pre-state Jewish community in the Land of Israel became the newly independent state's governing establishment.

1. Editor's note: This idea is linked to the idea of the "New Jew." See, for example, Anita Shapira, *Yehudim Ḥadashim, Yehudim Yeshanim* (New Jews, Old Jews) (Tel Aviv: Am Oved, 1997), pp. 155 ff.; Yitzḥak Conforti, "'The New Jew' in the Zionist Movement: Ideology and Historiography," *Australian Journal of Jewish Studies* 25 (2011), pp. 87–118; and in the various essays in volume 16 of the journal *Yisrael* (Hebrew).

Although there were those who opposed mass *aliya* for various reasons,[2] concern for the entire Jewish people and the future of the state prevailed, and the State of Israel absorbed large waves of immigrants. Entire communities were uprooted; their members immigrated and found themselves alienated and confused in a difficult and occasionally unfriendly environment. At the beginning, there were times when government institutions exploited the weakness of the immigrants to force them to adapt themselves to the secularist "melting pot." However, it did not take long for tensions to arise and for culture wars to erupt. These have not completely abated, but it seems that cooler heads have been prevailing.

Today, thank God, it seems that the majority of the Jewish people in Israel, even those who do not meticulously observe the mitzvot, have internalized the basic values of Jewish identity and share an affinity for national and religious symbols. Most of the Jewish public in Israel feels connected to its religious historical legacy.

There have been debates and polemics over the years, but it seems that we still have not held an orderly, sober, thoroughgoing, exhaustive discussion about the basic questions of the identity and character of the state, and for two main reasons: the frequent wars that the state has fought since the moment of its inception, and the prolonged process of the ingathering of the exiles, which changes the complexion and makeup of the population and prevents calm and deliberate crystallization of opinions. These conditions do not seem likely to change in the near future. The attacks on us have not ceased, and most of the exiles have yet to be ingathered. Nevertheless, we cannot postpone deliberation on these core questions indefinitely.

Democratic Values

In order to achieve practical agreement and cooperation between different segments of society, it is necessary to create opportunities for real dialogue between groups. This sort of dialogue will make it possible to

---

2. For documentation of the stormy debates about this issue, see Moshe Lissak, *HaAliya HaGedola BiShnot HaḤamishim: Kishlono Shel Kor HaHitukh* (Mass Immigration in the Fifties: The Failure of the Melting Pot Policy) (Jerusalem: Bialik Institute 1999). See, for example, pp. 64–65.

overcome the ever-deepening rifts and ever-widening chasms between the various groups. However, real dialogue is impossible if we do not understand the foundations of the thought processes of others and, more importantly, if we do not understand the foundations of our own thinking.

Sometimes, two people can use the same words and even agree on their lexical definitions, and yet they still engage in a dialogue of the deaf, in which each side uses the very same words to mean diametrically opposed concepts. This is because no concept exists independently, isolated from its historical, cultural, and social contexts. When parties to a debate do not have common principles, their dialogue cannot lead to agreement.

We can exemplify this with a discussion of values that have always been important to us, but which in recent generations have been emphasized and highlighted by the wider world, which views them as part of the modern democratic cultural tradition, as expressed in the motto of the French Revolution, "*Liberté, égalité, fraternité*" (liberty, equality, fraternity), and in the idea of human rights. Debate and disagreement about these values underlie a significant portion of the tensions within Israeli society.

Liberty

Our era is characterized, among other things, by the fact that most human beings view liberty as being more important than all other human needs. This is a positive development, as only one who cherishes the freedom of choice is able to use it for sublime spiritual purposes.

Maimonides writes with respect to the freedom of choice:

> Every person is given power over himself.... This is a major principle, the pillar of the Torah and the commandments, as it is stated: "See, I set before you this day life and goodness, death and evil" (Deut. 30:15)...that is, the power is in your hands. Whatever a person desires to do among human activities, he can do, whether they are good or evil...for the Creator does not compel human beings.... Rather, their hearts are their own.... It is [God's] wish that man has power over himself and discretion

> over all his actions. Nothing shall compel him or draw him in; rather, he, of his own volition, using the mind that God gave him, can do whatever he is humanly capable of doing.... Regarding this, Solomon said: "Rejoice, O youngster, in your youth...but know well that God will call you to account for all of these things" (Eccl. 11:9). That is, know that you have to power to act, but that you will eventually be called to account.[3]

The idea of free choice precedes the thirteen principles of faith. All of the other principles form the structure of the Torah's worldview, but the principle of free choice is the pillar upon which the entire magnificent building of the Torah and commandments stands. The Divine image is the power of choice imbued within man. The deeper and broader the scope of one's choice, the more one perfects the Divine image within. At first glance this is an early iteration of the motto of the French enlightenment: "*L'homme est né libre*"; "Man is born free."[4]

Yet there is a difference between these concepts and ideas. The Torah indeed places freedom at the center of its worldview, but it is paired with responsibility. A believer knows that the Creator wants man to act freely, without any power compelling him, but this gift to man – the freedom of choice – requires him to make an accounting of his choices to his Creator. Man is not freed of his duties toward God and his duties toward man simply because that is what he would like.

This is true not only on the personal plane, but on the public plane as well. In their fervent hope that the entire nation was progressing toward the sublime level at which they would serve God out of love and not fear, the Sages viewed limits on the application of coercive power as a step forward that prepared the whole world for willingly accepting God's kingship. To that end, they voluntarily relinquished the authority to enforce mitzvot and Torah law.[5] So too, society itself must minimize its use of coercive measures except in cases where the offender is causing

---

3. *Hilkhot Teshuva* 5:1–4, 7.
4. These are the opening lines of Jean-Jacques Rousseau's *The Social Contract.*
5. See above, the chapter titled "The Authority of Rabbinical Courts and the Torah View of Punishment," p. 117.

harm to others. On the other hand, it is necessary to educate people to assume responsibility. Privileges should certainly not be granted to one who chooses to deny or avoid his duties.

However, if man is nothing but the product of circumstance, then the fact that he has the power to choose is mere accident, and his liberty and freedom to choose have no goal or purpose beyond what each person determines for himself. It follows that he has absolute power to choose the goals that he sees fit. Man has no moral obligation beyond what he is willing to accept upon himself from his own volition. One who believes that man was – accidentally! – born with an inclination to do only good can take comfort in the hope that free people will usually choose good. But one who is aware that man also possesses a tendency toward wickedness and does not always instinctually choose goodness will understand that the idea of absolute free choice is essentially a license for anarchy. Moreover, in a world of unlimited freedom, anarchy can only be curbed by the violence of rivals in the struggle for survival, for they, too, have absolute freedom to pursue their own agendas. Consequently, there are religious worldviews – radical Islam, for example – that completely deny freedom, and there are worldviews like Communism that demand absolute freedom but descend into absolute dictatorship.

More broadly, this raises a fatefully problematic question for liberal society, which sees its purpose as providing to each individual the opportunity to pursue his personal benefit and realize his aspirations in achieving whatever goals he has set for himself. When there is no agreed-upon definition of what is good for everyone, then each individual has his own perception of what is "good." If everyone is entitled to achieve his own personal good, then to what extent can society intervene to limit the desires of one in favor of another? And to what extent is society responsible to provide each person with the means to attain the good he desires?

There are times when the rights of one individual, and certainly, then, the rights of a group of citizens, make demands of society in general. Of course, society has no resources of its own; it has only what it collects from the populace at large. In other words, sometimes granting the rights of one entails imposing obligations on others. This opens the door to friction and struggle between various groups within society, each of which demands entitlements at the expense of other groups.

Thus, for example, there are minority groups that seek recognition of their right to express their unique culture. While some states, like Switzerland, are structured as multinational states and recognize the unique expression of each of its constituent peoples, most progressive states are monocultural, at least foundationally. The United States, for example, is not willing to fund schools whose language of instruction is not English,[6] except in exceptional cases for new immigrants, and even then only in order to facilitate their rapid acquisition of English. Furthermore, state-funded schools may not be affiliated with any religious institution. The government does not prevent the establishment of various types of private schools, but it does not fund them, despite the fact that every citizen pays taxes toward educational needs, and it is on condition that the curriculum meets minimal standards in several subjects, to ensure that pupils are able to integrate into the broader society. The minority that chooses private education thus faces twofold discrimination: on the one hand, it pays taxes for educational services that are of no benefit to it, because it abstains from them, and on the other hand it builds and maintains an entire educational system at its own expense, without government assistance. In other words, according to the ostensibly self-evident will of the majority, the state views the agenda to preserve the English language as one that is incumbent on all of its subjects. Recently, in the wake of a large wave of Spanish-speaking immigrants, there is agitation from certain quarters to anchor the predominance of the English language in the Constitution.

Other countries, such as England, permit certain religious groups to administrate state-funded schools for their constituents. On the other hand, France has long prohibited the study of the languages of longstanding minorities in its school system, so as to hasten the integration of those minorities in the nation and its culture. Recently, it even passed a law preventing the excessive penetration of English terminology in the

6. Editor's note: See, however, Paul Ramsey, *Bilingual Public Schooling in the United States: A History of America's "Polyglot Boardinghouse"* (New York: Palgrave Macmillan, 2010).

media and the public sphere. Other states use other models to regulate the relationship between the society's basic values and educational freedom, but there is no modern democratic state that promotes full pluralism. The reason is simple: language and culture are central features of national identity in the modern state, and no social organism is willing to give up its identity.

This is not the case in contemporary Israeli society, though. Not only is the educational system divided by religion – there are Muslim and Christian schools as well as Jewish schools – but the primary language of instruction in non-Jewish schools is not Hebrew. We are fleeing from the idea that our culture is the regnant culture in Israel. This is all the more astounding in light of the fact that Israel is successfully combining Western scientific and technological development with Judaism's deep moral sensitivity. It is by virtue of this combination that our culture can exert a powerful gravitational pull. It would be better for us and for the minorities who live in our country if they would acclimate themselves to Israeli-Jewish culture. Of course, Jewish culture should not be forced on them, but if they only had the opportunity, presumably a significant segment of the minority population would choose to identify with us.

Such a development would clearly entail some risk, especially from a religious perspective. Only those with self-confidence and a profound sense of identity would be willing to take this calculated risk.

Equality

The mishna teaches about the value of equality:

> For this reason, man was created alone: to teach that anyone who destroys one Jewish life is considered as though he destroyed an entire world, and whoever sustains one Jewish life is considered as though he sustained an entire world; and for the sake of peace among men, so that no one can say to his fellow, "My father is greater than your father."[7]

7. Mishna Sanhedrin 4:5.

John Locke understood Scripture this way as well:

> ... reason ... teaches ... that being all equal and independent, no one ought to harm another in his life, health, liberty, or possessions: for men being all the workmanship of one omnipotent, and infinitely wise maker; all the servants of one sovereign master, sent into the world by his order.... Every one, as he is bound to preserve himself... so by the like reason ... ought he, as much as he can, to preserve the rest of mankind.[8]

However, even in ancient times, the Sages cautioned against the falsification of the idea of equality, illustrating this falsification with a parable about the people of Sodom: "They had a bed on which they let guests lie: if he was tall, they shortened him, and if he was short, they stretched him."[9]

In modern Western liberal society, there are likewise those who try to efface all difference in the name of equality. Thus, for example, with regard to gender equality,[10] there are those who deny the natural differences between male and female and the distinct functions that arise from these differences, instead trying to blur the differences. An example is the movement calling on women not to nurse their children, or, alternatively, those who seek to grant men an imaginary equality by advocating that they have children through surrogate mothers, thus destroying the natural bond between the birth mother and her child and turning these women into baby-making machines. Instead of building a healthy family, today they offer mass-produced children. The Torah's perspective is the diametric opposite. According to the Torah, both man and woman are God's handiwork, and both are responsible for the children.

Let us consider an example from a different realm, which illustrates the problems that arise with respect to the value of equality. Today, one in four Israeli citizens is not Jewish. It is clear that,

8. John Locke, *Second Treatise of Government*, §6.
9. Sanhedrin 109b.
10. See below, the chapter titled "The Status of Women: Vision and Reality," pp. 207 ff.

according to halakha, non-Jewish citizens deserve adequate representation in the administration of the state, because they are full partners in it. Consequently, they should be allowed to serve as government ministers, as we find with regard to the officers of King David.[11]

However, whereas we must extend equality and justice to minorities that live among us, we have not yet explicitly stated to the Arabs, ourselves, and other minorities, that in addition to rights, equality requires the acceptance of responsibility and the fulfillment of obligations. We have thus refrained from offering the minorities who live in Israel a choice of whether they want full citizenship or a limited status of temporary residency. It is true that very few Muslim Arabs living in the State of Israel would want to view themselves as loyal Israeli citizens, but when we fail to absorb the minority of Arabs that wishes to integrate into Israel's national framework, we distance them and help fan the flames of Arab nationalism.

Human Rights

Individuals and societies that view themselves as being bound by a covenant with the Creator take it for granted that this covenant, and the duties it entails, form the basis for all relations among individuals and between individuals and society. Each individual has rights that are implied by his covenant with God and by his participation in a covenant with the public – a social contract, in modern parlance – on which the government is founded. There are indeed absolute, inalienable rights, such as the right to life and liberty, but these, too, are conditioned on responsibilities and obligations.

The staunchly secular approach is diametrically opposed to this conception. We can illustrate the difference through the debate about abortion.

Those who advocate for abortion on demand claim that a person's body is his own, to do with as he pleases. As long as the fetus is still part of the mother's body, she has the exclusive right to decide whether to

11. Ittai of Gat (see Radak on II Samuel 15:19) and Uriah the Hittite (see *Responsa Rabbi Avraham ben HaRambam*, Freiman edition, 1938, §25).

raise and nurture it or to terminate it. No other party has any right to intervene in her freedom of choice.

What is a person's right over his body? What is its origin? From a completely secular perspective, this question is out of place. Man is completely independent, and he has the right to do as he pleases. This right can be limited if it impinges on the rights of others to act accordingly, but that limitation only applies when others can act independently, and a fetus cannot.

The theoretical basis for this view seems to be as follows: The human species, and each particular individual, was created by chance. Even parents who raise a child are given this particular baby by pure chance. It is true that when a human being becomes self-aware, he takes his fate into his own hands, and no one else has any right to make decisions about his life, but the claim with regard to a fetus is that it does not yet have the full right to life and is simply a part of the mother.

But a newborn also is dependent on others, so what is the difference? The premise is that a fetus is incapable of opposition if its mother wants to abort it, and therefore it also has no right to protest – indeed, it has no right to live beyond what its mother wishes to grant it. When the decision about the right to live is placed solely in human hands, it becomes dependent upon the wishes of those with power, and might makes right.

A believer, however, develops his attitudes based on entirely different premises. Humanity was created for a divine purpose, and as such, the Creator charges man to protect His world. The Torah's moral calculus is not based on rights, but on duties, from which rights stem as well. This does not refer only to the mother's duties toward her fetus, for there is a general commandment to save the life of a fetus and all are duty-bound to rescue it from harm. The duty to save the life of a fetus stems from the fact that a fetus is a human life *in potentia*. This is the way of the world; until the fetus emerges into the world, it exists as potential life, not as life *in realia*. This status is expressed in the Sages' statement: "The Torah said: Desecrate one Shabbat for it, so that it will observe many Shabbatot."[12] This is not merely license to desecrate Shabbat, but

12. Yoma 85b. See also what Nahmanides wrote in *Torat HaAdam*, in *Kitvei HaRamban* (Chavel ed.), vol. 2 (1964), p. 28. Likewise, see what I wrote in *Si'aḥ Naḥum* (Maaleh

a commandment to do so. The rights of the fetus, at the earliest phases of its existence, are anchored in the presumption that when it matures it will fulfill its duties.

In cases where abortion is permitted – to save the mother's life, for instance – the negation of the fetus's rights stems from the fact that it is in breach, already at this stage, of its duty not to endanger others. As the Talmud puts it: "It is a pursuer (*rodef*)"[13] – even though it endangers its mother unwittingly and innocently. For some reason, things went awry, and this fetus was diverted away from its designated purpose; it therefore lost its right to exist. Under normal circumstances, however, not only is it forbidden to harm the fetus, it is even obligatory to care for it and its welfare just as we care for its mother. Only divine law can determine which lives take precedence.[14]

When there is no agreement about goals, absolute equality and liberty for every individual and every group, which enable them to pursue opposing agendas as they see fit, leads to intolerable social tensions and eventually to social disintegration or anarchy.

On Democracy and Humility

Some people speak of democracy as a supreme value, but this is nothing but a vapid and erroneous slogan. The concept of "democracy," in itself, without any modifier, refers to nothing more than a type of governmental structure in which those in power are elected by the public. At times, even this is not so and a regime that calls itself democratic employs the term merely to perpetuate an illusion.

In fact, almost every society can adopt ostensibly democratic procedures without changing its basic values at all. A regime that is perfectly democratic in form is only a vessel, which is filled with the values that characterize that particular society. Let us not forget that Hitler, may his name be blotted out, was democratically elected. On

---

Adumim, 2008), §116.

13. Sanhedrin 72b; cf. *Hilkhot Rotze'aḥ* 1:9.
14. There are other cases in which abortion is permitted; for instance, when the fetus will have massive, severe defects that will prevent it from living any semblance of a normal life. A discussion of this is beyond the scope of this book.

the other hand, it stands to reason that if a perfectly liberal democracy would ever be established, it would quickly collapse, because absolute liberalism weakens societal adhesion and causes dissolution of those elements that work to unify and solidify society.

The leading contemporary Western states all have democratic regimes, but the built-in premises on which these regimes are founded – premises about the value and dignity of the individual – are rooted in Scripture. Alongside their declaration of the separation of religion and state, the founding fathers of the United States proclaimed, in the Declaration of Independence, their belief that human beings are "endowed by their Creator with certain unalienable rights." Without this solid foundation, there is no rational justification for the entire structure. From an intellectual perspective, it is suspended in midair, ungrounded, and so no cultural impulse would be strong enough to sustain it. Unless basic democratic values are rooted deeply in a nation's culture and traditions, democracy cannot survive. These values, which constitute the content and essence of democracy, are not derived from the structure of the regime, but without rootedness in those values, the governmental structure is unstable, liable to collapse easily under incidental circumstances. This is attested by all of the states that won independence after World War II and established democratic systems of government; many of those countries did not remain democratic for long.

Thus, the word "democratic" does not sufficiently describe the essence and character of a regime. To understand the essence of a state, one must be familiar with its cultural features. The character of most long-standing democracies may seem well known, but in truth, France is not like the United Kingdom, and neither of them is like other democratic states, despite a number of similar contours.

Many people think that the idea of democracy was conceived and born in Athens and the other city-states of Ancient Greece, ignoring the fact that Greek democracy was limited, not only in practice, but even in theory, to a very narrow segment of society. The freemen were a minority who lived and grew wealthy from the work of many slaves, whose status was as low as that of animals. Even the greatest Greek philosophers did not recognize the uniformity of the human race; they viewed slaves as subhuman, completely devoid of rights, a sort of animal that could be trained to serve the Hellenists. Aristotle cites Euripides in this context: "That is why the poets say, 'It is meet that Hellenes should rule over barbarians,' as if they thought that the barbarian and the slave were by nature one."[15] He goes on to define the master-slave relationship:

> The master is only the master of the slave; he does not belong to him, whereas the slave is not only the slave of his master, but wholly belongs to him.... He who is by nature not his own but another's man, is by nature a slave....[16]

He continues: "It is clear, then, that some men are by nature free, and others slaves, and that for these latter slavery is both expedient and right."[17] Later he returns to the same point: "It [is] expedient and right for the one to be slaves and the others to be masters: the one practicing obedience, the others exercising the authority and lordship which nature intended them to have."[18] He even describes "the art of acquiring slaves... justly" as "a species of hunting or war."[19] Slaves must labor according to their masters' whim, and maintaining proper relations between slave and master is good for both: "Those who are in a position which places them above toil have stewards who attend to their households while they occupy themselves with philosophy or with politics."[20]

There is no need to explain at length how distant the Torah is from the Greek way. Our Torah emphasizes that we were slaves in Egypt but were brought out to freedom. Our entire goal is to be subservient to God, not subservient to other humans, who are themselves slaves.[21] Moreover, all human beings were created in God's image and are equal in stature. We must be concerned for the welfare of all: "So that your male and female slave may rest as you do" (Deut. 5:14).

---

15. Aristotle, *Politics* I:2 (Everson trans.), p. 12.
16. Ibid. 4, pp. 15–16.
17. Ibid. 5, p. 17.
18. Ibid. 6, pp. 18–19.
19. Ibid. p. 19.
20. Ibid.
21. Kiddushin 22b.

The true recognition by a person that he is a servant of God brings him to humility. The Torah describes Moses with two related epithets: he is called a servant of God ("Not so with My servant Moses; he is trusted throughout My household" – Num. 12:7) and humble ("Moses was exceedingly humble, more so than any other man on earth" – ibid. 3). Moses had many virtues, of both intellect and character, but the Torah singles out just one of them: his humility.

Aristotle wrote at length and in profound detail about character virtues, and Maimonides copied many things from him verbatim. However, with respect to humility, Maimonides diverged from Aristotle's path toward the furthest extreme. According to Aristotle, excessive humility is almost a defect:

> For the unduly humble man, being worthy of good things, robs himself of what he deserves, and to have something bad about him from the fact that he does not think himself worthy of good things, and seems also not to know himself; else he would have desired the things he was worthy of, since these were good.[22]

Not so Maimonides. After describing the doctrine of the "golden path," in which he follows Aristotle, he makes an abrupt shift:

> There are some dispositions in regard to which it is forbidden to keep to the middle.... The right way in this regard is not merely to be humble, but to be lowly of spirit and very meek.... It was said of Moses our teacher that he was "exceedingly humble" – not merely "humble." Hence our Sages exhorted us, "Be exceedingly, exceedingly low of spirit," and they further said that one who swells his heart with haughtiness has denied the major principle [of faith], as it is written: "Your heart will be proud, and you will forget the Lord your God" (Deut. 8:14).[23]

---

22. Aristotle, *Nicomachean Ethics* IV:3, trans. W. D. Ross (Kitchener: Batoche Books, 1999), pp. 63–64.
23. *Hilkhot Deot* 2:3.

Humility is thus a necessary condition for remembering and serving God. Maimonides explains further:

> What is the path to love and awe of Him? When a man contemplates His great and wondrous deeds and creatures and from them sees His infinite and inestimable wisdom, he will immediately love... and when he contemplates those same matters, he will immediately recoil in awe and fear, and he will realize that he is a small, lowly, benighted creature of little and weak intelligence standing before Him of perfect intelligence.[24]

Moreover, the attribute of humility is itself ascribed to the Almighty:

> R. Yoḥanan said: Wherever you find the power of the Holy One, blessed be He, you also find His humility. This was written in the Torah, repeated in the Prophets, and repeated a third time in the Writings. In the Torah it is written, "For the Lord your God is the God of gods and the Lord of lords," followed immediately by, "who upholds justice for widow and orphan" (Deut. 10:17–18). It is repeated in the Prophets, as it is written, "Thus says the High and Lofty One, who lives eternally, whose name is holy," followed immediately by, "[I dwell...]with the contrite and low of spirit" (Is. 57:15). It is repeated a third time in the Writings, as it is written, "Extol Him who rides the clouds, God is His name," followed immediately by, "father of orphans, advocate of widows" (Ps. 68:5–6).[25]

Since we are commanded to imitate the characteristics attributed to God, as it says, "You shall walk in His ways" (Deut. 28:9),[26] we are commanded to be humble.

---

24. *Hilkhot Yesodei HaTorah* 2:1.
25. Megilla 31a.
26. See *Hilkhot Deot* 1:5–6.

God is described as being mighty, but His might is combined with humility. This is true mightiness, which man ought to cultivate – authentic concern for the other, which stems from real humility.

Even the king, whom all must honor, is commanded to be humble, as Scripture states: "So that his heart is not lifted above his brothers" (Deut. 17:20), and as Maimonides writes:

> Just as Scripture accords [the king] great honor and requires all to honor him, so it commands him to have a low and humble heart, as it states: "My heart is humble within me" (Ps. 109:22).... He shall be gracious and merciful to great and small alike; he shall conduct affairs according to their desires and benefit; he shall show compassion for the honor of even the smallest of them.... He shall always act with excessive humility. We have no one greater than our teacher Moses, who said, "What are we?" (Ex. 16:8), and he suffered their burden, troubles, complaints, and anger, as a nurse father bears an infant.[27]

His son, Rabbi Avraham, explained further:

> Necessity dictates what the tradition explains with respect to a king or prince when it interprets the verse "You shall place a king over yourselves" (Deut. 17:15) to mean "Fear of him shall be upon you"[28].... This is a deviation from outward humility – a deviation dictated by necessity, and only on condition that he maintains his inner humility, as He, may He be exalted, said: "So that his heart is not lifted above his brothers" (Deut. 17:20).... Because this is necessary for the good of the regime... the [Sages] mandated all that is stated in the halakha with respect to the honor accorded to a judge, chief, and king over the community of Israel.... How great is the danger if this is perceived as external haughtiness, which the Almighty so despises! Therefore... he shall hold the

27. *Hilkhot Melakhim* 2:6.
28. Mishna Sanhedrin 2:5.

> reins of power with the caution, concern, and self-discipline that grant him humility.... All of this is so that the ruler has a counterbalance to the outward honor that is necessary in some cases; he will thus be safe from straying away from inner humility, and he will (maintain his) humility before the Almighty.[29]

If this is true of a king, then it is certainly applicable to every individual.

Humility is the linchpin of Judaism. Only one who makes efforts to transcend himself and his desires, and tirelessly seeks the truth for its own sake, can appreciate the real value of another and accept the truth from whence it comes.[30]

In this context, of special interest is a responsum that Maimonides wrote with regard to the Karaites, a Jewish sect that denied the Oral Torah, and against whom he waged a fierce ideological battle over the course of decades:

> These Karaites who dwell here in No-Amon (i.e., Thebes), in Egypt, in Damascus, and elsewhere in the lands of Ishmael should be treated honorably and dealt with honestly; interactions with them should be with humility and in the manner of truth and peace – as long as they behave toward us in good faith and stop speaking intransigently and falsely, refraining from speaking perversely about the rabbinic sages of the day.[31]

29. *HaMaspik LeOvdei Hashem* (Dori ed.), pp. 71–72 (the chapter on humility).
30. *Shemonah Perakim*, Introduction, p. 36. It is worth noting the instructive comments of Rabbi Avraham, the son of Maimonides, in his "Essay on the Homilies of the Sages" (Margulies ed.), p. 88: "In truth, [R. Yehuda HaNasi] was called 'our holy rabbi' because a person who casts falsehood away from his presence while sustaining truth... and who changes his opinion when its opposite is demonstrated to him, is no doubt holy."
31. *Iggerot HaRambam* (Shilat ed.), p. 669. Rabbi Shilat raises questions about the ascription of this responsum to Maimonides, but the fact is that the greatest halakhists accepted this responsum as a matter of practical import. Here is not the place to expand on this.

One must act humbly even with ideological rivals. This does not mean one cannot have strong opinions, but rivals should debate one another fairly. This will advance both truth and peace. The attribute of humility is becoming not only of an individual, but also of an entire population. It ought to be the characteristic feature of our nation as a whole.

Throughout our history as a people, we have retained awareness that "you are the smallest of all peoples" (Deut. 6:7), as the Sages explain: "The Holy One, blessed be He, said to Israel: I love you because even when I bestow greatness upon you, you make yourselves small before Me."[32]

A Jewish democracy is possible only in a society characterized by two traits that stem from humility: the first is that even the greatest of the great recognizes his duty to respect and appreciate the smallest of the small, and the second is that each person is concerned for the well-being of others. The greater the person, the greater his responsibility to care for the property and welfare of his fellows.

In the absence of humility, democracy becomes merely a ruse, and nothing deters those with power from imposing their authority on the broader public through cynical exploitation of government institutions. Even somewhat free elections do not always achieve the transfer of real power and executive authority to elected officials. Instead of justice there is corruption. When the expected motive to run for office is the desire to grab the reins of power, then only the most arrogant and haughty individual can prevail. This is one of the most dangerous flaws of democracy – that it can lead to the rise of tyrants and demagogues, as Aristotle already recognized.[33]

The purpose of the Jewish people is to sanctify God's holy name. On the individual level, this is expressed in the fulfillment of the mitzvot, and the mitzva of Torah study in particular. The mitzvot grant inestimable worth as well as self-confidence to each individual, great and small, man and woman. A fine line separates extreme humility from self-negation and an inferiority complex. Only broad-mindedness can prevent the decline into self-effacement. When the Torah is the possession

32. Ḥullin 89a.
33. See *Politics* IV:4.

of the entire people, when each individual views Torah achievement as a personal challenge, then it will be impossible to neglect the inestimable value of each individual. Tyrannical regimes are established by undermining the uniqueness of the individual. Mass ignorance enables brainwashing and complete dependence on the leadership or the government. These are the tools that despots of every age have used to establish their absolute power. Such a system never succeeded among the Jewish people because the value of Torah study has penetrated and become deeply entrenched in public consciousness. The more one studies and learns, the more independent-minded he becomes.

The balance between intellectual independence and humility has contributed greatly to the strengthening of Jewish democracy.

Truth will show the way. The values of Tanakh, the legacy of halakha, and Jewish tradition are the content on which the Jewish state and Jewish democracy are founded, and they are what give it strength. Therefore, any attempt to undermine the Jewish essence of the state will also endanger its democratic identity.

A Model Society

The Jewish people entered into a covenant at Sinai: "You shall keep My covenant... and you shall be to Me a kingdom of priests and a holy nation" (Ex. 19:6). This is how Rabbi Avraham, the son of Maimonides, interprets this verse in his father's name:

> The priest of each congregation is the leader who is most eminent and is its role model, whom members of the congregation follow and thereby find the straight path. Thus, it says: You shall be, through observance of My Torah, leaders of the world. You will be to them as the priest to his congregation. The world will follow after you, imitating your actions and walking in your path. This is the explanation of the verse that I received from my father and master, of blessed memory....
>
> He promised the future fulfillment of this in His word to Isaiah (2:3): "And the many peoples shall go and say, 'Come let us ascend the Mount of the Lord, to the House of the God [of Jacob, so that He may instruct us in His ways, and so that we may

> walk in His path.' For instruction (Torah) shall go forth from Zion, and the word of the Lord from Jerusalem]."[34]

The Jewish people lives in constant tension between yearning for a life of sanctity and the need to provide for the material needs of individuals and society. The Torah's commandments serve as a guide; by implementing them, we can build a society of people whose lives express the Divine image in which they were created. Both individuals and society as a whole require principles that can serve as a foundation for a meaningful life. The covenant that God made with us at Sinai is what preserved the Jewish people throughout history. Now that we have been privileged to return to the holy land, our great challenge is to fulfill the command, "Observe justice and do what is right" (Is. 56:1), to build a society that will be a light unto the nations, a society in which each individual can develop all of his creative powers, in which everyone together realizes the prophetic vision: "And all your children shall be disciples of the Lord, and great shall be the peace of your children. You shall be established through righteousness; you shall be safe from oppression and shall have no fear from ruin, and it shall not come near you" (Is. 54:13–14). God's name will thus be sanctified throughout the world, as Maimonides described:

> Jeremiah said…"Thus says the Lord: Let not the wise man glory in his wisdom, neither let the mighty man glory in his might, let not the rich man glory in his riches; but let him that glories glory in this, that he understands and knows Me" (Jer. 9:22–23).… In this verse he makes it clear to us that those actions that ought to be known and imitated are loving-kindness, judgment, and righteousness. He adds another corroborative notion through saying "in the earth" (ibid.) – this being a pivot of the Law. For matters are not as the overbold opine who think that His providence, may He be exalted, terminates at the sphere of the moon and that the earth and that which is in it are neglected: "The Lord has forsaken the earth" (Ezek. 9:9). Rather it is as He made clear

34. *Perush HaTorah LeRabbi Avraham ben HaRambam*, ed. E. Weisenberg, p. 302.

> to us through the Master of those who know: "That the earth is the Lord's" (Ex. 9:29).... This is what He says: "That I am the Lord who exercises loving-kindness, judgment, and righteousness, in the earth" (Jer. 9:23). Then He completes this notion by saying: "For in these things I delight, says the Lord" (ibid.). He means that it is My goal that there should come from you loving-kindness, righteousness, and judgment in the earth.... Thus the end that He sets forth in this verse may be stated as follows: It is clear that the perfection of man that may truly be gloried in is the one acquired by him who has achieved, in a measure corresponding to his capacity, apprehension of Him, may He be exalted, and who knows His providence extending over His creatures as manifested in the act of bringing them into being and in their governance as it is. The way of life of such an individual, after he has achieved this apprehension, will always have in view loving-kindness, righteousness, and judgment, through imitation of His actions, may He be exalted.[35]

The return to Zion is not specific to the Jewish people only. Scripture states explicitly: "Let not the foreigner say, who has attached himself to the Lord, 'The Lord will keep me apart from His people'... for My House shall be called a house of prayer for all peoples" (Is. 56:3, 7).

Education

One of the most basic functions of public governance in Jewish communities throughout history was the establishment of educational institutions. The Sages, as summarized by Maimonides, threatened the most severe punishment for failure to fulfill this obligation:

> Teachers of children are installed in every country and in every region and in every city. The residents of any city that does not have [a school for] schoolchildren are excommunicated until it installs teachers for the children. If they do not install [teachers],

35. *Moreh Nevukhim* III:54, pp. 636–38.

> the city is destroyed, for the world continues to exist only due to the breath of schoolchildren [studying Torah].[36]

I know of nothing else in the realm of communal services that the Sages treated so stringently! It is worth noting that even the Western world's oldest civilized states only became truly democratic when they began to produce educated citizens, for only educated citizens have a sense of public responsibility and express judicious opinions about matters of governance. Among the gentile nations, this process took place during the past two centuries, and universal compulsory education likewise became a cornerstone of free countries. The more educated the public, the more it can take part in addressing problems of governance; on the other hand, when most citizens are uneducated, the country is fertile ground for tyranny. The more one learns and understands, the more independent-minded he becomes. When herd mentality prevails, democracy cannot succeed, but where there is a multiplicity of opinions, people will not settle for a repressive regime. The old saying, "Two Jews, three opinions," is not just a joke; indeed, throughout our history, we were unique among nations in that we emphasized widespread education. Thus, proliferation of different opinions has always been one of our hallmarks.

The school system must open the wellsprings of Torah and the wellsprings of secular sciences and disciplines before Israel's students. Children who do not study mathematical, logical reasoning cannot properly understand the Torah, either. Likewise, it is impossible to understand the Torah's system of reasoning without rudimentary understanding of the natural world. For this reason as well, various secular subjects should be taught broadly.

Commitment to educating the entire population must guide Torah leaders as well. We must work to broaden and deepen Torah education among all segments of the population, to each group according to its inclinations and lifestyles, in Israel and abroad. We must make education our highest priority.

---

36. *Hilkhot Talmud Torah* 2:1.

Parental involvement in schools should be encouraged, and there should be educational institutions of various stripes and with different emphases. Most importantly, we must foster a generation of educators who understand and love people and who are infused with a sense of mission, aware that they are doing sacred work.

We must view the Torah as "the heritage of the congregation of Jacob" (Deut. 33:4), with which every Jew has a connection. The religious school system must see itself as having a duty toward the entire public, and it must therefore compete successfully against other education systems to provide the needs of the entire people, not just the needs of the religiously observant population. These schools must teach Torah values without detracting from the cultivation of skills in every area of science and technology, which are so vital for individual livelihood and for the economic success of the entire state.

An interesting attestation is mentioned by Rabbi Yehuda ben Barzilai Al-Bargeloni, who cites a responsum from Rav Hai Gaon, from which it emerges that schools (which at the time were located in the synagogue) taught additional subjects: "It was said in the name of Rav Hai that it is permitted to teach children Arabic script and mathematics in the synagogue as a supplement to Torah study; however, without Torah, it is improper."[37]

The purpose of investing in education, in addition to the advancement of the spiritual dimension, is to give each child the opportunity to live a creative and productive life and to provide the skills and training that will enable him to earn a respectable living when he reaches adulthood.

Even among the non-observant public, there are many parents who are concerned about the permissiveness and licentiousness that has become so prevalent among youth; as a result, they seek ways to give their children a religious education.

We must create religious schools that are not only for children from families like these, but also for children whose parents seek excellence in computers, mathematics, art, and other subjects. Students in

37. *Sefer HaItim* §175.

these schools will also learn Torah; even if it is initially studied not for its own sake, eventually students will come to appreciate it for its own sake.

Over the past several decades, there has been a change in Israeli society. The mitzva-observant community is growing, and hopefully it will continue to grow. The process of secularization has halted, for the most part. Now is the time to open the ranks – "Enlarge the site of your tent" (Is. 54:2). Religious education can attract a large portion of Israel's children, if it can learn how to reach the various segments of Israeli society.

Legislation

The Torah teaches the most basic reason for commitment to Torah: "Be holy, for I, the Lord your God, am holy" (Lev. 19:2). Torah's purpose is twofold: not only the welfare of society, but also the welfare of the soul.[38] It is "directed toward speculative matters" and "gives heed to the perfecting of the rational faculty"[39] so that man can reach the realms of the Divine. About this, Scripture states:

> You shall observe and do, for it is your wisdom and your understanding in the eyes of the nations. For they will hear these ordinances and will say, "Surely this great people is a wise nation and understanding".... What people is there so great that it has righteous ordinances and judgments like the whole of this Torah which I put before you today? (Deut. 4:6–8)[40]

It emerges from these verses that the nations can recognize the superiority of the Torah's moral code. Since these nations presumably do not accept the fundamentals of Jewish faith, it is implied that they are able to recognize the utility of Torah law, even if they do not accept some of the specifically Jewish postulates about God that serve as the basis of the Torah. It stands to reason that the nations grant validity to the

38. *Moreh Nevukhim* III:27, p. 511.
39. Compare to *Moreh Nevukhim* II:40, p. 383.
40. Compare to *Moreh Nevukhim* III:31, p. 524.

Torah's moral code on the basis of other postulates; they relate to the Torah as a *nomos*, as Maimonides describes:

> If you find a Law the whole end of which and the whole purpose of the chief thereof, who determined the actions required by it, are directed exclusively toward the ordering of the city and of its circumstances and the abolition in it of injustice and oppression... the arrangement, in whatever way this may be brought about, of the circumstances of the people in their relations with one another and provision for their obtaining, in accordance with the opinion of that chief, a certain something deemed to be happiness – you must know that that Law is a *nomos* (i.e., promulgated by a human legislator).[41]

This attests that there are moral values that are recognized by the nations of the world and used as the basis of their laws – that is, that there are universal moral values. Laws that are derived from the moral principles that are common to us and to the nations of the world, and which have been implemented in situations that arose in the modern era, can be acceptable to us as well.

Where halakha did not set parameters, it is permissible to use the laws that have been accepted in progressive states and are based on the principles of justice and integrity. Even where halakha is explicit, the Torah recognizes the practical value of *nomos*, as long as these norms offer proper guidance.

For instance, the Torah has no law that protects intellectual property rights, but there is no doubt that had this been relevant in the ancient world, the Torah or the Sages would have introduced such laws. It is thus proper to produce such legislation today.

The social and economic conditions of our time, which are radically different from those of ancient times and which continue to change rapidly, have given rise to a reality in which broad areas of life are undefined by halakha. Furthermore, in much of civil law, as presented in the Talmud and codes, there are relatively few laws derived from explicit

41. *Moreh Nevukhim* II:40, pp. 383–84.

Scriptural passages; rather, most of it is deduced from principles of equity that are more or less universally acknowledged.

To fill the lacunae in halakha, to address the broad new demands of commerce, social legislation, economic planning, international relations, and other variables, it is possible to formulate laws based on principles of justice. In fact, there is ample precedent for incorporating various commercial rules of non-Jewish provenance into the corpus of halakha.[42] The generally accepted conventions of the commercial world are recognized by halakha because they serve a vital purpose in regulating an important area of activity – provided only that they do not conflict with halakhic principles.

The inclusion of such laws in halakha will grant them greater significance, as they will become part of the total halakhic system. To return to our example from the world of commerce, many deliberations in rabbinical courts in Israel and the Diaspora involve careful consideration of non-Jewish legislation, on the basis of which contracts, commitments, etc. are interpreted. In Israel, as in many other states, new legislation in these areas is frequently promulgated. However, even though rabbinical courts must take this legislation into account, under present conditions halakhists contribute nothing to the framing of the legislation. It would be proper for halakhists to play an active role in proposing legislation infused with the spirit of the Torah[43] that would also be acceptable to Israel's non-observant communities. Religious communities and Torah leadership must contend with the unique and very real problems that face the State of Israel and which have halakhic ramifications, from a broad social perspective that takes all the different parts of the Jewish people into consideration.

Another example from the economic domain is the policy of government-initiated inflation, which for a number of years was adopted by the Israeli government, as though wealth can be generated by printing more banknotes. However, each year, on the Shabbat before Tisha BeAv, when in every synagogue the words of the prophet, "Your silver

---

42. See *Hilkhot Mekhira* 7:6; *Shulḥan Arukh, Ḥoshen Mishpat* 201:2.

43. For one praiseworthy attempt at this, see the series of works on halakha-based economics and jurisprudence, published by the Keter Institute for Torah Economics.

has turned to dross" (Is. 1:22), are read aloud, no one noticed that his words were addressed to us.

Fostering a robust economy on every level – with respect to its material strength and stability, its ethical norms, and in terms of its social outcomes – is a religious obligation.

Are the religious parties willing and able to make their voices heard on this and other important issues?[44] Even if the religious representation in the Knesset remains silent, rabbis and halakhists must not. If the voice of the Torah is heard on these issues, it will ultimately resonate with the public.

A more urgent subject is that of traffic laws. Israel has earned low marks in this realm due to the carnage on its roads. There is an imperative need for studies that will lead to legislation to regulate highway construction, traffic control, vehicle safety standards, and related matters.[45] This ought to be a major priority for Torah-observant Jews. Joint efforts with other segments of the population will certainly meet with great success.

Undoubtedly, if the religious public were to focus on transportation issues, there could be a significant improvement, and in matters like these, improvements translate directly into lives saved.

Years ago, when it was proposed to install safety belts for all passengers in a vehicle, there were so many hesitations and reservations! When the law was ultimately passed, it mandated only that passengers in the front seat buckle in. Only after a trial period, in which it was demonstrated that seat belts indeed save lives, was the law expanded and applied to rear-seat passengers as well.

Yet this evidence had long been available in studies conducted in England, the United States, and other countries. Why did we need to lose more precious lives just so we could collect data specifically in Israel?

---

44. We must be very careful about adopting improper laws. Until recently, the British law subjecting debtors to imprisonment and foreclosure of all assets was still in effect in Israel. This outrageous injustice is in complete opposition to what the Torah states explicitly: "You must remain outside... and if he is a needy man... you must return the pledge to him" (Deut. 24:11–13). This law still has not been amended properly.
45. Editor's note: This has greatly improved over the years; see recent WHO-estimated road traffic death rate reports.

The Sages established a general rule: "Danger should be [treated] more stringently than ritual prohibitions."[46] Accordingly, they enacted several regulations against hazardous practices. The time has come for us to acknowledge that there is a religious and moral duty to address such problems, and we ought to be at the forefront of efforts to improve public safety.

Promotion of moral principles that lead to moral action is regarded by halakha as virtuous in its own right, for even where there is no acknowledgment of any divine command, the very observance of and engagement with the Torah's moral code is beneficial. It also generates opportunities to cooperate with segments of the population that are not yet prepared to accept the Torah's authority, but for whom ethical considerations are important. "R. Ḥiyya b. Abba said: 'They have forsaken Me' (see Jer. 16:11) – I will forgive this, for perhaps they have kept My Torah. For if they forsook Me but kept My Torah, the leaven in it would bring them close to Me."[47]

The state of Judaism in our time is such that some parts of our people are apathetic about religious values but deeply committed to the values of justice and integrity. It matters not whether this dedication is a vestige of Jewish tradition or rooted wholly within modern culture. From a practical standpoint, the way to ensure the unity of our people and to renew its loyalty to the covenant with God is by strengthening shared moral values within the framework of Torah.

Although halakha, for pragmatic reasons, cannot yet serve as the accepted source of jurisprudence for the entire nation, we must strive to work together and build a wide consensus, at least in realms where common concerns and shared conceptions of justice prevail. Our faith in the eternal posterity of Israel must be such that if we can make progress slowly, one step at a time, the day will come when the Torah fills every part of our lives.

---

46. Ḥullin 10a.

47. Y. Ḥagiga 1:7. Some variants have "the light (*ma'or*) within it" instead of "the leaven (*se'or*)."

The Light of Torah

The challenge facing Torah Judaism today is immense. From the Emancipation until the last half-century, there was a constant decline in the number of Jews who were ready and willing to recognize the binding value of the Torah and mitzvot. This process caused a crisis of halakhic authority, that is, a situation in which the Torah and halakha are no longer a major authoritative factor in shaping communal life.

In Diaspora lands, religious Jews could react to these new conditions by disengaging from the rest of the Jewish population and creating their own, isolated environments where they could live life according to the Torah.

However, now that we have been privileged, by the grace of God, to return to our land and establish the State of Israel, such isolationism constitutes a denial of God's goodness and the abandonment of precious Jewish souls. Today, the choice to secede from society and state demands a stricter, more extreme form of isolation than what was required in the Diaspora. Consequently, this form of isolationism has harsher ramifications. About those who tread this path we learn: "The blows of the sectarians consume the world."[48] The rebirth of Jewish statehood makes us responsible for building, strengthening, and protecting all of the social and economic institutions that a modern state needs.

However, the way to restore the crown of Torah to its former glory and to renew the authority of halakha is not by means of standard partisan and political activity. As a result of partisan maneuvering and political tensions involving religious political parties, the grandeur of the Torah has been diminished in the eyes of many.

We should recognize that many Jews today see the Torah as nothing but a slogan of small political parties, which exploit it for their narrow, sectarian interests. Marshaling the Torah for the political activities of a minority group will not restore the grandeur of the Torah. On the other hand, the voice of the Torah is unfortunately not heard with respect to precisely those crucial issues to which Torah values can and should contribute to the public discourse.

---

48. Mishna Sota 3:4.

The Torah does not need political power or disciplinary authority. If we want Jews to identify with the Torah's values, they must first discover their identities within the Torah. To that end, the Torah's messages must be directed toward the authentic murmurings of every Jewish heart, religious and secular alike. Scripture states: "For the commandment is a lamp, and the Torah is light" (Prov. 6:23). This verse should be understood straightforwardly: the attraction of light stems from the fact that everyone recognizes why it is preferable to darkness. Thus, we must enable each individual to see the light of Torah in himself, and then to follow its path of his own free will.

The light of Torah can be fully expressed only when the Torah is for the entire public and not when it is observed as a private, individual Torah. The challenge facing Torah scholars is to demonstrate how beneficial the Torah can be for society.

Our commonalities greatly outweigh our differences. If we manage to disclose the total scope of the Torah, which encompasses all of life, that shared heritage will again be revealed. The Torah has a great deal to teach. It can contribute to the advancement of the society we live in and repair its flaws – after all, one of the Torah's two goals is "welfare of the body," which means the welfare of society. The Torah has something to say about citizenship and leadership, and about social and economic issues; Torah scholars should be teaching these lessons to every segment of the Israeli public, but unfortunately they have not spent much time on such endeavors. The light of Torah, which illuminates all of the complex problems of the modern state, can bring even those who are the furthest and most alienated from the Torah to identify with our heritage. Thus, each Jew will gain the self-respect and self-esteem that comes along with a strong, stable identity.

The basic question is: Will an Israeli culture develop that is strongly rooted in Torah values and historical Jewish culture, but which looks toward the future? It is not enough that there are more students of Torah today than ever, even more than there were during the era of the talmudic Sages. Of course, we must not downplay the significance of this fact, but it is insufficient. If the Torah community remains in its isolation, overseeing only its internal affairs and not concerning itself with the cultivation of the spiritual stature of the nation as a whole, the contribution of this community will likely be minor and inconsequential.

There is presently a real opportunity to spread the light of Torah to vast swaths of the Israeli public – and ultimately almost the entire population – if we could but break down the sectarian and partisan political barriers. This is no simple task, and each side has those who try to reinforce those barriers because they simply want to protect their narrow interests. Nevertheless, we must face up to this task.

The proliferation of political parties causes us to overemphasize our differences. Debate about the most marginal of issues becomes overheated, at the expense of cooperation on matters of consensus. Woe to us that the Torah can become the subject of political horse-trading, identified as it is with the partisan objectives of small groups that can never hope to realize their political aims.

It would certainly be better if we could reform government in a way that would result in the elimination of small, marginal parties and force parties to think beyond narrow partisan issues and take broader social responsibility. This will also make government more stable. Will the politicians agree? Perhaps not, but we do not have to leave all decisions in the hands of politicians!

The Torah can be a powerful positive influence on Israeli politics, if only we could present it as the Torah of the entire Jewish people, addressing the members of every party and every segment of the population – anyone who is truly seeking the memory of our collective past and who is drawn to a vision of human well-being. Such ideas can unify us.

Teachers of Torah must speak the Torah's teachings loudly and clearly, especially on matters of ethics and justice. They must try to show the people that the Torah has solutions to difficult problems. This must all be done with a pleasant demeanor, a display of full partnership, and a commitment to share in the public burden. I believe that many parts of the Israeli public yearn to hear the words of the living Torah. Let us join them in a real and honest partnership to build a society that will realize the purpose of the Torah: "The well-being of the states of all its people according to their capacity."[49] Achievement of this goal will

49. *Moreh Nevukhim* III:27, p. 510.

result in spreading the light of the Torah, which will guide us toward the ultimate perfection: the perfection of the soul.

Democratic Jewish Identity

Shaping the Jewish and democratic identity of our state is the most urgent challenge facing us, because this is the only way to provide the social adhesiveness without which the entire endeavor will come undone. We must clarify and internalize the notion that Jewish identity does not mean there is no place for non-Jewish minorities. On the contrary, justice, the precondition for God's presence in human society, must be manifest through the establishment of a society that is attentive to the needs and concerned for the welfare of every resident of the state. However, we must emphasize the *sine qua non* that no minority group has the right to a hostile foreign culture that plans to take control by violent means; such a culture weakens the identity of society as a whole. But if we have the self-confidence of every other independent nation that dwells in its land and has control over its own fate, then we will understand the powerful attraction of a Jewish culture that is rooted in the past and oriented toward the future, and we will be able to assimilate different minorities willingly, without any coercion at all.

Individual liberty is the cornerstone of Jewish democracy, but each individual must be socially responsible, for there are no rights without responsibilities. The individual's greatest right and privilege is to be part of a society in which each person can realize the Divine image within. The tradition of mutual responsibility and full partnership, combined with the powerful drive to advance science and wisdom, constitute the features of Jewish culture. The sense of mission of a kingdom of priests, coupled with the awareness of our covenant with the Almighty, are the calling cards of Jewish identity. A culture that deepens this awareness is worthy of being the heir and successor of our glorious past.

When culture is characterized by spiritual and moral atrophy and the education system deprives students of their Jewish heritage, society thereby empties meaning from the lives of its youth and alienates them from their eternal roots – whether they are a descendant of Abraham, Isaac, and Jacob or a gentile who chooses to live in the state of their descendants. Such a society undermines the foundations of our existence, harming not only us but all of humanity's culture, for our duty toward all of humanity is to set an example and promote the understanding that man has intrinsic worth. In this we will realize the prophet's words: "Nations shall walk by your light, kings by your shining radiance" (Is. 60:30).

Chapter 9

Toward a Torah-Based Economic Policy

Introduction

In any discussion of the Torah's approach to questions of economic policy, a central issue is the tension between striving to prevent poverty and the harsh reality that perpetuates it, despite attempts to overcome it. The Sages were well aware of this tension:

> "There shall be no needy among you" (Deut. 15:4), yet later it states, "For there will never cease to be needy ones in your land" (ibid. 11). When you do the will of the Omnipresent, the needy are among the others, but when you do not do the will of the Omnipresent, the needy are among you.[1]

In ancient times, it was very difficult to generate enough sustenance for the productive laborers and the rest of society. Occasionally, a single year of famine could diminish yields to the point that many lost their sources of livelihood. Today, thank God, conditions are greatly improved, but until we arrive at the End of Days, when "there will be neither famine nor war.... Goodness will abound, and luxuries will be

---

1. *Sifrei Devarim* 111.

as common as dust,"[2] there will never cease to be needy people in our land. Nevertheless, we can achieve great improvements by acting in accordance with the will of God. This is not dependent upon supernatural miracles, but is the essence of the promise that "the Lord your God will bless you in the land that the Lord your God is giving you as an inheritance" (Deut. 15:4). The Sages expounded in *Sifrei*:[3] "This teaches that the blessing depends on the land alone," and the land only yields its bounties through hard work, as it is written: "By the sweat of your brow you will eat bread" (Gen. 3:29). We can therefore explain the verse about poverty as follows: "There shall be no needy among you" if you fulfill the commandment stated in the previous verse, "but from that which you have with your brother you shall remit your claim" (Deut. 15:3), as well as the other mitzvot to support those in need, as explained in that passage in the Torah. Additionally, you must observe all of the mitzvot whose purpose is to encourage us to understand the laws of nature and to learn how to use them to make the land yield fruit when we cultivate it properly; thus our work will not be in vain. Maimonides explains:

> [The idolaters] connected idolatry with agriculture, the latter being necessary for the subsistence of man and of most animals. Accordingly the priests of idolatry preached to the people... that through the practices of this cult, rains would fall, the trees would bear fruit, and the land would become fertile and populous.... God, may He be exalted, wished in His compassion for us to efface this error from our minds and to take away fatigue from our bodies through the abolition of these tiring and useless practices and He gave us the Torah through Moses our Master....[4]

It follows that when we fulfill God's will we will have good enough control of social and economic factors to provide for the needs of even society's most needy individuals.

---

2. *Hilkhot Melakhim* 12:5.
3. Ibid.
4. *Moreh Nevukhim* III:30, pp. 522–23.

The Torah provides several general principles for governing socioeconomic life in a way that enables us to address the social problems with which other nations have had to grapple as well. In this chapter, we will look at several such problems through a halakhic lens.[5] This is not a historical study and is certainly not comprehensive. Rather, it is a brief survey of several halakhot that express the Torah's socioeconomic policy. We will attempt to garner perspectives from the individual, communal, and national realms. The common denominator of these halakhot is that they exemplify, on the one hand, the societal duty to help individuals obtain their basic, existential needs, and, on the other hand, the responsibility of each individual to do everything in his power to provide for himself, as well as the awareness that economic equality should not be artificially imposed.

Societal Support and Personal Responsibility

In Egypt, all the land belonged to Pharaoh (Gen. 47:20), and consequently, the entire people was "slaves to Pharaoh" (ibid. 25), not only in the symbolic sense, but in the real sense that they were slaves whose entire livelihood depended on the will of the ruler. The Torah overthrew this conception and revolutionized private land ownership when it determined that each family would have its own homestead in the Land of Israel, from which it could subsist through manual labor. Even if economic necessity forced an individual to sell his ancestral property, it would not be a permanent sale: "The land shall not be sold in perpetuity" (Lev. 25:23). It is the responsibility of the individual's relatives, members of his natural support group, to redeem the land that he has sold; this essentially means that the extended family has the responsibility to help their needy kinsman. If they fail at this task, the law of the Jubilee year allows the next generation to start over from roughly equal positions. Possession of land gave each individual the means to support himself by his own power. However, this applied only in an agrarian society where almost everyone had to cultivate the soil in order to subsist. The purpose of the law of the Jubilee year, which returns land to its original owners and releases slaves from bondage, is clear: to give

5. We will base ourselves primarily on Maimonides' *Mishneh Torah.*

the new generation an opportunity to rise up from the indignity of poverty, whether one lost his homestead for reasons out of his control, or because of indolence or mismanagement, or because his greed led him to thievery and ultimately to slavery.

Moreover, this law prevented the concentration of vast tracts of land in the hands of the few or of the Temple, for even lands that were consecrated and were not redeemed were given to private priests. This was in complete contrast to the contemporary practice of other nations.

Scripture shows that the law of the Jubilee year, which is an ideal law in its essence, was not observed meticulously in practice, nor was the oppression of debtors truly uprooted. The woman cries to Elisha: "The creditor is coming to take my two children as slaves" (II Kings 4:1). Nevertheless, Scripture teaches us that awareness of the principles behind this law had become so firmly rooted that even when King Ahab of Israel sought to take the vineyard of Naboth, Queen Jezebel had to come up with a nefarious plot so that Ahab's deed would have the veneer of lawfulness (I Kings 21). Where else in the ancient world was a king unable to simply appropriate land to his heart's content without any need for pretexts?

Even in later eras, and even during the exile, a person's unquestioned right to his home was not completely erased. One's lands are mortgaged to his creditor, and they can be repossessed, but his home cannot. Even if the debtor has no money to repay his loan, it is not possible to evict him from his home onto the street.[6] Furthermore, the Talmud states: "We make arrangements for a debtor," meaning that one cannot collect the personal effects of the debtor or the tools of his trade, so that he can continue practicing his profession and earning a livelihood from his own labors.[7]

Indeed, townspeople are obligated to provide food and clothing to the extremely poor from public charity funds, and Jewish

---

6. See *Responsa Rambam* §96: "If it is his residence, and he has no other, it should not be sold to him; they may collect from its rent, if there is what to rent out in addition to his residence." See also *Hilkhot Malveh VeLoveh* 2:2, and my *Yad Peshuta* commentary ad loc.
7. See *Hilkhot Malveh VeLoveh* 1:7 and my *Yad Peshuta* commentary ad loc.

communities throughout the ages have done so, as Maimonides attests: "We have never seen or heard of a Jewish community that has no charity fund."[8] In addition to the individual mitzva of charity, which is incumbent on each and every Jew, the Torah imposes obligatory gifts to the poor from all agricultural produce. With respect to these gifts "there is no benefit of gratitude to the owner; rather, the poor come and take against the owner's wishes. We even take [these gifts] from the poorest Jews."[9] The poor come on their own, pick the produce from the corners of the fields (*pe'ah*) and gather the stray (*leket*) and forgotten (*shikheḥa*) ears.[10]

This contrasts with the priestly gifts: "It is forbidden for priests and Levites to assist in the granary in order to receive their gifts. Anyone who assists has profaned the holy unto God, and of them it is stated: 'You have corrupted the covenant of the Levites' (Mal. 2:8). It is forbidden for an Israelite to let them help him; rather, he gives them their portion with respect."[11] The reason for this distinction is straightforward: The priestly gifts are "in return for the services that they perform, the services of the Tent of Meeting" (Num. 18:21). They were also given another task: "They shall teach Your laws to Jacob, and Your Torah to Israel" (Deut. 33:10). They receive their gifts from the owner, and the owner has the benefit of gratitude, the right to give the gifts to the priests and Levites with whom he is spiritually connected and whom he knows well. This is not the case with respect to gifts to the poor. These gifts belong to the poor; the Torah granted the gifts to them directly, making them partners in the produce. Just as the landowner works during the harvest and the gathering seasons so that he may eat, so does the pauper, and the landowner has no right to prefer one pauper over another. Even one who has become completely impoverished has a right to agricultural produce, but he must work to obtain it, for this is what preserves his independence and dignity.

---

8. *Hilkhot Matnot Aniyim* 9:3.
9. Ibid. 1:8.
10. The pauper's tithe (*maaser ani*), which is indeed given by the owner to the paupers of his choice, is different. See ibid. ch. 6.
11. *Hilkhot Terumot* 12:18.

This principle applies to the mitzva of *Shemitta*, the agrarian Sabbatical year that occurs once in seven years. The fruits of the *Shemitta* year are ownerless: "But in the seventh you shall let it rest and lie fallow. Let the needy among your people eat of it" (Ex. 23:11). However, during the *Shemitta* year, it was necessary to do the work of picking, harvesting, pressing, and all other necessary labors, not just the gathering and collecting of the leftovers after the landowner had already done the bulk of the labor. In this situation, the license for anyone to enter the fields caused only damage, and when the Sages saw that violent men were breaking into fields, inflicting damage, and grabbing all of the produce without leaving for anyone else, they made an enactment:

> When the date harvest arrived, agents of the court would hire workers to harvest the dates, to press the dates into cakes, to gather them into barrels, and to bring them to storehouses in the city; when the grape harvest arrived, agents of the court would hire workers to harvest the grapes, to trample them in the wine press, to gather them into barrels, and to bring them to storehouses in the city; when the olive harvest arrived, agents of the court would hire workers to harvest the olives, to crush them in the olive press, to gather them into barrels, and to bring them to storehouses in the city. They would distribute them before each Shabbat, to each according to his household.[12]

We learn from here that in order to ensure that everyone received according to his needs, the Sages had to give up on the principle that each would enjoy the fruit of his labor, but they nevertheless preserved the key concept by hiring the poor to do the labor on the court's behalf, so they subsisted from their own labors even during the *Shemitta* year.

Over the years, other arrangements were created in the same spirit. These include sharecropping, contract labor, and transactions that are part loan and part joint venture, all of which allow the needy to earn their livelihoods in a dignified way, from their own efforts. Alongside agriculture, other crafts developed, which, unlike farming, did not require

12. Tosefta Shevi'it 8:1.

land to be productive. Achieving the requisite level of craftsmanship demanded specialized training; craftsmanship is a form of human capital that can be utilized, just as land is a form of material capital that can provide a living. In addition to this, the realm of commerce evolved, in which it was often possible to achieve success from an initial investment of relatively little money.[13] The goal of nurturing the independence and responsibility of each individual to meet his own needs is the declared purpose of the entire mitzva of charity:

> The highest level, exceeded by none, is that of one who supports an impoverished Jew by giving him a gift or a loan, or by entering a partnership with him, or by giving him work, to the point that he does not need the support of others and does not ask for it. Of this it is said: "Strengthen the stranger and sojourner, so that he may live with you" (Lev. 25:35) – that is, strengthen him so that he does not fall into neediness.[14]

Despite the supreme value of the mitzva of charity, the Sages were aware of the danger of creating a class of "professional paupers" who demand support from the community and become a burden on the public. The Sages therefore commanded:

> Even one who is wise and respected, if he has become poor he should engage in a trade, even a disgusting trade, rather than become dependent on others. It is better to strip skins off carcasses in the street than say to the people, "I am wise, I am great, I am a priest – support me."[15]

The Sages maintained that engagement in productive labor is important not only for the poor, but also for the rich; sometimes it was one's wealth

---

13. See *Hilkhot Matnot Aniyim* 9:13.
14. Ibid. 10:7.
15. Ibid. 18.

specifically that would cause his lack of productivity and creativity and output: "People who are wrapped in silver and gold... do not do work."[16]

Public Services

The public was responsible for providing various services to citizens. In some cases the public hired workers, who were paid from communal funds or by the direct beneficiaries of their services. In other cases the residents were conscripted into meeting a common need, such as digging water channels. In order to achieve the status of a city or community, it was necessary to ensure the provision of vital services. Under conditions that prevailed then, ten such needs were listed: "A court that metes out punishment, a charity fund that is collected with two [officials] and dispensed with three [officials], a synagogue, a bathhouse, a lavatory, a physician, a blood letter, a scribe, a school teacher, and a water source."[17] Some added a slaughterer, guards, copyists, a planter of trees, and other functions, all depending on the time, the place, and the need.[18] We may thus conclude that basic needs were determined according to the yardstick established by Maimonides: "The Law as a whole aims at two things: the welfare of the soul and the welfare of the body (i.e., society)."[19]

Wage policy seems to have been fashioned in accordance with the model developed in Jerusalem for determining the wages of judges: "In accordance with their needs, along with their wives, children, and grandchildren."[20] It should be noted that, with respect to the possibility that wage-earners would not be satisfied with their allotment, the Talmud comments: "Are we dealing with wicked people?"[21] For common labors, they would hire workers at market value, and unless it was

16. Shabbat 54a. See later in that passage for the explanation of the word "wrapped" ("*kavul*").
17. See Sanhedrin 17b and the variant texts there, and cf. Maimonides, *Hilkhot Deot* 4:23 and the sources cited in *Yad Peshuta* ad loc.
18. See *Hilkhot Shekhenim* 6:1–7, and *Hilkhot Shekalim* 3:8.
19. *Moreh Nevukhim* III:27, p. 510.
20. *Hilkhot Shekalim* 4:7.
21. Ketubbot 105a.

urgent, the preference was to undertake these public works during Ḥol HaMoed:

> All public works were undertaken during the festival. How so? They would repair water damages in the public domain; fix roads and streets; dig wells, cisterns, and caverns; dredge rivers to make them potable; gather water into public cisterns and caverns and repair their cracks; remove thorns from roads; measure *mikvaot* (ritual baths); and divert water to complete any *mikve* that was found to be deficient.[22]

The Talmud explains why specifically the intermediate days of the festival were chosen for the undertaking of public works: "R. Yoḥanan said: Because the wage of laborers is lower then [due to a dearth of private work]."[23] We can infer from here that the Sages understood that custody over public funds demands thriftiness.

A higher level of responsibility was demanded of public appointees. They were required to accept more responsibility than tradesmen working in the private sector, in that they were required to repair losses that they caused:

> A planter of trees for the townspeople who caused ruin, a town slaughterer who rendered animals non-kosher, a blood-letter who caused injury, a scribe who made mistakes on documents, a school teacher who was negligent toward children and did not teach them, or taught them mistakes, and likewise any craftsman who cannot restore the losses he caused may be dismissed without warning; they are considered forewarned, so that they are meticulous in their work, since the public appointed them over it.[24]

Public services are funded by the public. Some of them are for "the welfare of the body," providing the basic necessities without which life

22. *Hilkhot Yom Tov* 7:10.
23. Moed Katan 6a.
24. *Hilkhot Sekhirut* 10:7.

is unlivable, but which not everyone can obtain on their own. Some of them are intended to provide the younger generation with the skills and training to earn a living from non-agrarian occupations. And some public services are for "the welfare of the soul" – to strengthen spiritual life through Torah study and the fulfillment of mitzvot. Originally, duties toward the next generation devolved upon the father: "The mitzvot on behalf of the son that are incumbent upon the father are six. They are: to circumcise him, to redeem him, to teach him Torah, to marry him to a woman, to teach him a trade, and to teach him to swim in a river."[25] If there was no father present, these duties devolved upon the public at large. Over time, the Sages institutionalized several of the father's duties toward his son and transferred responsibility to the community as a whole.

One clear example of this, for our purposes, is the communal obligation to hire schoolteachers. The presence of a school was the identifying mark of a Jewish community, and without one, it had no right to exist.

> Teachers of children are installed in every country and in every region and in every city. The residents of any city that does not have [a school for] schoolchildren are excommunicated until they install teachers for the children. If they do not install [teachers], the city is destroyed, for the world continues to exist only due to the breath of schoolchildren [studying Torah].[26]

A source that has survived from the geonic era shows that in the schools, which were located within synagogues, they studied other subjects as well, so as to train the children in a trade. Thus writes Rabbi Yehuda ben Barzilai Al-Bargeloni:

> It was said in the name of Rav Hai that it is permitted to teach children Arabic script and mathematics in the synagogue as a supplement to Torah study; however, without Torah, it is improper.[27]

25. Maimonides, *Commentary on the Mishna*, Kiddushin 1:7.
26. *Hilkhot Talmud Torah* 2:1.
27. *Sefer HaItim* §175.

The purpose of investing in education, in addition to the spiritual dimension, is to give each child the opportunity to live a creative and productive life and to provide the skills and training that will enable him to earn a respectable living on his own.

Labor Relations

The Torah forbids us to enslave one another, and the Sages derived from this law that under normal circumstances, an individual is free to stop working for his employer, even if he has not completed his work:

> If a laborer began his work and then reneged, even in the middle of the day, he is permitted to renege, for it is stated: "For the Israelites are slaves unto Me" (Lev. 25:55), and not slaves unto slaves. What is the law of a laborer who reneged after he began? We assess what he has accomplished, and he takes [his wage].... To what does this apply? To something that will not be ruined, but with regard to something that will be ruined... he may not renege unless he is forced to, such as if he took ill or heard that a relative died. However, if he is not forced, one may hire against his wages or mislead him.[28]

On the other hand, the employer has no such liberty:

> If one hires a laborer to work for an entire day, and the work was finished at midday, then if he has another task that is similar or easier, [the laborer] works for the rest of the day, but if he has nothing for him to do, he pays his wages as an idle worker.[29]

Moreover, laborers of a particular trade may set general procedures for all members of that trade:

> Craftsmen may arrange among themselves that no one may work on the day that his colleague works, etc., and that anyone who

28. *Hilkhot Sekhirut* 9:4.
29. Ibid. 7.

> violates this stipulation shall be fined a certain amount. To what does this apply? To a country that does not have a distinguished sage to order the affairs of the polity and foster prosperity among its inhabitants. However, if it has a distinguished sage, their stipulation is ineffective, and they may not punish or cause loss to one who does not accept the stipulation, unless he stipulated with them and they did so with the knowledge of the sage. One who caused a loss through a stipulation that did not have the consent of the sage – must pay.[30]

It is our duty to look after laborers, who are generally of limited means, but the laborer likewise must not perpetrate injustice. It is impossible to determine fixed, invariable laws to govern employer-employee relations in all times and places, since circumstances change from one era to the next. However, we must heed the Torah's moral demands in order to establish justice, and we therefore need to consult with Torah sages in addition to public representatives. In this way, state action will be improved and bring success to its inhabitants.

Economic Oversight

The Torah commands us: "When you make a sale to or buy from your fellow, you shall not take advantage of one another" (Lev. 25:14). This mitzva demands strict adherence to fair weights and measures, about which we were commanded separately in a positive mitzva as well as a negative mitzva: "You shall not falsify measures of length, weight, or volume. You shall have an honest balance, honest weights, an honest *ephah*, and an honest *hin*" (ibid. 19:35–36). It is about these and similar mitzvot that it is said: "The court is obligated to set standards and appoint marshals to enforce them. No one shall take whatever profit he wishes; rather, one-sixth shall be allocated to them as profit, and no seller shall profit more than one-sixth."[31] The Sages also enacted laws whose purpose is to prevent monopolies and speculation on food staples:

---

30. *Hilkhot Mekhira* 14:10–11.
31. Ibid. 14:1.

> One may not hoard produce that is vital to life in the Land of Israel or anywhere that there is a Jewish majority, for this brings suffering to Israel.... In years of famine, one should not even hoard a *kav* of carob, because it brings calamity upon market prices. One who destabilizes market prices or hoards produce... is like a usurer.[32]

With respect to these goods, the Sages saw fit to permit competition, because it ultimately benefits the public: "This one brings from his granary to sell, and this one brings from his granary to sell, so that they will be sold cheaply."[33] Similarly: "He may undercut market prices to increase his customers, and the others in the market may not stop him."[34] However, they also set boundaries to prevent unfair competition, such as between taxpayers and those who are exempt from taxes:

> If a migrant from another country comes to open a store next to another's store, or a bathhouse next to another's bathhouse, they may prevent him; however, if he would pay his duty to the king alongside them, they may not stop him.[35]

With regard to nonessential commodities, the Sages did not see fit to limit the profits of traders, but they were insistent on the protection of the rights of both buyer and seller, so that neither can deceive the other. If goods with a fixed market price were traded at a price significantly higher or lower than the accepted market price by means of exploiting the buyer's or the seller's ignorance, the buyer or seller who lost on the deal is considered to have been defrauded, and he may cancel the deal. "If the price-gouging exceeded one-sixth... the sale is null, and the victim may return the object and need not repurchase it."[36]

---

32. Ibid. 5–6.
33. Ibid. 4.
34. Ibid. 18:4.
35. *Hilkhot Shekhenim* 6:5.
36. *Hilkhot Mekhira* 12:4.

National Economic Regulation

Thus far we have addressed municipal or local communal issues – what might be called "microeconomics." During the era of the Mishna and the Gemara, macroeconomic activity, pertaining to the entire country and beyond, was in the hands of foreign rulers, and even though the Sages understood the importance of various government actions, the Jews had barely any influence over them. For example, the Gemara recounts:

> R. Yehuda began: "How good are the works of this nation [Rome]! They have installed markets, baths, and bridges!" R. Yose remained silent. R. Shimon b. Yoḥai responded: "Whatever they installed was for their own needs. They installed markets to situate prostitutes in them, baths to pamper themselves, and bridges to collect tolls!"[37]

During the Second Temple era, large construction projects were undertaken to improve transportation. For instance, public wells were installed, especially for pilgrims to Jerusalem. This was a large investment with an obvious economic utility, and because it encouraged the fulfillment of a religious commandment, the Sages even introduced several halakhic leniencies in the Laws of Shabbat.[38]

In earlier eras – during the times of King Solomon, for instance – there were several impressive national projects, with the construction of the Temple, the royal palace, and the walls of Jerusalem and other fortified cities foremost among them. However, they were built by conscripted labor (I Kings 5:26). Solomon also built the port of "Etzion Gever, which is beside Elot, on the shore of the Reed Sea" (ibid. 9:26), and assembled a fleet of ships to set out from there and develop trade ties with lands outside the Mediterranean Basin, which until then had been the boundary of the natural commercial area of the Israelites. This undertaking doubtlessly contributed to the general welfare and won the king accolades from his subjects. Even in those days, one of the functions

---

37. Shabbat 33b.
38. See Eiruvin 20b: "Wooden strips around wells were permitted only for [the animals of] festival pilgrims." Compare to *Hilkhot Shabbat* 17:30.

of the government in the eyes of the people was to promote the national economy, for the benefit of all.

Conclusions

Despite the immense gap between the conditions that prevailed in ancient times and our present ones, and despite the dearth of sources that can teach us about the economic problems of that era and their solutions, we can still derive several general principles and attempt to implement them:

1. Each individual should be given the basic tools to generate his own material or human capital that will enable him to earn a decent living and live a life of spiritual elevation.
2. It should be made feasible for every family to purchase its own home.
3. There should be a "safety net" for those who have temporarily or permanently been displaced by the economic system. Their needs should be provided at public expense. Nevertheless, the principle of working for oneself should be preserved to the degree possible.
4. Employer-employee relations should be regulated such that the employee is not completely economically dependent on his employer; rather, his independence and liberty shall be preserved.
5. Free-market competition should be encouraged for public benefit; monopolies in the trade of basic and vital goods should be prohibited.

In sum, as a Jewish society, we must invest effort in the "welfare of the body," that is, in the attainment of economic well-being, but also in the "welfare of the soul," by enshrining the values of social justice and Jewish ethics.

Chapter 10

The Status of Women: Vision and Reality

The Uniqueness of Woman: The Mother of All Life

At the beginning of Genesis, the Torah presents two different potential relationships between man and woman, and they portray different models of the status of woman. One relationship is a model worthy of aspiration, while the other one is less than ideal.

At the time of creation, the proper relationship between man and woman was presented as a supreme value. The Torah states: "He created them male and female... and He named them 'Human' when they were created" (Gen. 5:2). This is a description of complete partnership between man and woman, a partnership in which the value of each partner is equal. Both of them together constitute the ideal "Human," and neither is complete without the other. It is together that they are supposed to bear and raise the next generation.

However, each of them has a unique role embedded in their nature; this is an expression of their complete codependency, the purpose of which is to produce the generations of the future. God created a world that will endure and develop; many things are necessary for this to happen, but the main one is that human beings create a society whose members get along with one another, are devoted to one another, and build a better world together. The incubator of this type of interpersonal relationship is the family.

The woman's unique status in the realization of this purpose was recognized by her spouse, who called her "Eve (*Ḥava*), for she was the mother of all life (*em kol ḥai*)" (Gen. 3:20). The precise timing of this naming within the creation narrative is of great significance. After the episode of Adam's sinful eating from the Tree of Knowledge, the Torah states, as a synopsis of the story of his fall, "Now man has become like one of us, knowing good and evil" (ibid. 22). Maimonides cites the translation of Onkelos, who renders the verse as follows: "This man was unique in the world; it was within him to know good and evil."[1] He explains: "This species, mankind, is unique in the world. There is no other species like man in this respect, in that he autonomously, with his intelligence and understanding, knows good and evil."[2]

The appearance of "evil" here is understandable. When Adam chose to disobey God's command not to eat from the Tree of Knowledge of Good and Evil (Gen. 2:16–17) and, on top of that, to feign innocence and blame God and the woman ("The woman You put at my side – she gave me of the tree, and I ate" [ibid. 3:12]), he demonstrated his capacity for evil. But what is the "good" that Adam knew? When did he demonstrate his knowledge of good?

When Adam heard his sentence, "Cursed be the ground because of you" (Gen. 3:17), along with his wife's bitter punishment, he did not argue or grumble about his curse. He did not answer at all. Rather, his response to being condemned to "return to the ground" (ibid. 19) was: "Adam named his wife Eve, for she was the mother of all life (*em kol ḥai*)" (ibid. 20). The meaning of this response is that it seems to have suddenly dawned on Adam that he had sinned grievously against his wife. He therefore turned directly to her, out of love and concern for her well-being. By calling her this name, he offered her comfort, as

1. *Shemonah Perakim*, ch. 8, p. 92.
2. *Hilkhot Teshuva* 5:1. Onkelos' translation parses the verse differently than most: "Man has become one (i.e., unique)" is separate from "it is within him (*mimenu*) to know good and evil." Man has not become like "one of us (*aḥad mimenu*), knowing good and evil," but "unique" in that "it is within him to know good and evil." See also *Moreh Nevukhim* I:2, pp. 23–26.

though to say, "Don't worry, you are 'the mother of all life,' and you will yet build a better world."

The description "mother of all life" is not begrudging and does not describe a suboptimal reality; it is a description that acknowledges a status that was intended from the beginning. It represents man's discovery of woman's unique virtues, as the Talmud says: "She rises with him [to a higher station], but she does not descend with him [to a lower station]. R. Elazar said, this [is derived from] here: 'She was the mother of all life.' She was given for life, not for pain."[3] Adam's eyes were opened to the injustice he had perpetrated when he blamed his wife. Therefore, he was no longer concerned about his own fate, only that of his wife. He thereby demonstrated that it was in his power to "know good" as well.

However, there is another possible type of relationship between man and woman, as described in God's rebuke to woman in the immediate aftermath of the sin: "Your desire shall be to your husband, and he will rule over you" (Gen. 3:16). This describes a relationship of rivalry and power. It is a punishment – she will desire him, and he will rule over her. This is not good for either of them. It expresses the curse of Eve.

The goal is to rise above the sin and its punishment, to achieve a life in which each spouse fulfills their individual role, and in which together they fulfill their shared role. They improve the world as a couple, as the Sages said: "Man and woman: if they are worthy, the Divine Presence dwells with them."[4]

The uniqueness of woman is also discovered by considering the nature of the world that God created. Regarding the verse "Hannah spoke in her heart" (I Sam. 1:13), the Gemara says:

> R. Elazar said in the name of R. Yose b. Zimra: She spoke concerning her heart. She said before Him: Master of the Universe, among all the things that You have created in a woman, You have not created anything without a purpose: eyes to see, ears to hear, a nose to smell, a mouth to speak, hands with which to work, legs with which to walk, and breasts with which to nurse. These

3. Ketubbot 61a.
4. Sota 17a.

> breasts that You have put above my heart, are they not to nurse with? Give me a son, so that I may nurse with them![5]

It emerges from here that the function of the limbs defines their purpose. A mother's purpose is not simply the sum total of pregnancy, birth, nursing, and even child-rearing. Rather, she accompanies her child for her entire life, providing love, guidance, and support. By her very existence, she serves as a model of maternal responsibility, as Moses described the role of a mother: "Have I conceived this people [and]...given birth...that You should tell me: Carry them in your bosom" (Num. 11:12).

Rabbi Meir Simha of Dvinsk, in his commentary on the Torah, explains that a woman's exemption from the mitzva of procreation is connected to her maternal role:

> It makes sense to say that the reason the Torah exempted women from [the mitzva of] procreation and obligated only men is that God's laws and ways are pleasant, and all [the Torah's] paths are peace. It did not impose on a Jew what the body cannot tolerate.... Therefore, women, who are endangered during pregnancy and birth... are not commanded by the Torah to be fruitful and multiply. It is thus permissible for her to imbibe contraceptives.... But to sustain the human race, He embedded in her nature a stronger desire to bear children than that of a man. We find that Rachel said: "Give me children, or I shall die" (Gen. 30:1).... It may also be that the Torah exempted women from procreation because, in truth, desire is embedded in nature, even more so for women... and what she is compelled by her nature to do is sufficient.[6]

God embedded within His world a natural drive to procreate. A woman's natural inclination and desire to bear children and build a family is extremely deep and strong. This is manifest even in the natural structure of a woman's body, which carries the fetus from the moment of conception and later nourishes the newborn. Since this is a natural orientation,

5. Berakhot 31b.
6. *Meshekh Ḥokhma* on Genesis 9:7.

there is no need to command it, because women find intense satisfaction from having children. An expression of this natural tendency can be seen nowadays in the case of women who, unfortunately, cannot have babies naturally but are willing to undergo cumbersome and painful treatments in order to become pregnant.

This is not the case with respect to the father, who can even deny his paternity. This almost happened with Judah until Tamar said: "Please recognize" (Gen. 38:25). For this reason the command to "be fruitful and multiply" was given to men specifically.

Nevertheless, in general, both parents love their children and take care to guide them on their paths. Ralbag addresses this in his commentary to the Torah (Lev. 19:3): "Parents will discipline their children and imbue them with the morals that will keep them from destroying themselves and others; this quality of loving their children is natural in parents." Even regarding areas from which women are exempt, such as the mitzva of Torah study, the Sages said: "How do women merit? By bringing their children to the synagogue,"[7] where the schools were located in those days. There is no drive more powerful than a mother's concern for her children, their upbringing, and their education.

In His abundant kindness, God endowed man and woman with many physical, cognitive, and spiritual powers. None of this was created for naught, and it is clear that people must develop and use these powers. But people were blessed with many powers – more than they can realize in their lifetimes even if they were to live long and healthy lives. People must recognize their limitations and choose where to invest their energies. Naturally, when one chooses one possibility over another, there is a cost that can be painful, if only because of the talent that remains undeveloped. But if one is successful in fulfilling the role that God had in mind, the person experiences great satisfaction.

The possibility of self-fulfillment is also connected to historical processes. Human culture develops slowly and gradually. In the past, building a family and providing the basic necessities of food, health, and security demanded most of man's time; he had very little time to develop his spiritual capacity, and therefore it was impossible, for men

---

7. Berakhot 17a.

and women alike, to realize every potential. The man, who worked to provide for the family, and the woman, who raised the children, could not develop all of their talents. However, the ideal is that both men and women realize their full potential, while both being involved in raising the family. The point of equilibrium between these two realms must change as history progresses.

The full partnership between man and woman is described by the last of the prophets as follows: "She is your companion and the wife of your covenant" (Mal. 2:14). The aim is obvious: *for man and wife to be partners in an everlasting covenant.* The covenant between God and the Jewish people has the same aim; in the words of the prophet: "On that day, says the Lord, you will call Me 'my husband,' and you will no longer call Me 'my master'" (Hos. 2:18).

Vision and Reality: Personal Status

The Torah occasionally presents an aspirational idea even though it will be impossible to realize for a long time. Alongside these, the Torah sets minimum standards, so that the very existence of individual and society is not threatened. These standards are associated with both the constraints of reality and the path of the Torah, and their goal is to advance society step by step.[8] Let us now address several examples relating to the status of women, which reveal the tension between historical realities and the path toward realization of a vision.

The Marital Covenant

The Torah's first words about male and female illuminate the nature of their relationship: "Male and female He created them" (Gen. 1:27) – that is, one male and one female. "Hence a man leaves his father and mother and clings to his wife, so that they become one flesh" (ibid. 2:24) – husband and wife form an enduring structure. This is what God implanted in the very nature of creation. Unlike some other species, human births

8. For additional examples, see "The Role of the Commandments," in my *Pathways to Their Hearts: Torah Perspectives on the Individual* (Maggid and Me'aliyot, 2023), pp. 39 ff.

are half male and half female.[9] Clearly, then, the optimal situation is the coupling of one man with one woman, and such pairing is exactly what God had in mind, as expressed by Adam when he said: "The woman You put at my side" (ibid. 3:12).

The same idea that appears in the Torah is repeated in the Prophets and the Writings. "You cover the altar of the Lord with tears, weeping, and moaning, so that He refuses to regard the gift anymore and to accept what you offer. But you ask, 'Because of what?' Because the Lord is a witness between you and the wife of your youth with whom you have broken faith, though she is your companion and the wife of your covenant" (Mal. 2:13–14). You have but one partner – "Only one is my dove, my perfect one" (Song. 6:9) – and the covenant you made with her is an everlasting one: "I am my beloved's, and my beloved is mine" (ibid. 3).

This principle is reflected even more intensely in the prophetic words that describe God's covenant with Israel, which is modeled on the covenant between husband and wife. God says to Israel: "I will betroth you forever" (Hos. 2:21); He will never replace us with another people,[10] nor will He divorce us and cast us out: "Where is your mother's bill of divorce, with which I sent her away?" (Is. 50:1). Scripture is clear in its disapproval of one who divorces his wife: "For I hate divorce – said the Lord, the God of Israel" (Mal. 2:16). The Sages expounded: "R. Yoḥanan says: One who divorces is hated [by God].... R. Elazar said: When one divorces his first wife, even the altar sheds tears."[11]

This invites a question: If one who divorces is hated, why does the Torah permit divorce?[12] Not only is divorce permitted, but there are even several positive and negative mitzvot governing divorce and its implementation under various circumstances. Moreover, if each man has only one wife, why does the Torah permit polygyny? It is only about the high priest that the Torah says: "To make expiation for himself and

9. See Yevamot 119a.
10. See Pesaḥim 87a.
11. Gittin 90b.
12. This contrasts with the Catholic Church, which does not recognize the possibility of severing the bonds of marriage.

his household" (Lev. 16:11) – from which the Sages derive that he may have only one household, no more.[13]

To answer we must first understand that, ideally, marriage is permanent, and we aspire to reach that ideal. Nevertheless, reality does not always match our lofty aspirations; not everyone finds the right match, and it is impossible for two incompatible people to live together without ultimately descending into a constant stream of quarrels and fights.

In addition, even if births are half male and half female, in ancient times there were several variables that threatened the integrity of the family: infertility, the need for large, strong families, wars that decimated the male population and left large numbers of widows and single women, yet other reasons for which the divine wisdom saw fit to permit polygyny. However, the Torah also saw fit to caution against the discord that can result from polygyny, and no case is more instructive than the story of Joseph and his brothers.

In contrast to all of this, the Torah instituted betrothal, marriage, and the mutual duties of spouses, and their purpose is to shape marital life so as to cultivate sanctity within the Jewish family, imbue the institution of marriage with spiritual content, and create functional relationships within the family.[14] This preserves crucial values and sets the tone for the future generations.

Some people mistakenly think that since the Sages used the term "*kinyan*" (which often denotes "acquisition") with respect to betrothal and marriage, the implication is that the husband "acquires" his wife as though she were an object. This is completely erroneous, as a woman cannot be betrothed unwillingly.[15] The term "*kinyan*" describes an act that generates obligations. When we say that the man "acquires," it means that he performs the act that creates the duties. It is a legal term and is not used here in the sense that one buys something in the market. All

13. Yoma 13a.
14. See *Hilkhot Ishut* 12:1–3, *Moreh Nevukhim* III:49, pp. 601–13.
15. Kiddushin 2b, *Hilkhot Ishut* 4:1. See also Nahmanides' novellae to Gittin 9a, where he wrote: "This woman is not her husband's property; rather, she marries of her own volition."

obligations are formalized by means of a *kinyan*,[16] and the substance of the betrothal *kinyan* is that it generates mutual obligations.

The Torah mandates that where divorce is necessary, it is the man who gives the bill of divorce to his wife. This law stems from the fact that, according to Torah law, it is the man who performs the act of betrothal. In the past, this fact provided women with shelter and protection, since it made it possible to betroth and marry a minor – a girl under the age of twelve – and in the ancient world, young unmarried girls were at risk of exploitation and abuse. Where there was no urgent need for such marriages, the Sages cautioned against betrothing a minor.[17]

Nevertheless, the Sages found it necessary to establish parameters and enactments to prevent wicked men from exploiting their power in order to embitter the lives of their wives or to cruelly divorce them for no reason. They therefore instituted the *ketubba* (marriage contract), which imposes financial liabilities on the husband in cases of divorce, "so that it is no light matter in his eyes to divorce her."[18] The *ketubba* is the husband's liability so that he cannot control his wife by threatening to divorce her. This was the primary purpose of instituting the *ketubba*, and indeed, no one party should be able to break up the family over minor issues.

Long ago, halakha incorporated other ways to protect women. Maimonides,[19] following the *Geonim*, rules that a woman who claims that she finds her husband repulsive can sue for divorce, and the *Geonim* even made various enactments with respect to her *ketubba*.[20] A woman who feels that she cannot live a normal life with her husband may sue for the termination of their marital bond. In Ashkenaz, in contrast, Rabbeinu

16. This is the meaning of Ruth 4:7. The ancient Israelite practice whereby "one man would take off his sandal and hand it to the other" was, in fact, a *kinyan*.
17. Kiddushin 41a; *Hilkhot Ishut* 3:19; see also *Avot DeRabbi Natan* 48: "R. Shimon says: One who marries off his minor daughter restricts procreation, loses his money, and ends up shedding blood."
18. Ketubbot 39a.
19. See *Hilkhot Ishut* 14:8.
20. See the responsum of Rabbi Sherira Gaon in *Teshuvot Geonim – Shaarei Tzedek*, vol. 4, §15.

Tam opposed this enactment vehemently; it seems that his opposition stemmed from practical concerns as well.[21]

Likewise, in the early medieval era, Rabbi Gershom Me'or HaGola (the Light of the Diaspora) saw that the time had come to forbid divorce against a woman's will[22] and to ban polygyny.[23] His enactments applied to the communities of Ashkenaz, but by now they have spread to the entire Jewish people.

Such enactments are examples of the work of sages who have recognized that as time passed, sensibilities became more refined and sanctity has spread. As the values that the Torah trains us to espouse have taken root, it has become possible to introduce new legislation that raises even those who are on a lower level to a higher level.

Unfortunately, in our day we have not managed to update the duties required in the *ketubba*, as was done in some places in the past. However, there has been a recent trend in which a prenuptial agreement, which strengthens the woman's status in the event of a breakup, is signed alongside the *ketubba*. In addition, the laws governing the division of property have been altered to reflect the changes in society and the fact that, in many cases, both spouses work. Therefore, just as they share the burden of earning a livelihood, so they should share equally in the division of property.[24] However, there is more to be done in this realm and Torah leaders must lead the way in instituting new norms that are suited to modern realities.

Rabbinic leaders enacted many innovations throughout history, but they did not simply invent things out of thin air, as their enactments applied values that had been established in the Bible. However, in the biblical era, the time was not yet ripe and the people were not ready to realize the ideal vision in its entirety. Over time, as a result of being educated in light of the Torah, our hearts became more attuned to this ideal, and it was then possible to come closer to the goals set by the Torah.

---

21. See, for example, *Responsa Rosh* 43:8.
22. See Rema, *Even HaEzer* 119:6.
23. Ibid. 1, 10.
24. See the article by Rabbi Shlomo Daichovsky, "The Laws of Partnership – Is It the Law of the Land?," *Teḥumin* 18 (1998), pp. 18–31.

Spiritual Purpose

With regard to the ideal vision of the pursuit of lofty spiritual heights, there is no difference between men and women. Even young men and women will achieve high spiritual and intellectual levels, revealing hidden truths on their own,[25] as promised by the prophet: "After that, I will pour out My spirit on all flesh; your sons and your daughters shall prophesy" (Joel 3:1). This has already occurred historically, as there were several women who achieved the level of prophecy.[26]

Though we are far from realizing these aspirations, women certainly have a share in the Torah. Women, like men, are commanded to love and fear God, and these mitzvot require study, contemplation, and intellectual and emotional development to the extent of one's capabilities, whether one is a man or a woman. Maimonides affirmed the ability of women to study intricate talmudic discussions, of which he wrote: "They are the great good that God has bestowed to promote social well-being in this world and thereby enable people to obtain life in the hereafter. All are capable of knowing them – great and small, man and woman, and those with broad or limited intelligence."[27] Therefore, "A woman who studied obtains reward."[28]

The following passage from *Pirkei DeRabbi Eliezer* is also worth quoting:

> R. Pinḥas says: On the eve of Shabbat, when Israel stood at Mount Sinai, the men camped by themselves and the women by themselves. The Holy One, blessed be He, said to Moses: Go ask the daughters of Israel if they want to accept the Torah. Why did He ask the women? Because it is the way of men to follow the opinion of women. As it is stated: "Say thus to the House of Jacob" (Ex. 19:3) – this refers to the women; "and tell the sons of Israel"

25. Compare to *Moreh Nevukhim* II:32, pp. 360–63.
26. See Megilla 14a.
27. *Hilkhot Yesodei HaTorah* 4:13.
28. *Hilkhot Talmud Torah* 1:13.

(ibid.) – this refers to the men. They all responded as one: "All that God has said – we will do and we will heed."[29]

Although there is also a dictum that expresses negative attitudes about teaching girls Torah, going as far as to say that one who teaches his daughter Torah "has taught her frivolity,"[30] Maimonides notes that this is related to the social reality of the past: "Because the minds of most women are not directed toward study."[31] Note that he writes "most" – not all. Some of the other dicta about women in our sources can be explained similarly. In contrast, commenting on the verse describing how the prophetess Deborah sat beneath a palm tree (Judges 4:5), *Seder Eliyahu Rabba* states:[32] "Deborah would sit beneath the palm tree and teach Torah publicly."[33]

Nevertheless, women are not commanded to study Torah, and moreover, they are exempt from several positive commandments. "Regarding all positive commandments that are at particular times and not constant, women are exempt, with the exception of the sanctification of the [Shabbat and festival] day, eating matza on the night of Passover, slaughtering and eating the Paschal offering, *Hak'hel*, and rejoicing [on festivals], which women are obligated to fulfill."[34]

It is not hard to imagine what would happen to babies and children who need attending to if their God-fearing mother was meticulous about every time-bound positive mitzva. Since women are designated "the mother of all life," the Torah exempted them from most of these obligations, and the Sages likewise did not require them to pray at fixed times each day.[35] Certainly the mitzva of Torah study, which is so great that we are instructed not to interrupt it even for the sake of procreation,[36]

29. *Pirkei DeRabbi Eliezer*, ch. 40.
30. Mishna Sota 3:4.
31. *Hilkhot Talmud Torah* 1:13.
32. *Seder Eliyahu Rabba* (Ish-Shalom ed.), section 10, p. 50.
33. See *Pitḥei Teshuva, Ḥoshen Mishpat* 7:5, which addresses the status of women as halakhic decisors. See also my *Si'aḥ Naḥum* §60 (Maaleh Adumim, 2008).
34. *Hilkhot Avoda Zara* 12:3.
35. *Magen Avraham, Oraḥ Ḥayim* 106:2.
36. *Hilkhot Ishut* 15:2–3.

would conflict with her role as the mother of all life. At the very least, it would generate tension and feelings of guilt about neglecting Torah study. Women are therefore not obligated in Torah study as men are. However, when Torah study does not disturb her primary task, which is her true glory, then she may engage in Torah study and is rewarded for doing so, as long as she knows that there is no defect if she neglects Torah study. The same applies to other time-bound mitzvot from which she is exempt: if she fulfills them, she has performed a mitzva, and has earned reward.

In recent generations, when it has become commonplace for women to become educated, it is important, valuable, and virtuous that women study Torah. Rabbi Yisrael Meir Kagan, the Ḥafetz Ḥayim, writes that times have changed and things are no longer as they were.[37] It is unthinkable that women can be educated in every discipline except for Torah, which is the tree of life for all who steadfastly grasp it!

Thanks to the massive technological advances that followed the Industrial Revolution, it is possible to earn a respectable living without investing as many hours as in the past. Economic growth has allowed for a high standard of living, and concomitantly, advances in medicine have raised human life expectancy to unprecedented heights. This has afforded men and women alike the opportunity for extensive Torah study for many years once they conclude the formative stages of child-rearing. The vision of the prophet Joel is no longer so astonishing, and there is no surer path to its realization than by building a multi-generational family in which both father and mother feel responsible for the spiritual guidance of all of their descendants, including their grandchildren and great-grandchildren.

Vision and Reality: The Public Sphere

It is not only matters of personal and intra-familial status that have undergone major changes; in the public sphere, the changes have been even greater. We will consider several examples that reflect how to address differences between the law as it applies to men and the law as

---

37. *Likutei Halakhot* (Warsaw, 1899), Sota, ch. 3, n. 3, pp. 21–22.

it applies to women – differences that hinge on the conditions of life and on societal norms.

Testimony

Historically, in Jewish as well as in other societies, there were differences between men and women regarding occupational opportunities and expectations. Men engaged in agricultural and other forms of manual labor while women primarily worked within the home. The Torah therefore recognized the need to distinguish between them with respect to legal and juridical matters as well.

The laws of evidence and testimony are the basis for any legal system that aspires to impose order. It is vital not only that witnesses tell the truth, but that those with information come to court to testify. Maimonides rules: "A witness is commanded to testify in court whatever he knows, whether the testimony will implicate or vindicate his fellow… as it says: 'A witness who has either seen or learned of the matter – if he does not give information, he shall bear his iniquity' (Lev. 5:1)."[38] For women, who generally did not engage in business or commerce and were not involved in the events that produced the sorts of problems that ended up in court, the duty to testify in court was liable to cause not only discomfort but sometimes even real danger, which is the case even today in some undeveloped countries.

To preserve the woman's status as a "woman of valor," it was necessary to isolate her from the influences of the marketplace. There are still countries in which this situation prevails. However, honesty dictates that if one is not required to testify, then even if he testifies, his testimony is not accepted, as he can always refuse to testify on the grounds that it will be personally damaging, and agree to testify only when it suits his needs. The rule, then, is that one who does not have the obligation to testify does not have the right to testify either. Thus, it was established as a matter of law that the testimony of women is not accepted.

38. *Hilkhot Edut* 1:1.

It is clear that the fact that women are not eligible to testify has nothing to do with their credibility, because whenever a single witness is acceptable, women can testify as well.[39]

Even in ancient times, there were issues about which women could testify, since they were main actors in those realms. Thus Maimonides writes: "Three may testify about a firstborn: the midwife, the mother, and the father."[40] Likewise, a woman could testify that another woman's husband had died.[41]

The fact that the Torah did not invalidate the testimony of a woman absolutely, that a woman is credible, and the fact that a woman's testimony is accepted in court if the litigants both agree that her testimony should be admissible, indicate that women are not fundamentally disqualified. On the contrary, the Torah considered the possibility that the time would come when the testimony of women would be needed. It follows that even when there is a difference in status between women and men, the Torah does not distinguish between them with respect to the significance of their actions: a woman's credibility is the same as a man's, but the Torah did not require her to testify. Her testimony is not accepted because the requirement to testify and the acceptability of testimony are contingent on one another. However, if times were to change, and the testimony of women would be necessary to restore justice and improve society, it would be possible to accept the testimony of a woman.

Indeed, over the course of history, the acceptability of women's testimony has been broadened. Rema wrote: "The early authorities enacted that where men are not normally present, such as in the women's synagogue or anywhere else that it so happens that women frequent but not men... women are deemed credible.... One [authority] wrote that even one woman, a relative, or a minor is believed with respect to assault, the humiliation of a Torah scholar, other quarrels, or informants, because it is unusual to have kosher witnesses available at such incidents...."[42] *Pitḥei Teshuva* adds that "it is the practice of all Jewish courts to send

39. Ibid. 5:3.
40. *Hilkhot Naḥalot* 2:14.
41. *Hilkhot Geirushin* 12:16.
42. *Ḥoshen Mishpat* 35:14.

communal trustees to collect testimony from honored women,"[43] so that those "honored women" would not have to humiliate themselves by appearing in court. We see here that as times changed, the sages saw fit to make enactments that advance the Torah's stated purpose: that a woman should be able to contribute her share to strengthening social institutions and reinforcing justice. Without the enactment to accept the testimony of women in monetary cases, it would be impossible to adjudicate commercial law justly now that women engage in commerce, and the goal of the Torah is the pursuit of justice: "Justice, justice you shall pursue" (Deut. 16:20).

Inheritance

The Torah states that where there are male children, only they inherit, not daughters. This law was necessary given the highly tribal structure of life in the ancient Middle East, and the Torah itself emphasizes that this law prevents estates from passing from one tribe to another.[44] However, we find that some of the earliest enactments of the *ketubba* were made so that women would inherit.[45] The Sages further enacted the *benin dikhrin* clause of the *ketubba*[46] and a document that gave daughters half of the share of each son.[47] It is clear that equality is desirable and necessary for some matters.

Women in Public Roles

The status of women in communal leadership roles and in the rabbinical court system is a hotly debated issue today in our communities. In truth, it was a matter of great interest in the distant past as well. For the most part, *Rishonim* and *Aḥaronim* dealt with these questions in the context of the Scriptural story of Deborah: "Deborah was a prophetess, the wife of Lapidot; she was judging Israel at that time. She would sit under the palm tree of Deborah, between Rama and Beit El on Mount Ephraim,

43. Ad loc. 10.
44. Num. 36:7.
45. Ketubbot 52b.
46. Mishna Ketubbot 4:10. This clause ensures that the male children of a woman will inherit their mother's *ketubba* even if she predeceases her husband.
47. Rema, *Even HaEzer* 90:1.

and the Israelites would come to her for judgment" (Judges 4:4–5). There is a disagreement among *Rishonim* when it comes to characterizing Deborah's status. Some maintain that women are not fit to judge, and Deborah was an exception; others maintain that women are fit to judge just as men are. *Sefer HaḤinukh* summarizes these two opinions:

> We can say that the leaders of Israel accepted her to judge for them, and following them everyone would decide cases by her word. For upon acceptance all are properly fit [to sit in judgment], since any condition [accepted] in monetary matters takes effect. In any case, though, all this that we have said, that [women] do not judge, is according to the view of some authorities, and by the ruling of the Jerusalem Talmud.... In the view of certain other authorities, however, they are properly fit to act as judges; and they asserted that this is an explicit verse, since it is stated: "She was judging."[48]

Tosafot state:

> We see that a woman is fit to judge, as it is written about Deborah: "She was judging Israel at that time." And at the end of the first chapter of Bava Kamma (15a) it is expounded: "That you shall place before them" (Ex. 21:1) – Scripture equates women to men with respect to every penalty in the Torah. And just as this verse refers to those who are judged, it also refers to those who judge, as is expounded in Gittin (88b): "'Before them' – and not before idolaters."[49]

According to this view, women are fit to judge and do not require any special acceptance by the litigants.

Maimonides, it seems, has a different view, as he writes:

48. *Sefer Hahinnuch: The Book of [Mitzva] Education*, trans. Charles Wengrov, vol. 1 (New York: Feldheim, 1978), §77, pp. 309–11.
49. *Tosafot* to Nidda 50a, s.v. *kol hakasher ladun*, and *Tosafot* to Bava Kamma 15a, s.v. *asher*.

> Women are not installed as monarchs, as Scripture says: "King" (Deut. 17:15) – and not a queen. Likewise, only men are appointed to all offices in Israel.[50]

However, one can see that Maimonides was speaking of a different concept of appointment, because he continues:

> Once a king is anointed, the privilege belongs to him and his sons forever, for the monarchy is hereditary.... Not only the monarchy, but all authority and all appointments in Israel are an inheritance to his son, and his grandson, forever.[51]

Maimonides did not relate to the case of Deborah at all. Even in his view, Israel can accept whichever judges they want. This includes women.[52] However, such appointments cannot be permanent, and they are certainly not hereditary.

Yet even according to Maimonides, we cannot appoint a king nowadays, because the monarchy is reserved for the Davidic dynasty, and we cannot identify David's patrilineal descendants today.[53] Our contemporary leaders are elected for fixed terms, and women may be appointed to such positions as well. This also applies to judges who are appointed for limited terms.

Men and Women: Who Takes Precedence?

The need to set priorities when allocating limited resources raises many weighty questions, even more so when decisions impact lives directly. Given the fundamental importance of this issue, we will broaden the discussion and grapple directly with the relevant talmudic passages.

---

50. *Hilkhot Melakhim* 1:5.
51. Ibid. 7.
52. Compare to *Hilkhot Sanhedrin* 7:2–3.
53. *Hilkhot Melakhim* 1:7, 9.

The mishna lists the order of preferences between men and women with respect to various matters:

> A man takes precedence over a woman when it is necessary to sustain life or to return a lost object, and a woman takes precedence over a man with respect to clothing and ransom from captivity. When both are given to degradation [in captivity], the man takes precedence over the woman.[54]

Maimonides explains the reason for these orders of preference:

> You have already learned that all mitzvot are incumbent upon males, whereas females are only obligated in some of them, as explained in Kiddushin.[55] He is more sanctified than her, and therefore the man takes precedence with regard to sustaining life. It says, "Both are given to degradation," meaning that if both are in captivity, and sexual demands are made on both, the man is redeemed before the woman, since this is atypical for men, as they demand from him what is not in his nature.[56]

Maimonides' explanation of the case when "both are given to degradation" is based on the Yerushalmi: "When both are given to degradation, the man takes precedence over the woman. Why? Because it is normal for women but not normal for men."[57] However, the first part of Maimonides' comment demands explanation, especially in light of the fact that Maimonides discusses these laws in his *Mishneh Torah*, yet, surprisingly, he seems to entirely omit the mishna's statement that a man takes precedence over a woman with regard to sustaining life or returning a lost object.[58]

---

54. Mishna Horayot 3:7.
55. Mishna Kiddushin 1:7.
56. *Commentary on the Mishna* ad loc.
57. Y. Horayot 3:4. Editor's note: The meaning is that if both the male and female captives are in danger of being raped, homosexual rape is considered more severe.
58. Many commentators have addressed this omission. I discuss it in *Yad Peshuta* on *Hilkhot Gezeila VaAveida* 12:1–2 and *Hilkhot Matnot Aniyim* 8:15.

To understand Maimonides' position, we must first understand that the two laws in the first part of the mishna address two distinct issues: a) sustaining life, which refers to providing food in a time of famine;[59] b) return of lost property. Given the structure of *Mishneh Torah*, since these are two fundamentally different laws, we would expect to find them cited in different places.

Maimonides cites most of the laws that appear in the mishna in Horayot in *Hilkhot Matnot Aniyim*. However, instead of writing "A man takes precedence over a woman when it is necessary to sustain life," as it appears at the beginning of the mishna, he writes the opposite: "A woman takes precedence over a man with respect to providing food." He then adds an explanation:

> A woman takes precedence over a man with respect to providing food, clothing, and ransom from captivity, because it is normal for a man to beg but it is not normal for a woman to beg; her humiliation is greater. If they were both in captivity and sexual demands were made on both, the man's ransom takes precedence, because this is not normal for him.[60]

However, when he presents the law concerning the return of a lost object, he completely ignores the mishna in Horayot, not even mentioning a woman's lost object separately, even though the mishna does. He thus asserts:

> One who lost an object and then found his object and his fellow's object: if he can restore both, he must do so. If he can restore only one, his own lost object takes precedence, even over the lost object of his father or his rabbi; his takes precedence over that of any other.[61]

59. See *Tosafot Rid* on Ketubbot 67a and Meiri on Horayot 12b.
60. *Hilkhot Matnot Aniyim* 8:15.
61. *Hilkhot Gezeila VaAveida* 12:1.

Commentaries throughout the generations have attempted to explain why Maimonides reversed one part of the mishna and omitted another. We will content ourselves with the explanation of Rabbi Yosef Rosen, the Rogatchover Gaon, in his *Tzofnat Paane'aḥ*.[62] He proposes that Maimonides rejected the mishna in Horayot on the basis of another mishna and the Talmud's discussion of it:

> If a man [on his deathbed] says, "If my wife bears a male, he shall receive 100 zuz," and she bears a male, he receives 100 zuz. "And if she bears a female, 200 zuz," and she bears a female, she takes 200. "If a male 100, and if a female 200," and she bears a male and a female, the male takes 100 and the female 200.[63]

The Gemara explains this mishna as follows:

> Does this imply that a daughter is preferable to him than a son?... Who is [the *Tanna* of this mishna]? It is R. Yehuda ... for we learned in a *baraita*: "It is a mitzva to provide for one's daughters, *a fortiori* one's sons, who engage in Torah study. These are the words of R. Meir. R. Yehuda says: It is a mitzva to provide for one's sons, *a fortiori* one's daughters, so that they do not face ignominy.[64]

In *Hilkhot Matnot Aniyim* (10:16), Maimonides explains the expression "so that they do not face ignominy" to mean "to direct the daughters on the right path, so that they not be shamed."

Maimonides rules in accordance with the mishna in Bava Batra in *Hilkhot Zekhiya UMattana*:

> A person on his deathbed who ordered that a gift be given to the unborn child in his wife's womb, the unborn child receives the gift. If he said, "If my wife bears a male, he shall receive 100 zuz, and if a female 200," then if she bears a male, he takes 100 zuz, if

62. *Hilkhot Matnot Aniyim* 8:15.
63. Mishna Bava Batra 9:2.
64. Bava Batra 141a.

> she bears a female, she takes 200, and if she bears a male and a female, the male takes 100 and the female 200.[65]

This law accords with R. Yehuda that parents prefer daughters. It follows, argues the Rogatchover Gaon, that the mishna in Horayot, which states that a man takes precedence over a woman, accords with R. Meir.[66] Maimonides therefore ruled in accordance with R. Yehuda that a woman takes precedence based on the rule that "[in a dispute between] R. Meir and R. Yehuda, the law is in accordance with R. Yehuda."[67] It therefore seems that even the Sages deliberated the proper balance between male and female.

However, I would humbly suggest that this explanation is not so simple, because it is unthinkable that R. Meir and R. Yehuda disagreed over what all or most parents want. There are many and varied reasons for parents to prefer a son or daughter, and those preferences can even change with time and circumstance. It stands to reason that parents who have many sons will want a daughter, and vice versa. After all, the mitzva of procreation is fulfilled by having a son and a daughter!

Moreover, the dispute between R. Yehuda and R. Meir in the *baraita* is about future hopes and providing for children. Indeed, Rashbam there notes that the Gemara embeds its own comments within the *baraita*: "[The words] 'who engage in Torah study' and 'so that they do not face ignominy' are explanations and are not part of the *baraita*." Thus, in Bava Batra it is inferred that Torah study is R. Meir's highest value, but the subject of the mishna in Horayot is the order of precedence between adult men and women. Therefore, Maimonides explained that the man's precedence is due to his being obligated in more mitzvot.

Before drawing conclusions from these passages, let us comment on what I mentioned above, namely, that Maimonides explains the Gemara's formulation, "so that they do not face ignominy," to mean "to direct the daughters on the right path, so that they not be shamed."

---

65. *Hilkhot Zekhiya UMattana* 8:5–6.
66. According to the rule that "an anonymous mishna is R. Meir," as explained in Sanhedrin 86a.
67. Eiruvin 46b.

How does he know this? To explain, let us look closely at the passage in Bava Batra and a difficulty that emerges from it.

It could have been explained that a parent of daughters may feel obligated to provide for them lest they stave off hunger by descending into the shame and ignominy of prostitution.[68] In this context, R. Meir focuses on hopes for the sons' future Torah study, and he gives precedence to sons so that they may achieve something virtuous. R. Yehuda, on the other hand, speaks to the fear of the daughters' moral degradation, giving precedence to providing for daughters so that they stay out of trouble. If this is the proper understanding of the dispute, how could the Gemara propose that R. Yehuda maintains that "a daughter is preferable to him than a son"? The daughters' precedence according to R. Yehuda is not a question of preference, but one of concern for her degradation.

Maimonides therefore concludes that the Gemara means to say that in addition to the greater risk that applies to daughters, there is also a positive element that counterbalances the sons' advantage – that is, that daughters, too, can achieve great moral virtue, though if the parents fail to guide them properly, they are at risk of falling into ignominy. This is the meaning of "to direct the daughters on the right path, so that they not be shamed."

In my opinion, Maimonides understands that the dispute between R. Meir and R. Yehuda is about one's expectations of his children. According to R. Meir, most fathers' greatest hope is that their sons study Torah. In contrast, R. Yehuda maintains that most parents' aspiration to keep their daughters on the "right path" equals their goal of raising their sons to study Torah. However, since daughters also carry the risk of ignominy, their needs take precedence over the needs of the sons. Thus, "a daughter is preferable."

R. Yehuda believes that these two aspirations, that one's sons engage in Torah study and that one's daughters tread the right path and build a Jewish family, are equivalent. Neither of these values is preferable to the other. However, the daughter is at greater risk, so if it is impossible to achieve both aspirations, the daughter takes precedence. The law accords with R. Yehuda, but there is no disputing that both aspirations

68. On the meaning of the "right path," see also *Hilkhot Sota* 4:19.

are worthy. The disagreement is about whether, when the two aspirations conflict, one is of greater value than the other and about which aspiration can be attained and which is most likely to become a false hope.

An example of this principle emerges from another mishna: "I might think that honoring the father is greater than honoring the mother. Therefore Scripture states, 'A man shall revere his mother and father' (Lev. 19:3), which teaches that they are equal. However, the Sages said that the father nevertheless takes precedence, because son and mother are obligated to honor the father."[69] That is, in certain cases, an additional consideration changes the order of precedence.

Thus, if one asks whether people prefer sons to daughters or daughters to sons, the clear answer is that there are no hard-and-fast rules. Nevertheless, R. Meir decided the law in favor of the sons based on *a fortiori* reasoning, so that they study Torah, and R. Yehuda derived from *a fortiori* reasoning that the daughters take precedence, so that they do not fall into ignominy. Under routine circumstances, however, there is no reason to prefer sons or daughters; just as mothers and fathers are of equal status, so too sons and daughters. Thus, Maimonides rules, without invoking *a fortiori* arguments, that sons and daughters are of equal status when it comes to sustenance:

> One who provides sustenance for his sons and daughters... so that the sons study Torah and to direct the daughters on the right path, so that they not be shamed, and likewise one who provides sustenance to his father and mother – this is classified as *tzedaka*.[70]

Maimonides explains the mishna similarly:

> One is obligated to provide for his children... and we compel him and take his money for their sustenance according to his wealth, just as we do for the maintenance of his parents.... There is no

69. Mishna Keritot 6:9.
70. *Hilkhot Matnot Aniyim* 10:16.

> difference with regard to sustenance between male and female children.[71]

Maimonides is teaching us that just as father and mother are equal, in that we have been commanded to honor and revere both of them as one, so too sons and daughters are equal, as both can reach great spiritual heights – in his words, "so that the sons study Torah and to direct the daughters on the right path." Neither of these values is greater than the other. However, even though men and women are equal in principle, there are constraining circumstances, such as when resources are limited and their needs cannot all be met, in which case it is necessary to determine an order of precedence. For that reason, the third factor is decisive: "so that they not be shamed," which alludes to the Gemara's "so they do not face ignominy."

We can now return to Maimonides' ruling in *Hilkhot Matnot Aniyim*:

> A woman takes precedence over a man with respect to providing food, clothing, and ransom from captivity, because it is normal for a man to beg but it is not normal for a woman to beg; her humiliation is greater.[72]

The reason that a woman takes precedence is "because it is normal for a man to beg but it is not normal for a woman to beg." The source for this reasoning is the Gemara:

> Our Rabbis taught: An orphan boy and an orphan girl who have come for provisions – we provide for the orphan girl and then we provide for the orphan boy, because it is normal for a man to beg but it is not normal for a woman to beg.[73]

---

71. *Commentary on the Mishna,* Ketubbot 4:6.
72. *Hilkhot Matnot Aniyim* 8:15.
73. Ketubbot 67a.

The fact that it is not normal for a woman to beg is related to her greater humiliation even in the presence of one person; certainly in the presence of many. Her humiliation is greater than that of men, and therefore this factor is decisive. Maimonides alludes to his method for arriving at a decision when he emphasizes that "her humiliation is greater." The source of this is likewise the Gemara:

> Our Rabbis taught: A share of *teruma* is given neither to a slave nor to a woman at the threshing floors, but in places where a share is given, it is to be given to the woman first, and she is immediately dismissed. What does this mean? It is saying that where the pauper's tithe is distributed, it is to be given to the woman first. Why? Because of her degradation (i.e., if she is forced to wait, she will be humiliated).
>
> Rava said: Formerly, when a man and a woman would come before me for judgment (each with their own claim), I would dispose of the man's lawsuit first, reasoning that a man is obligated in [more] mitzvot. However, once I heard this [*baraita*], I dispose of the woman's lawsuit first. Why? Because of her degradation.[74]

Initially, Rava gave precedence to the man because "he is obligated in mitzvot," and Maimonides explains the precedence given to men in the mishna in Horayot in the exact same way. Rava believed that even according to R. Meir a reason is needed to tip the scales and decide who takes precedence. Since R. Meir gave precedence to the son to that he could study Torah, it would seem to follow that an adult man should likewise be given precedence over an adult woman, since men are obligated in more mitzvot, an advantage equivalent to Torah study. Later, however, based on the *baraita* regarding the pauper's tithe, Rava changed his mind and thought that a judge must give precedence to the woman's hearing "because of her degradation." Indeed, when Maimonides cites Rava's law, he uses the exact same language that he uses in *Hilkhot Matnot Aniyim*: "A woman's case takes precedence over a man's because her

74. Yevamot 100a.

humiliation is greater."[75] The *baraita* also explicitly gave precedence to women over men out of consideration for the woman's greater humiliation: "An orphan boy and an orphan girl who come (separately) in order to marry – we marry off the orphan girl and then we marry off the orphan boy, because a woman's humiliation is greater than that of a man."[76] Maimonides rules accordingly: "An orphan boy and an orphan girl who come in order to marry – we marry off the orphan girl before the orphan boy, because a woman's humiliation is greater."[77]

Rava decided the law against the mishna of R. Meir and even gave a woman's court case precedence over a man's court case. He did so because it is evident from a *baraita* that deals with the distribution of the pauper's tithe that even though men and women are equal, the woman's humiliation is the decisive factor, because if the judge hears the man's case before the woman's, it will hurt and offend her. Maimonides therefore rules in accordance with the *baraita* and rejects the mishna in Horayot.

Accordingly, the reason that Maimonides, in his *Commentary on the Mishna*, explains that the reasoning of the *Tanna* in Horayot, "that all mitzvot are incumbent upon males, whereas females are only obligated in some of them," is to teach us that this reason is not accepted as practical law, as the law in fact accords with R. Yehuda that men and women are equal, unless there is a special reason to give one of them precedence.

We can now understand the omission from *Mishneh Torah* of the law concerning the return of lost objects. Humiliation is not a factor when it comes to returning a lost object, because the woman does not know who found the object. The greater number of mitzvot for men, in contrast, does not supersede the equality between men and women because a woman can keep to the right path. Maimonides therefore omits the second part of the mishna in Horayot because when it comes to returning lost objects there is no set precedence to either men or women; they are equal.

---

75. *Hilkhot Sanhedrin* 21:6.
76. Ketubbot 67a–b.
77. *Hilkhot Matnot Aniyim* 8:16.

Maimonides also rules as follows: "The meal offering of a man takes precedence over the meal offering of a woman."[78] The Rogatchover Gaon proposed that the source of this law is a passage in Yoma (44a), where it is derived from a verse, "And he will make expiation for himself and his household" (Lev. 16:17), that "his expiation precedes the expiation of his household," "household" referring to his wife. The fact that even the law that sets an order of precedence with respect to offerings must be derived from a verse proves that in the typical case, men and women are equal. For one to take precedence over the other, a special reason is needed.

Based on this approach, we can understand another of Maimonides' omissions – a *baraita* that appears in the Gemara:

> They said to him: If his wife gives birth to a male, he says, "Blessed is He who is good and bestows good."[79]

However, Maimonides rules:

> In sum, over anything that is good for him and others, he blesses, "Who is good and bestows good."[80]

The reason is that since sons and daughters are equal according to halakha, the blessing should not be ordained only for the birth of a son. Rather, he must recite the blessing upon the birth of a daughter as well.[81]

The mishna in Horayot indeed presents orders of precedence between men and women, but these orders accord with the view of R. Meir, who views the obligation in the mitzvot as the exclusive and decisive consideration. However, a different approach, that of R. Yehuda, emerges from several *baraitot*. In this view, it is not the number of mitzvot that determines the orders of precedence, because the spiritual value of

78. *Hilkhot Temidin UMusafin* 9:10, based on an explicit ruling in Tosefta Zevaḥim 10:4 (Zuckermandel ed.).
79. Berakhot 59b.
80. *Hilkhot Berakhot* 10:7.
81. See my explanation in *Yad Peshuta* ad loc.

a man or a woman hinges on their keeping to the right path, and Rava decides the halakha in accordance with this view.

Equality and Self-Fulfillment

There were times when women suffered discrimination on multiple levels, and this inequality persists even until today. There is a certainly basis for the demand for equality, and a healthy society must allow every woman to be a full partner in every field to which she can contribute to the betterment of society.

Some people are drawn to hollow slogans that pretend it is possible to create absolute equality in every facet of life. But the physical, emotional, and psychological differences between men and women cannot be ignored. Human existence depends on these distinctions, and ignoring the different natural roles of men and women is potentially disastrous.

The revolutionary idea of modern times, to equate men and women in every way, can lead to absurdities. It is self-evident that even one whose worldview has been so skewed by extreme individualism that he views pregnancy, birth, and nursing as a form of injustice, as violations of women's rights, cannot transfer these functions to men in order to create an imaginary equality.

Doctors today have recognized that a mother's milk is better for newborns than any artificial substitute, and that babies who nurse are the recipients of numerous health benefits, including antibodies against various diseases. Half a century ago, however, the prevailing opinion in the Western world was that there was no reason to breastfeed, and that women could be liberated from this function. Only later was it revealed that this foolish attempt at equality caused the proliferation of allergies and sensitivities among children and health problems among mothers.

Nevertheless, there are still extremists who view with suspicion anyone who attempts to emphasize the woman's privilege of being "the mother of all life." For those who maintain that individuals ought to be self-centered, society and its future are unimportant, and so having and raising children are not pursuits that offer satisfaction. If we wish to prevent discrimination against women, then in contradistinction to these views, we must ensure that social institutions take the differences between men and women into consideration and seek ways to enable a woman to realize a better integration of all of her abilities without requiring her to give up her purpose as "the mother of all life."

In recent years, a new battlefront has appeared: the integration of women into every part of the military. Of course, no one demands the integration of women on men's basketball teams because everyone understands that differences in physical strength are critical,[82] but when it comes to the military, this consideration is ignored.[83]

In addition to the physiological aspects, there is also an essential moral angle. Those who champion imaginary equality scream that women must be drafted into the military – an outrageous denial of the ideal of becoming "the mother of all life." There is no greater example of "using something that gives life for that which takes life"[84] than integrating women into combat units. The value of life is replaced by the value of bringing about death. We are pained by the necessity of sending our sons into battle, and they want us to send our daughters, too! Instead of limiting the military to what is essential, they establish militarism as a basic foundation of society, thus sacrificing the mother, the universal symbol of life, on the altar of Molekh.

Misplaced demands for equality threaten the existence of the human family unit. A woman who is fortunate to have and raise sons and daughters, to build a sound, solid family grounded in good character and lofty values, will merit seeing that her grandchildren, great-grandchildren, and beyond are all impacted by her personality.

Past and Future

The world has progressed, and we are fortunate enough to live in societies of plenty. Today it is possible to raise a family and also to take advantage

---

82. Editor's note: See, however, *Sex Integration in Sport and Physical Culture: Promises and Pitfalls*, ed. Alex Channon, Katherine Dashper, Thomas Fletcher, and Robert J. Lake (New York: Routledge, 2017).
83. Editor's note: Regarding the debate on this issue, see *Women and Gender Perspectives in the Military: An International Comparison*, ed. Robert Egnell and Mayesha Alam (Washington DC: Georgetown University Press, 2019), particularly chapter 8 discussing the Israeli military.
84. See Rashi on Exodus 20:22.

of improvements in the conditions of life in order to develop talents and abilities that in past generations only the privileged few had the opportunity to cultivate. Nevertheless, we must maintain the proper balance. The choice is in the hands of each individual, whether man or woman, but we must consider the purpose and goal of individual and society alike.

We must recognize natural limitations. It is certainly impossible for anyone, man or woman, to fully develop each of their talents and potentials. Human beings pay a price for their decisions, which perforce leave roads that are not taken and never will be. We must therefore set priorities that will determine what we focus on and which inclinations to try to develop.

However, for many people, the problem is more basic. It is not that they struggle to develop the potentials they have chosen to focus on; they have not even decided which potentials they wish to develop, because they have never given much attention to setting their priorities. It is only once one has a defined scale of priorities that he can focus on fulfilling the potential he has chosen to develop. The Sages said: "Who is rich? One who is happy with his portion."[85] This does not refer to monetary wealth only but rather also to one who is discontented with his portion; one who does not acknowledge his lot in life will be miserable in whatever he does.

This balance cannot be prescribed with any specificity. It is likewise impossible to prescribe to a married couple how many children they must have. Each family has its own structure, needs, and challenges. Of course, there is value in having many children, but it is also clear that it is not an absolute value; it can be superseded by other values. This has been addressed in the Talmud and in the writings of Jewish sages throughout history. Rav Saadia Gaon, for example, wrote:

> Others, again, are of the opinion that [men] ought to dedicate themselves earnestly to the begetting of children.... Now I considered this allegation on their part carefully and I noted that it was correct so far as those children are concerned whom the Creator grants to His servant in accordance with His wish. The mistake

85. Mishna Avot 4:1.

> of the advocates of this theory lies in their requirement that one pay attention to this matter alone, to the exclusion of everything else. I say, however: Of what benefit are children to a person if he is unable to provide for their sustenance, covering, or shelter? And what is the good of raising them if it will not be productive of wisdom and knowledge on their part?... Furthermore, what about the pains of pregnancy and the pangs of childbirth and the birth itself?[86]

It is impossible to prescribe one principle for everyone in such matters. However, the very institution of the family is the foundation, created by God, on which a healthy society is built. He requires us to establish families and thereby become His partners in the creation of the world. Every couple must balance between different values and considerations, and when husband and wife have a strong relationship, they will certainly come to an agreement about what is right for them.

We live in a generation of sea change. The change in the status women is but one of many dramatic shifts that are taking place. If we can guide our educational efforts and our communal aspirations toward recognizing the unique creativity of each woman in maximizing her every potential and in the family that she builds with her husband, humanity as a whole will be the better for it. This is the solid foundation of society itself; the individual is not supposed to be isolated. The basic building block of society, the unit from which it is composed, is the family. The biological companionship of husband and wife, not competition between them, serves as a model relationship for most aspects of life. Every person, man or woman, needs companionship with others in various realms. No one can arrive at perfection alone.[87] But if we are seduced by empty clichés that demand artificial equality and view the individual, man and woman alike, as rivals and competitors with every other individual, it will lead to fragmentation and, ultimately, ruin.

---

86. Saadia Gaon, *The Book of Beliefs and Opinions,* trans. S. Rosenblatt (New Haven: Yale University Press, 1948), pp. 381–82.
87. Maimonides (*Moreh Nevukhim* II:40, p. 381) writes that man, in contrast to animals, is "political by nature." That is, he needs society.

As a general rule, the Torah gives us signposts by which we are to navigate our spiritual development, as men and women, as individuals and as spouses, as members of families and societies, as part of the Jewish people and of mankind. In addition, the Torah guides the actions of every generation toward the ultimate destination, even as it remains far off. We need but incline our ears to hear the majestic voice of God and open our eyes to see that the world is not, God forbid, haphazard. We must answer the call of our Creator and accept responsibility for our actions as individuals, as spouses, and as members of society.

Chapter 11

"This People I Formed for Myself": Israel and the Nations

Determinism, Freedom, and Meaning

To the best of our knowledge, of all known species, only man can ask himself: Where did you come from and where are you going? Then, once he recognizes that he had no choice but to be born and will have no choice but to die, he realizes that "even if [he] lived a thousand years twice over... all are bound for the same place" (Eccl. 6:6), and a troublesome question emerges from the recesses of his consciousness: "What does man gain for all his toil?" When man expands his perspective and contemplates all of humanity, his question becomes still deeper: "What is man that You should notice him, mortal man, that You take him into account?" (Ps. 144:3).

As man becomes more curious and asks more penetrating questions – about himself, about society, and about the substance and essence of the world around him – he discovers that all of these fundamental questions are interconnected. Even more surprisingly, although it seems that different answers to these questions have been given over time, the theoretical underpinnings of most of the solutions proffered are nothing but different combinations of the same small set of basic premises.

Although these premises take on varying forms in different cultures and in the works of various thinkers, their essence has remained unchanged since the dawn of history, despite revolutions and upheavals in the social, scientific, and intellectual climates.

The most bothersome question is this: "Do life and the world have meaning?" If so, all of the questions that follow this initial question also take on meaning, since even if man cannot fully grasp the world, he can nevertheless experience it? If the history of the universe, or at least the history of mankind, leads toward a purposeful goal, it seems that the human mind cannot identify it, define it, or articulate it fully, even after many generations. However, the sense that there is such a purpose is never far from man's consciousness. Is there any human experience that can confirm this feeling?

Alternatively, perhaps we should not attempt to understand why. It is better to avoid inquiries that can only cause agony, melancholy, and doleful musings about the worth of mankind. This approach is sometimes presented as denying that reality has any meaning or purpose – thus the view that the entire universe can ultimately be reduced to the product of random chance. This approach can also reflect a conception of man as a caged bird, for whom the world remains sealed off, rendering man no better than animal. Such perspectives lead to one of the following practical conclusions: one can be reconciled, out of despair, to the bleak reality that man is incapable of lifting a finger out of free will, because free will itself is a mere illusion. This will generally lead a person to be very passive and to not plan out his next steps and actions. Alternatively, one can join the fight for survival that typifies all of nature, and become an unbridled hedonist – eating and drinking, for tomorrow we die! For one unfortunate enough to experience pain and suffering and who expects that reality to continue, the understanding that life is meaningless may lead him to end the battlefield of suffering by taking his own life.

The problem is that the same blood that flows in man's veins does not let him spill that blood. Self-awareness is precisely what forces man to continue bearing life's burden. What is this natural impulse to stay alive? Where does it come from? Beyond the question of meaning is an even more profound question. Presuming that there are only two possible basic worldviews, how can one decide between them?

There are two ways to answer this question. According to one, the world is everything and includes all existence – creator and creatures, source and derivatives, influencer and influenced. Beyond the world there is nothing, for it includes every cause and effect, catalyst and result, stimulus and response, god and man. If nature has laws, they are inscribed within it from within. Even if random chance reigns supreme, it, too, is inscribed.

This feature of randomness characterizes Darwin's theory of evolution. The law that governs the world is survival of the fittest. Random chance produces innumerable different combinations; those that are of use will remain, while all others will be replaced and disappear. The world thus becomes increasingly complex. Animals contend unceasingly over vital but limited resources, and might makes right. Entire species and their individual members are born, procreate, and die, but new, improved species develop from among their descendants. This is how Darwin begins his *The Descent of Man*:

> Man may be excused for feeling some pride at having risen, though not through his own exertions, to the very summit of the organic scale; and the fact of his having thus risen, instead of having been aboriginally placed there, may give him hope for a still higher destiny in the distant future.[1]

According to Darwin, advancement is not the result of any active force; it is completely passive. New configurations form randomly, and the ones that can best adapt to the conditions of life endure. Darwin did not explain why life always evolves toward greater complexity, but others have suggested that matter contains some hidden impulse that drives it forward. According to both views, the struggle for survival is the sole driving force shaping the future, since only the victor in this struggle, even if the victor is but a single individual, will survive to be subjected to further changes.

---

1. Charles Darwin, *The Descent of Man and Selection in Relation to Sex* (New York: Appleton, 1874), p. 619.

However, it is clear that the process of evolution does not happen to individuals only. Most animals cannot exist on their own, only in groups and packs; this is all the more true of human beings, as the life of an individual human depends on family and society. There are struggles for survival within a society, and societies compete against one another. The struggle against an outside society differs fundamentally from the struggle that transpires within a social unit – a clan, a tribe, a nation, a group of nations, or any other collaborative group. The wars between hostile clans and tribes, and certainly between rival classes and races, are much crueler, and can become wars of extermination.

In the ancient world, belief in gods of war was widespread. This belief has taken on new, secular forms, which are prevalent around the world to this very day. In European thought of the past few centuries, these ideas have been integrated into the positivist tradition, and under its pseudo-scientific influence, revolutionary totalitarian regimes arose, on the right and the left, promising a new, improved world, all the while flooding the world with rivers of blood and fire.[2] The idea of a materialistic god of progress, whether he is supposed to lead to an imaginary equality (communism) or to engineer a master race, was exposed in all its horrific, terrible ugliness in the fury of destruction that it inflicted on most of the world, and especially upon the Jewish people during the Holocaust. Even Jewish history, saturated with death and destruction, had experienced nothing that compares to the Holocaust.

In an apparent response to the focus on society and the collective that characterizes totalitarianism, a strain of thought that views the erosion of society as the salvation of the individual emerged. The individual became an end in himself. The yardstick by which both progress and justice are measured is the fulfillment of the individual's appetites. If society and its institutions fall victim to the exploits of an individual, then this, too, will be considered good, because any restraint on the spirit and freedom of the individual is nothing less than the embodiment of evil. This all occurred while the dystopia of *Animal Farm* was merely the fanciful imagining of a science fiction writer.

---

2. For a summary, see Eric Voegelin, *From Enlightenment to Revolution* (Durham: Duke University Press, 1975).

Now that the age of genetic engineering is upon us, who can predict what will be? We are already hearing voices that welcome the possibility, which some pretend to see on the horizon, that the wish of extreme individualism will be fulfilled, and that it will be possible for an individual to achieve immortality on this earth, without the need for a spouse or a family. Nietzsche spoke of the *Übermensch*, the superior human who has no need for society except inasmuch as he can enslave and rule over it.[3] The natural order will soon be overturned, and an aging individual will be able to clone himself as a newborn. Human evolution will thus grind to a halt, as it will have already achieved its peak!

But there is another way.[4] "The people that walked in darkness have seen a brilliant light; on those who dwelt in a land of the shadow of death, a light has shone" (Is. 9:1). What sort of light is this, and what vision is revealed to the people from amidst the darkness? The Torah teaches us: "Moses said, 'I will turn aside to see this marvelous sight'.… When the Lord saw that he had turned aside to look, He called to him" (Ex. 3:3–4). The Sages explained: "What is the meaning of 'to him'? This teaches that there were people with Moses, and no one saw but him."[5] God's glory fills the world, but it can only be seen by one who grasps that the source of existence lies beyond the sensory world, that space and time cannot contain the one true God. In the recesses of the human soul is a wondrous spark that can be ignited by the fire that flows from eternity. Within the gloom, the shadow, the fog – immortality can flourish. This spark, with which man has been graced, is hidden, for this is the Divine within man, and no man can see the Divine and live. It is not easy for everyone to recognize and acknowledge this uniqueness. By

---

3. "A great man – a man whom Nature has built up and invented in a grand style – What is such a man?... He asks for no 'compassionate' heart, but servants, instruments…." Friedrich Nietzsche, *The Will to Power*, book 3, §962, vol. 15 of *The Complete Works of Friedrich Nietzsche*, trans. Oscar Levy (Edinburgh: Foulis, 1910); "The great man is conscious of his power over a people" (ibid. §964).
4. For most people, the distinctions are not so clearly and sharply drawn. Most people have complicated views that are not always entirely consistent. In many cases, we are not aware of the internal contradictions in our worldviews. In addition, there are all sorts of middle positions that reflect attempts to include different values within one system.
5. Exodus Rabba 2:5.

recognizing it, one becomes, like Saul, a different person, called to stand before God, to know Him: "Teach me the path of life; in Your presence is perfect joy. Delights are forever in Your right hand" (Ps. 16:11). Man, who is formed of matter, is not capable of grasping spiritual essences, and he certainly cannot define the purpose and plan of all life. However, he knows that it is incumbent on him to somehow become part of that plan and advance that purpose.

The world does not move on its own toward perfection; only human beings who recognize their Creator and try to cleave to Him can advance themselves along with the whole world. There is a constant tension between good and evil; man must choose to open his soul to the light of the Almighty.

When one knows before whom he stands, his thoughts, speech, and, of course, actions and behaviors reflect the divine light that shines upon him. He walks upright, as God created him to do, and avoids the distractions that derail many people.[6] This task may occasionally be daunting, frustrating, and even painful: the ability to choose exposes man to the fear of responsibility. The very realization that human actions have significance makes demands on us, though it contains a perplexing paradox: on the one hand, this realization confronts man with far-reaching expectations, as befits one who is "a little less than divine" (Ps. 8:6). On the other hand, it confronts him with the truth that he is nothing but a small creature, formed of dust, whose life is fleeting as a shadow. How dare he dream of things so much greater and more marvelous than him?

Furthermore, "sometimes the truth flashes out to us so that we think that it is clear as day, and then matter and habit in their various forms conceal it so that we find ourselves again in an obscure night.... And even this small light that shines over us is not always there, but flashes and is hidden again, as if it were the flaming sword which turned every way."[7] Yet every man is capable of bearing this responsibility. "The reason man was created alone...is to proclaim the greatness of the Supreme King of kings, the Holy One, blessed be He – for if a man mints a hundred coins with one mold, they are all similar to each other, but

---

6. See *Hilkhot Shemitta VeYovel* 13:13.
7. Introduction to *Moreh Nevukhim*, p. 7; translation emended.

the Supreme King of kings, the Holy One, blessed be He, fashions every man in the mold of Adam, yet none is similar to his fellow. Therefore, everyone can proclaim: 'The world was created for me.'"[8]

On Meaning in History and the Covenant

Only the individual human being has any hope of achieving eternal life beyond this world, free from the shackles of time and place. This is not the case of any social organism, like a family, tribe, or nation. These are unique to the material world, on which their entire existence depends. Indeed, "the spirit of man is the lamp of the Lord" (Prov. 20:27), but a nation has no soul. The social framework that everyone needs, though comprising individual human beings who have glimpsed eternity, is itself entirely of this world. A nation is a social organism composed of people, and though its existence may span many generations, it is limited to this world.

Nevertheless, history is the chronicle of societies and cultures, nations and empires, movements and factions, which span centuries. If history has meaning, it should be sought here, no less than in the accounts of the lives of individuals!

The presumption that man is a divine being necessarily implies that the development of humanity and its institutions, with all of its diverse cultures and lifestyles, has an essence and a purpose. Is a life of meaning possible only at the individual level? How does one who has not personally experienced divine illumination attain spiritual elevation?

Indeed, even if history has a direction and a Director, can they be discovered? The tools and instruments of natural science are wholly unfit to investigate purposefulness. On the contrary, the great leap forward of modern science began only after scientists stopped looking for purpose, a fundamentally speculative exercise, and focused on describing empirical evidence. The study of history would therefore seem to be incapable, even in the best case, of yielding anything but an improved version of materialism. Surprisingly, though, this brings us to a turning point.

The individual's grasp of the eternal is in his heart; eyes of flesh have not beheld it. However, the survival of the Jewish people, God's

---

8. Mishna Sanhedrin 4:5.

nation, is an enduring fact. In contrast to the spiritual anchor of an individual's soul, which cannot be investigated nor perceived with the senses, the vital records of the Jewish people are scattered all across the civilized world. As they were persecuted, so they would multiply and thrive. Pretentious philosophies that remove God from their theories of history crash against the shoals of this cold, hard fact. It is for this reason that some tried to ignore Jewish history or demean it as something insignificant, negligible in the context of the broad fabric of all of human history.[9]

The survival and endurance of the Jewish people is a historical anomaly that attests to man's superiority over beast. It cannot be proven in a laboratory that the human spirit transcends the mere material, but empirical experience, which shows that God will not abandon His people, teaches us that the human spirit comes from God, its Giver. This was all true even before God remembered Zion and returned the remnants of His people to its land, where they experienced rejuvenation; it is even more obvious today, now that we have experienced this remarkable historical process.

The Torah bases human history on the notion of covenant. It is the covenant that gives meaning to the lives of individuals, to Jewish history, and thus to all of human history. The first covenant was made with Noah, from whom all the diverse nations descended, each with its own land and language. "The devisings of man's mind are evil from his youth" (Gen. 8:21), yet God's esteem for man is so great that He commands him, admonishes him, and designates him with a most sublime honorific: "But for your own life-blood I will require a reckoning... for He made man in the image of God" (ibid. 9:5–6).

It is with this covenant in mind that Moses, many generations later, could exhort his audience to consider history and learn its lessons:

---

9. Compare to Toynbee: "If we cast our eye over all the civilizations that were still alive in A.D. 1952, we shall see... all the eight then extant civilizations had churches for their chrysalises, and the seven then extant fossils of extinct civilizations were all preserved in ecclesiastical integuments. This was true alike of Jewry, a fossil of an extinct Syriac Civilization that had come to be dispersed throughout the World." Arnold J. Toynbee, *A Study of History*, vol. VII (London: Oxford University Press, 1954), p. 393.

"Remember the days of old, consider the years of ages past" (Deut. 32:7). The Sages explained: "There is no generation that has no people like the people of the generation of the Deluge, and there is no generation that has no people like the people of Sodom. However, each and every one is judged in accordance with his actions."[10] There are definitely cyclical phenomena that characterize the rise, flourishing, and fall of societies on the stage of history, for no matter the culture or civilization, man is still man. However, these are not arbitrary processes devoid of meaning, but rather the hand of God that directs history and enforces justice. There is justice and there is a Judge beyond the physical reality of the world, and therefore each and every individual can transcend his time and place, and imbue his life with an eternal purposefulness. The covenant with Noah is with each individual human being, and, as a consequence, with all mankind.

Even though eternity beckons to each individual, and the Divine Presence and grace fill the entire universe, so that whoever wishes to experience it may come and do so, between these moments of illumination, man requires a great deal of support, whether to establish stable lifestyles, clear principles of conduct, or to move every member of society toward higher goals.

Every man lives in a material reality that does not allow even the greatest individuals to disconnect from their environment and social setting. Furthermore, in order to cultivate greatness and excellence, it is necessary to create a community in which all aspire to closeness with God. Abraham was indeed alone, but even he could not survive his sojourns without his household. And when Elijah fled alone to the cave, God demanded of him harshly: "What are you doing here, Elijah?" (II Kings 19:9).

Maimonides explains[11] the development of idolatry at the dawn of human history, and the activities of our father Abraham on behalf of monotheism. In earlier generations, the more people became aware of the wonders of creation, and the more they realized the dependency of human beings on the powers of nature, like the sun, the heavenly bodies,

10. *Sifrei Devarim* 310.

11. See the beginning of *Hilkhot Avoda Zara*.

wind, rain, etc., the more they worshipped and feared these phenomena. As a result, they began trying to influence these supernal powers to deal beneficently with man; belief that these forces of nature and celestial entities have independent power took root, and they ultimately viewed them as deities. They developed an entire cultic system whose purpose was to influence the gods to act for man's benefit. Since man's needs are many and diverse, and since his ability to produce food and provide shelter and clothing hinges on a range of variables, the cultic system spread through the entire world, to the point that they believed "that through the practices of this cult, rains would fall, the trees would bear fruit, and the land would become fertile and populous."[12]

Powerful, deceitful, and corrupt people then rose up and took control over others, helped by the claim that they knew how to appease the gods:

> That by means of these practices they drove away harmful animals...from the villages, and...warded off various sorts of damages from plants.... Those that set up these false opinions, which have no root or any utility, in order to fortify belief in them, use the device of spreading among the people the belief that a certain calamity will befall those who do not perform an action perpetuating this belief.... Now it is known that it is the nature of men in general to be most afraid and most wary of losing their property and their children.[13]

This process reached a turning point thanks to Abraham, who discovered the truth on his own, whereupon the Master of the World revealed Himself to him. Abraham was able to transmit his knowledge of God to his family, which developed into a nation. Nevertheless, when Israel was exiled in Egypt they learned from their ways. "The doctrine implanted by Abraham was, in a very short time, almost uprooted."[14]

---

12. *Moreh Nevukhim* III:30, p. 522.
13. *Moreh Nevukhim* III:37, p. 542, 545–46.
14. *Hilkhot Avoda Zara* 1:3.

It is not enough to preach pure faith. Even clear evidence, proofs, and demonstrations are not enough, because not everyone is capable of understanding those proofs. Just as false beliefs took root because a complete system of law and cultic practice formed around them, so too it is necessary that pure faith does not remain a matter of mere cognitive awareness but is translated into deeds and actions that foster a recognition of truth and project sanctity into every aspect of life. Thus, "because of God's love for us, and because He kept His oath to our father Abraham, He appointed Moses to be our teacher and the teacher of all the prophets, and He sent him.... God chose Israel as His heritage, coronated them with the mitzvot, and showed them how to worship Him."[15]

Our teacher Moses was charged with the task of shaping an entire people to be able to live with the reality that God speaks to man. This nation had common origins and familial ties, and it was bound by the cords of the faith that was imparted to it at Mount Sinai. This people lives in constant tension between longings for a life of sanctity and the pressure to provide food for the children, meet the threat of large and powerful surrounding nations, and address other vital needs.

The commandments of the Torah are the road signs by which we can clear a path to the Source of spiritual light. They determine the routines of daily life that guide the individual through the long, confusing, frightening lulls between peaks of illumination. The implementation of these mitzvot builds a society that cultivates individuals who reflect the Divine image within. Torah law creates a productive balance that moderates the constant tension between the individual and the public; between the individual's aspiration for self-actualization and his acceptance of the yoke of societal needs; between "If I am not for myself, who is for me?" and "When I am for myself, what am I?"[16] Individual and society are dissimilar, but there is a common denominator: both require legal principles on which a life of meaning can be based. The heart is most devious, and it is dangerous to rely on the rare flashes of spiritual illumination to make the heart upright. Powerful yearnings for the Source of existence can propel man's search for his Creator, but recoiling from

15. Ibid.
16. Mishna Avot 1:13.

His presence can cause man to flee to places where he will never see eternity, to hide where sin constantly lurks, ready to entrap him.

The covenant that God made with us at Sinai is what allows us to face those who stand against us in every generation. We have always been smaller in number than all other peoples, and even after pogroms and persecutions, the surviving remnant would be ravaged again. Yet, through it all, "like the terebinth and the oak, of which stumps are left even when they are felled" (Is. 6:13), the holy seed remains. It is of the eternity of the Jewish people that Maimonides said: "This, to my mind, is likewise an indication of the eternity of the Law because of which we have a special name."[17]

A Kingdom of Priests

Unlike the covenant with Noah, which was made with an individual, an entire people entered into the covenant at Sinai: "You shall keep My covenant... and you shall be to Me a kingdom of priests and a holy nation" (Ex. 19:6). This is how Rabbi Avraham, the son of Maimonides, interprets this verse in his father's name:

> The priest of each congregation is the leader who is most eminent and is its role model, whom members of the congregation follow and thereby find the straight path. Thus, it says: You shall be, through observance of My Torah, leaders of the world. You will be to them as the priest to his congregation. The world will follow after you, imitating your actions and walking in your path. This is the explanation of the verse that I received from my father and master, of blessed memory....
>
> He promised the future fulfillment of this in His word to Isaiah (2:3): "And the many peoples shall go and say, 'Come let us ascend the Mount of the Lord, to the House of the God [of Jacob, so that He may instruct us in His ways, and so that we may

17. *Moreh Nevukhim* II:29, p. 342.

> walk in His path.' For instruction (Torah) shall go forth from Zion, and the word of the Lord from Jerusalem]."[18]

We must understand the significance of this role. As far as we know, there does not seem to be any genetic difference between Jews and non-Jews. It also emerges from Maimonides' writings that he does not think there is any genetic difference between Jews and non-Jews. We learn in Genesis that all human beings are created in the Divine image, and the mishna says:

> For this reason, man was created alone in the world: to teach that anyone who destroys a life[19] is considered as though he destroyed an entire world, and whoever sustains one life is considered as though he sustained an entire world; and for the sake of peace among men, so that no one can say to his fellow, "My father is greater than your father." And so that the heretics do not say that there is more than one power in heaven. And to proclaim the greatness of the Supreme King of kings, the Holy One, blessed be He – for if a man mints a hundred coins with one mold, they are all similar to each other, but the Supreme King of kings, the Holy One, blessed be He, fashions every man in the mold of Adam, yet none is similar to his fellow. Therefore, everyone can proclaim: "The world was created for me."[20]

---

18. *Perush HaTorah LeRabbi Avraham ben HaRambam*, ed. E. Weisenberg, p. 302. Compare this to the commentary of Rabbi Ovadia Sforno ad loc.: "In this you will be treasured above all, for you will be a kingdom of priests, understanding and teaching all of mankind to call out in God's name, so that they may stand shoulder to shoulder. Thus it shall be for Israel in the future. As it says: 'You shall be called priests of God' (Is. 61:6), and as it says, 'For Torah shall go forth from Zion…' (ibid. 2:3)."
19. Some variants add the words "in Israel" here, but this word does not appear in the version of the mishna that appears in Maimonides' manuscript, nor in other manuscripts of the mishna. For a survey, see E. E. Urbach, "'Anyone Who Saves a Life…': The Evolution of a Textual Variant, the Vicissitudes of the Censor, and the Business of Printing" (Heb.), *Tarbiz* 40:3 (1971), pp. 268 ff.
20. Mishna Sanhedrin 4:5.

Maimonides explains: "The mold of Adam – the essence of humankind, which makes human beings human, and which all humans share."[21]

According to Maimonides, the potential to reach great spiritual heights has been given to all people, as he writes: "Among the foundations of religion is the knowledge that God prophesies to human beings."[22] It is likewise stated in *Tanna DeVei Eliyahu*: "With heaven and earth as My witness, whether gentile or Jew, whether man or woman, whether slave or maidservant, in accordance with one's deeds, so the holy spirit rests upon him."[23]

Maimonides further writes at the end of *Hilkhot Shemitta VeYovel* (13:13):

> ... any individual in the world whose spirit moves him; who has understood, in his wisdom, to set himself apart and stand before God, to serve Him, to worship Him, and to know God; who walks upright, as God created him to do; and who has cast away the burden of the many calculations that people pursue – is sanctified with the utmost holiness. God will be his portion and his inheritance forever and ever.

We find that the Sages stated characteristic virtues of Israel: "This nation has three identifying marks: They are merciful, bashful, and kind."[24] Maimonides elaborated:

> Anyone who possesses brazenness and cruelty, who hates people and is not kind to them, is extremely suspect ... for the marks of Israel, the holy people, [is that they are] bashful, merciful, and kind.[25]

21. *Commentary on the Mishna*, ad loc.
22. *Hilkhot Yesodei HaTorah* 7:1.
23. *Tanna DeVei Eliyahu* §10 (Ish-Shalom ed.).
24. Yevamot 79a.
25. *Hilkhot Issurei Bia* 19:17.

He even asserts with absolute certainty: "This is the way of the seed of Israel and their proper heart."[26] However, he explains further:

> The children of our patriarch Abraham, that is, Israel, upon whom the Holy One, blessed be He, bestowed the Torah's goodness and whom He commanded with just laws and statutes, are merciful to all.[27]

A people that absorbs the ideas and values of the Torah over the course of generations develops a certain personality, and this can be discerned in the Jewish people. This cultural DNA transmits the nation's characteristic features from one generation to the next, and the vestiges of these traits endure, at least for a few generations, even among those who have abandoned the Torah's framework.[28]

The uniqueness of the Jewish people lies in its mission, responsibility, and duty to lead the whole world to recognize Torah values and morals, just as the role of a priest is to teach Torah and morals to the Jewish people. At the same time, this idea can only come to fruition if we remain separate, as a "kingdom of priests," that is, by building a nation that knows God and follows the Torah, which will cause the rest of the world to want, on their own, to learn from Jewish conduct and

26. *Hilkhot Teshuva* 2:10.
27. *Hilkhot Avadim* 9:8.
28. Researchers hesitate to investigate this phenomenon further due to their revulsion for anything that has even the slightest resemblance to the vile racism that provided the pretext for so much of the world's suffering in recent centuries. Nevertheless, there have been some modest preliminary studies of specific issues like alcohol and drug addiction. According to these studies, alcohol consumption, for example, is more moderate among Jews who observe the Torah and mitzvot, and their habits persist among their second- and third-generation descendants, even those who became nonobservant. However, the power of restraint grows weaker as the generations grow more distant from the Torah. See C. R. Snyder, "Culture and Jewish Sobriety," in C. R. Snyder and D. J. Pittman, *Society, Culture and Drinking Patterns* (New York: Wiley, 1962), pp. 188–225; Eldar and Weiss, "Three National Surveys on Non-ritual Drinking Practices of the Israeli Jewish Adult Population in the 1980s," *Israel Journal of Psychiatry and Related Sciences* 27(1) (1990); Rachel Ehrenfeld, "From Lawful Deviance to Unlawful Deviance," *Delinquency and Social Deviance (Avaryanut UStiya Ḥevratit)* 11 (1983), pp. 25–28 (Heb.).

morals. The relationship and mutual understanding between Israel and the nations is what brings progress toward the ultimate goal – that all of mankind recognize that we are all descended from one man, who was created in the Divine image, and that we are all children of one God.

The Influence of Biblical Heritage on the Nations

The Jewish people was chosen to bring about the vision articulated by the prophet Isaiah: "And the many peoples shall go and say, 'Come let us ascend the Mount of the Lord, to the House of the God of Jacob, so that He may instruct us in His ways, and so that we may walk in His path.' For Torah shall go forth from Zion, and the word of the Lord from Jerusalem" (Is. 2:3). This vision will be fully realized at the End of Days, when the Jewish people dwells in its land and the Temple is rebuilt. Nevertheless, it remains incumbent upon the Jewish people to work toward this vision even during its wanderings in exile.

This is a prolonged, arduous process, and at times both the Jews and the nations of the world, consciously or otherwise, wish they could ignore it. However, scrutiny of history's meandering path in light of the covenant leads to the conclusion that, despite all the obstacles and delays, God is leading His world toward its higher purpose:

> But it is not in man's power to comprehend the thoughts of the Creator of the world, for our ways are not His ways, and our thoughts are not His thoughts. The entire matter of Jesus of Nazareth and of the Ishmaelite who came after him are only to pave the way for the King Messiah and to improve the whole world so that it will worship God as one, as [Scripture] states: "For then I will restore pure speech to the nations, so that they may all call God's name and worship Him, shoulder to shoulder" (Zeph. 3:6). How so? The world has become filled with speech about the Messiah, with the words of the Torah, and with talk of mitzvot. They have spread to remote islands and to many nations with insensitive hearts, who now discuss these matters as well as the mitzvot of the Torah. These say: "The mitzvot were true, but they have now been annulled and were not applicable for all time." Those say: "They contain esoteric matters that are not

> straightforward, and the messiah has already come and revealed their secrets." But when the true King Messiah arrives and is exalted and uplifted, they will all repent; they will know that their fathers bequeathed them falsehoods, and their prophets and fathers misled them.[29]

It was precisely while the Jewish people was in exile, scattered among the nations, persecuted, and scapegoated, that the foundational ideas of their Torah spread and won adherents. The Torah came to be espoused by much of the world, albeit with dangerous misinterpretations that found expression in the intensification of their hatred for the eternal nation.

As times changed, especially in the Western world, a fresh look at Scripture gave rise to – or at least accompanied – movements for social and cultural renewal. Scripture's impact was far-reaching and profound. The Bible was a central component of educational systems in many countries until modern times. Even today, in many areas of the United States, familiarity with the Jewish Bible and its heroes is culturally ubiquitous.

The influence of the Torah can be discerned at the most basic levels of modern society.[30] For instance, there was a fundamental difference between the theory and practice of democracy in England and the US, on the one hand, and on the European continent, on the other.[31] Even the most cursory survey of the writings of major thinkers reveals the traces of Scriptural ideas and concepts. This was already noted in 1867 by the great man of letters, Matthew Arnold:

> But nothing more strongly marks the essential unity of man than the affinities we can perceive, in this point or that, between members of one family of peoples and members of another, and no affinity of this kind is more strongly marked than that likeness in the strength and prominence of the moral fibre, which,

29. *Hilkhot Melakhim* 11:4 (this passage was censored from the standard editions of *Mishneh Torah*).
30. Editor's note: See Fania Oz-Salzberger, "The Jewish Roots of Western Freedom," *Azure* 13 (2002), pp. 89–131.
31. Editor's note: See Jacob Talmon, *The Origins of Totalitarian Democracy* (London: Secker & Warburg, 1952).

> notwithstanding immense elements of difference, knits in some special sort the genius and history of us English, and our American descendants across the Atlantic, to the genius and history of the Hebrew people.[32]

Let us consider an example from the discipline of political philosophy. The governing power has two basic functions: to ensure the security and protect the rights of all its subjects, without exception, and to establish justice in its territory, which is the key to keeping the peace among the population. These two functions are, in essence, two sides of the same coin. Government is the means of ensuring survival against internal conflict and external threats. As Maimonides states concisely: "A king is appointed in the first instance only to do justice and make war, as Scripture says, 'And our king will judge us and will go before us and fight our wars' (I Sam. 8:20)."[33] A king who protects the rights of all his subjects is worthy of his reign and must be obeyed, but a king who evades his duty to protect even a small part of the nation loses his right to reign.

We cannot ignore or avoid the struggle for survival; it is indeed a law of nature that God implanted in His world. Among the nations of the ancient world, and even those of today in some instances, the purpose of the struggle was not only to survive, but to dominate everything, to the extent that others have no right to exist except as slaves to the master nation. This is how violent men, the heroes of old, men of renown, became kings, struck fear in the hearts of their people, and took from them whatever they wanted.[34] They then made war on other nations, to exterminate and enslave them, tyrannizing peoples with their fury and causing distant nations to tremble. Kings became so haughty that they said, "I am a god; I sit enthroned like a god" (Ezek. 28:2). This was a typical feature of royalty.

This was not the case in Israel. In contrast to the accepted norms of the ancient world, and even of parts of the world today where rulers

32. Matthew Arnold, *Culture and Anarchy*, ed. J. Dover Wilson (Cambridge: Cambridge University Press, 1966), pp. 141–42.
33. *Hilkhot Melakhim* 4:10. See also above, chapter 5, section "The Authority of the King," pp. 59 ff.
34. See Genesis 6:2–4.

place themselves above the law in accordance with the Greek adage, "The law was not written for the king," a king of Israel is not only responsible for the law, but he is also subject to it, for the law is God's, and it was not created by the word of the king or ruler. "Behold, a king shall reign in righteousness, and ministers shall govern with justice" (Is. 32:1). This principle was so strongly emphasized that the Sages applied it to the King of kings, God Himself, even though His deeds cannot be compared to the actions of mortal kings. "R. Lazar said: '*Para basileos ho nomos agraphos*' (for a king, the law is unwritten)[35] ... but the Holy One, blessed be He, is not like that. Rather, He issues a decree and is the first to uphold it.... 'They shall observe My observances.... I am the Lord' (Lev. 22:9). I am the first to observe the commandments of the Torah."[36]

Only a king who wages war fearlessly stands a chance to defeat external enemies and to ensure the survival of a nation compared to a lamb among seventy wolves. However, he must resist the temptation to wage war for the sake of victory alone or to establish an empire. He certainly must not use his power to subjugate his own people by force. The struggle for survival is inevitable, but life acquires meaning thanks only to the unceasing tension between the forces that drive the struggle and the forces that restrain it, which obey a higher command.

The covenantal model is the foundation of the law of the Israelite monarchy. This is repeated several times in Scripture: "All the tribes of Israel came to David at Hebron...and King David made a covenant with them at Hebron before the Lord, and they anointed David king over Israel" (II Sam. 5:1–3). This covenant was bilateral, binding on both the king and the people.[37]

John Locke (1632–1704), the philosopher who laid the foundation of modern democratic thought, drew ideas from Scripture and cited

---

35. *HeArukh HaShalem*, s.v. *agraphos*: "This is entirely Greek, and it means to say: A flesh and blood king dictates law and makes enactments but does not follow them. The Holy One, blessed be He, is not like that. The literal Greek meaning of '*Para basileos ho nomos agraphos*' is 'For kings, the law is unwritten,' which means that kings abrogate the laws that they themselves decreed." (See n. 3 ad loc.)
36. Y. Rosh HaShana 1:3.
37. This monarchical structure fits with the idea of a constitutional monarchy, which is the model espoused by most Western European democracies.

it frequently. I do not know if he was familiar with Maimonides' Laws of Kings,[38] but it is interesting that he writes in a very similar style. He asserts that government was created to serve two purposes: establishing a just social order, and defending against external enemies. He also concludes that a government that wages war against its own people and a ruler who denies natural and divine law lose all legitimacy.[39]

Likewise, English socialism, as opposed to the French and German varieties, drew heavily upon Scriptural sources. Its thinkers spoke of Christian influences, but they refer mainly to the prophets of Israel. Anthony Benn writes the following about the legacy of the British Labour movement and its founding fathers:

> [They] went beyond the authority of the Bible and began to develop out of it... a humanist buttress for their social philosophy, without losing its moral force. They were, in a special sense, bridge builders: constructing a bridge that connects Christian teaching with humanism and democratic socialism.... That bridge is still there for anyone who wishes to cross it in either direction. Some use it to go back to trace one of the paths leading to the Bible. Others... cross that same bridge... to social action and democratic socialism.[40]

---

38. It is not impossible that Locke was familiar with Maimonides' writings. The religious and political ferment in Locke's England can be characterized, *inter alia*, by serious engagement with Jewish sources, even though there were not many Jews in England at the time. The writings of the English statesman and jurist John Selden, who published a translation of parts of Maimonides' *Mishneh Torah*, were influential in this respect. For our purposes, most significant is his book on the Sanhedrin and the Israelite monarchy, *De Synedriis Veterum Ebraerorum*, published in 1653. Locke's work, from which the quote in the next note is extracted, was published in 1689.
39. Compare the following statements in particular: "For the king's authority being given him only by the law, he cannot impower any one to act against the law, or justify him, by his commission, in so doing" (John Locke, Second Treatise on Government, §206); "The delivery also of the people into the subjection of a foreign power, either by the prince, or by the legislative, is certainly a change of the legislative, and so a dissolution of the government: for the end why people entered into society being to be preserved one intire, free, independent society, to be governed by its own laws" (ibid. §217).
40. Anthony W. Benn, *Arguments for Socialism* (London: Penguin, 1980), p. 28.

Another prominent Scriptural influence can be seen in attitudes toward the return to Zion. It is well known that the Balfour Declaration had its roots in the influence of Scripture over key decision-makers in England. The dream of return to Zion was cultivated among English writers and thinkers even before Herzl and political Zionism appeared on the scene.

On a deeper level, the secularist revolt against Christianity, which strengthened nihilism and other negative phenomena, was most prevalent in those areas where the Christian faith had grown most distant from its Jewish roots. Those who based their faith directly on the Bible, absorbing its emphasis on the value of the individual and on man's moral duties in this world, were not so attracted to the new idols. On the contrary, their focus on Scripture refined and sublimated Christianity, weakening its syncretic Greek components and, in some circles, eliminating it altogether. At the same time, they became more aware of the intrinsic value of man, fashioned by the Creator. Liberty and justice were given the highest political priority, and government became more friendly and humane. This was in complete contrast to what happened in states dominated by revolutionary secularism – the god that promised so much but ended up being a bitter disappointment.

Christianity and Islam

Over the centuries, wars repeatedly erupted between the nations of Europe, and it was only after the entire continent was set ablaze during the bloodbath of World War II that a period of relative calm arrived. The reconciliation of the nations of Western Europe in the wake of World War II was largely the result of cultural and political developments that brought about the establishment of democratic governments that espoused values common to all the nations in the region – values that originated in the reformist religious movements that were directly influenced by Scripture.

One of the side-effects that is of particular interest to us as Jews is the transformation of Christian conceptions. The pagan heritage, which viewed war as an ideal, was barely tempered as long as Christianity encompassed all the nations of Europe and it harbored aspirations to impose Christianity on the whole world by means of the sword. For centuries, memories of the Holy Roman Empire fueled the dreams and aspirations of kings and tyrants to dominate many nations, until the realization that there is another way finally broke through.

Judaism and Christianity have a long adversarial history. They have profound religious disagreements, and over the centuries, the Jews have suffered greatly from persecution at the hands of Christians. The major claim of Christianity is that all of the mitzvot were annulled upon the appearance of Jesus of Nazareth, with the exception of moral mitzvot, whereas we believe that the mitzvot apply for all times. It is for this reason that Maimonides was careful to include, among his thirteen fundamental principles of faith, that the Torah would never be replaced. Christianity further claimed that since Jews did not accept Christianity, they are no longer God's chosen people. However, we know that God made an everlasting covenant with the Jewish people, and "the Eternal One of Israel neither lies nor changes His mind" (I Sam. 15:29).

Moreover, faith alone does not provide for all of man's needs. Spiritual and intellectual perfection is not true perfection if it is not expressed in the world of action. Had intellectual perfection been sufficient, the Almighty would have had no need to place man in this world; He could have created disembodied souls capable of learning and understanding. God created man and placed him in this world so that he would grapple with the challenges of mundane human life and work to improve this world and to improve human life in this world. It is through this – and this alone! – that one merits life in the next world as well. To that end, we are required to devote ourselves to building a just society. As the prophet says, "I am the Lord who exercises loving-kindness, judgment, and righteousness, in the earth, for in these I delight, says the Lord" (Jer. 9:23). The mitzvot are the realization of loving-kindness, judgment, and righteousness. Faith is the basis for observing the mitzvot, and at the same time, the mitzvot are the application of faith. One who has faith, but does not work to implement his faith practically, has a barren faith. If the mitzvot are annulled, then all that is left is nothing but a mirage.

Nevertheless, despite the enduring religious and spiritual disagreements with Christianity, there is no ignoring recent changes to Christian doctrine. Even the Catholic Church, known for its conservative stances, has all but abandoned its triumphalism – its pretension to be the exclusive and eternal replacement of Judaism.[41] This concession reflects an internalization of the value of peace – a cardinal value of Judaism.

There are Christian denominations that have made great progress in their love of peace and in performing acts of kindness for fellow human beings. This is especially true in Western states, which were influenced by the English model and by English thinkers (the United Kingdom, the Netherlands, Denmark, Sweden, and, of course, the United States). The culture of these states recognizes the liberty and stature of man.

On the other hand, most of the Muslim world has been left behind, in various stages of a declining medieval culture. We can see how the artificial states, created in the wake of the departure of European colonialism and overtaken by tyrants, are still stuck in their never-ending conflicts. As for Islam's attitudes toward Judaism, the Muslims have long accused us falsely, as Maimonides already writes: "They were compelled to accuse us saying, 'You have altered the text of the Torah, and expunged every trace of the name of Mohammed therefrom.' They could find nothing stronger than this ignominious argument, the falsity of which is easily demonstrated to one and all by the following facts. First, Scripture was translated into Syriac, Greek, Persian, and Latin hundreds of years before the appearance of Mohammed."[42] The exact same denial of historical evidence continues to grease the wheels of the Arabic propaganda machine in its attempts to accuse us of being foreign invaders.

Interestingly, Maimonides himself notes a basic difference between Christianity and Islam with respect to their attitudes toward Scripture. On the one hand, Christian monotheism, unlike Islamic monotheism, was defective – "The Ishmaelites are not idolaters at all… and they unify God properly and without error."[43] As a result, we share similarities with them with respect to faith. Nevertheless, when it comes to Torah study, they have a completely different status:

---

41. "Nor did the Jews in large number, accept the Gospel…. Nevertheless, God holds the Jews most dear for the sake of their Fathers; He does not repent of the gifts He makes or of the calls He issues – such is the witness of the Apostle" (*Nostra Aetate*, Declaration on the Relation of the Church to Non-Christian Religions, Proclaimed by His Holiness Pope Paul VI on October 28, 1965, section 4).
42. *Epistle to Yemen* (ed. Cohen and trans. Halkin), p. vii.
43. *Responsa Rambam* §448.

> ...it is permissible to teach the commandments to Christians and to draw them close to our religion. This is prohibited with respect to Ishmaelites, because, as you know, they reject the divine origin of Torah, and if they are taught any of its writings, they will find that it contradicts that which they invented due to the jumble of stories and confused perspectives at which they have arrived, and they will not deem it evidence that their version is mistaken.... The uncircumcised (i.e., Christians), on the other hand, believe the text of the Torah has not changed, although they interpret it improperly in their inferior commentaries.... If they were presented with the correct interpretation, perhaps they would recant.[44]

Christianity is thus easier to repair, because its cure is already at hand. Nevertheless, the process of refining Christianity has already taken hundreds of years and has centered primarily on England and its satellites. It has not had much influence on other states and their churches, and consequently on their political regimes.

On the other hand, we see how deeply entrenched tyranny and corrupt governance are in most Arab states, and how thoroughly they loathe and abhor anyone who is not one of them. In addition to the ancient hostilities, many Muslims view the State of Israel as the representative of Western modernity, with all of its decadent maladies, which threatens their heritage.

The Return to Zion and Historical Transformation

Our generation has been blessed in a way that many generations only dreamed about: we have been privileged to witness the realization of God's promise with the return of the Jewish people to its land. This opportunity is also a challenge to fulfill the historic aim of the selection of Israel, "You shall be to Me a kingdom of priests and a holy nation" (Ex. 19:6), and to become a "light unto the nations" (Is. 49:6).

In every epoch, it is necessary to consider afresh how to carry out our historic mission. We must comprehend the responsibility that we have been given as the generation of return to our ancestral land.

44. *Responsa Rambam* §149.

This means that we must confront issues that we have not addressed for many centuries or that we have addressed only tangentially, from vantage points that had long ceased to have any practical application. There are topics we addressed as victims of persecution, which we must now address as a free people, having absorbed and considered the implications of the opportunity and privilege we have been granted through the realization of God's promise to return us to our land.

The Torah teaches us that the relationship between the Jewish people and the nations of the world is an important issue, and that we must carefully consider and establish the appropriate relationship in each generation and era. Of course, to ensure our survival we must remain vigilant and prepare to defend ourselves, lest other nations and religions trample us. At the same time, we must cultivate positive attitudes toward all human beings and cooperate with the nations of the world.

It is true that there are statements from the Sages and prominent rabbis throughout the generations that express an approach that sees an unbridgeable chasm between the Jewish people on the one hand and non-Jews on the other. However, we must understand that some of these statements relate to the moral and religious condition of the idolatrous gentiles of those times and to the struggle against these cults and their attendant corruption. Other statements stem largely from historical conditions, in which Jews were persecuted by other nations over the course of centuries. The sages of each generation understood the necessity of keeping our distance from gentiles, and they occasionally expressed the need to be wary of them. This was especially true when we were not living as a nation in our homeland, because it was necessary to be exceedingly vigilant about the physical and spiritual survival of the Jewish people. Even today, after our return to our land, we must assure not only our physical security but also our unique identity as Jews and our religious and moral values.

On the other hand, we must consider that several changes have occurred: the cultural advancement and development of nations and religions, the penetration of the Bible among the nations, and the fact that we are a national group in our land all generate opportunities to become a light unto the nations. Throughout history, great sages who took an expansive view recognized the importance of the exposure of

Jews in the world. They therefore cautioned against placing too much distance between Jews and other nations, because proximity between Jews and gentiles makes possible the realization of our mission – to be a kingdom of priests and a holy nation, to advance toward the fulfillment of the prophetic vision: "I will make you a light unto the nations, so that My salvation may reach the ends of the earth" (Is. 49:6).

Let us consider several examples that reflect the complex relationship between Israel and the nations, and the transformation that this relationship has undergone.

The Seven Noahide Laws and Monotheism

The Torah imposes duties and responsibilities on gentiles as well. "Sons of Noah" – that is, all gentiles – were given seven mitzvot. Maimonides writes: "Although they are all traditions that have come down to us from our teacher Moses, and they are reasonable, it is implied by the words of the Torah that [man] was indeed commanded in their respect."[45] That is, even though the Torah nowhere directly commands the sons of Noah regarding anything but the prohibitions of murder and eating the limb of a live animal, it is evident just from reading the Torah's stories that human beings were punished for transgressing these seven laws, even before the giving of the Torah.[46]

Since these seven commandments are the foundation of human morality, there is necessarily much common ground between the Noahide laws and the mitzvot that apply to the Jewish people; there is nothing that is permitted to a Jew but prohibited to a gentile,[47] even if there are differences in the specifics and consequences of the respective sets of laws. Adam, the first man, was commanded regarding six things:

45. *Hilkhot Melakhim* 9:1.
46. See *Bereshit Rabbati, Vayeshev* 37:26 (Jerusalem: Mekitzei Nirdamim, 1967), p. 176. See also *Moreh Nevukhim* III:50 (pp. 613–14): "Know that all the stories that you will find mentioned in the Torah are there for a necessary utility for the Law; either they give a correct notion of an opinion that is a pillar of the Law, or they rectify some action so that mutual wrongdoing and oppression should not occur between men.... In the same way the story of the Flood and the story of Sodom and Gomorrah were recounted in order to bring proof for the following correct opinion."
47. Sanhedrin 59a.

idolatry, blasphemy, murder, incest and adultery, robbery, and setting up a system of justice. When it became permitted for the sons of Noah to eat meat, they were given a seventh commandment: not to eat the limb of a living animal.

However, there is a fundamental difference between the seven Noahide laws and the mitzvot incumbent upon the Jewish people. The Noahide laws are very general. Each law encompasses several issues. With respect to the Jewish people, though, we learn in a mishna: "R. Ḥananya b. Akashya says: The Holy One, blessed be He, wished to confer merit on Israel; He therefore gave them an ample Torah and numerous mitzvot, as it is said: 'The Lord wanted, for the sake of [Israel's] righteousness, to magnify and glorify the Torah' (Is. 42:21)."[48] The Jewish people thus has an abundance of specific mitzvot that are not just general principles. As Nahmanides writes:

> The reasonable explanation is that the sons of Noah were admonished with respect to their mitzvot generally, not in the specifics... whereas for Israel, [God] increased the number of prohibitions and restraints by giving a separate admonition for each one. They therefore count many mitzvot.[49]

This difference is most glaring with respect to the one Noahide law that requires positive action – the command to set up a justice system.[50] Israel has clear instructions about how to appoint judges, the authority of the various courts, court procedure, and court rulings. However, the sons of Noah were given no specific directives about judges or about the laws they must adjudicate, because the presumption is that every nation has its own political system, its own juridical establishment, and its own laws. The Torah only requires that gentiles apply the principles

48. Mishna Makkot 3:17.
49. Nahmanides' glosses to Maimonides' *Sefer HaMitzvot*, at the end of the fourteenth introductory rule.
50. See *Yad Peshuta* on *Hilkhot Melakhim* 9:14, where I explain Maimonides' view of the severity of the Noahide obligation to appoint judges and magistrates and the scope of their responsibilities.

of the seven mitzvot, which are primarily admonitions (negative commandments), within their justice system.

The prohibition against idolatry is listed first among the seven Noahide laws, and separation from idolatry is a central issue in the Israelite system of mitzvot as well, as Maimonides writes:

> You know from texts of the Torah... that the first intention of the Law as a whole is to put an end to idolatry, to wipe out its traces and all that is bound up with it....
>
> For the foundation of the whole of our Law, and the pivot around which it turns, consists of erasing these opinions from [people's] minds and of these [idolatrous] statues from existence.[51]

Many specific laws pertain to idolatry. Some were established based on the conduct of the nations at the time of the giving of the Torah, and over the course of history, in response to epochal transformations, cultural development, and changing patterns of gentile conduct, these laws had to be considered afresh.

The Talmud states that gentiles living outside of the Land of Israel are not idolaters; rather, "they uphold the customs of their ancestors."[52] What is the meaning of this statement? When discussing attitudes toward a sinner, we must distinguish between one who knowingly rebels and one who sins because he does not understand profound matters, and although he sins he still acts nicely toward others and does not cause harm to his fellow out of hatred or passion. Furthermore, over the course of history, various idolatrous ceremonies have developed that contain no cruelty or malice, and these have become part of the cultural heritage of various peoples. Alongside their superstitious beliefs, they also developed a sense of responsibility and a desire to foster peace among men. In most civilized nations, most people cannot distinguish between false beliefs and the good character traits that have been tied to them. This is what the Sages mean when they say: "They are not idolaters; rather, they uphold the customs of their ancestors." Therefore, even as

51. *Moreh Nevukhim* III:29, pp. 517, 521; translation emended.
52. Ḥullin 13b.

we must recognize the danger inherent in their misleading beliefs, we must relate and act toward these people in a manner that advances "ways of peace,"[53] which is the main feature of our holy Torah – "Its ways are ways of pleasantness, and all its paths are peace" (Prov. 3:17).

Meiri writes likewise:

> These statements were made for those times, when those nations were idolaters, tainted in their actions and of repulsive character, as stated in brief: "You shall not copy the practices of the land of Egypt where you dwelt, or of the land of Canaan..." (Lev. 18:3). However, other nations, which are bound by the paths of the laws and are free of the repulsiveness of these traits – on the contrary, they mete out punishment on account of them – are doubtlessly not the object of these statements.... This has been repeated many times in our words.[54]

And Rav Kook writes:

> We follow the opinion of Meiri, that all nations who are bound by proper conduct between man and his fellow are considered resident aliens ("*gerei toshav*") in terms of all civil obligations.[55]

Christians and the Status of "Resident Aliens"

Christian monotheism has been flawed from the start. Nevertheless, the Tosafists long ago addressed the status of Christians, writing that oaths that they take are in the name of a syncretic, not purely monotheistic god (lit. "with inclusion," meaning that pure monotheism is adulterated by the inclusion of other divine beings). They explain that gentiles were never admonished against practicing syncretic forms of monotheism.[56]

53. See *Hilkhot Melakhim* 10:12.
54. Meiri on Avoda Zara 22a. He repeats this several times in his commentary.
55. *Iggerot HaRe'ayah* 1:89. I thank my close friend Rabbi Eli Reif for bringing this source to my attention.
56. See Tosafot to Sanhedrin 63b, s.v. *asur*; Bekhorot 2b, s.v. *shema*. This is a matter of dispute among early modern authorities. See *Pitḥei Teshuva, Yoreh De'ah* 147:2,

Accordingly, they concluded that Christians do not have the status of idolaters.[57]

This is an important assertion, as it enabled a practical change of approach and the development of economic ties between Jews and Christians. Some did not accept this ruling and wished to be stringent, but in practice, Ashkenazic communities were lenient in this regard. Moreover, it is clear from Tosafot's presentation of the lenient approach that it is based on an understanding that religions undergo historic transformations, with important halakhic implications. It is also worth noting that several Christian churches have undergone major changes throughout history, and there are even some that adopted pure monotheism.

In this context, it is worth citing the words of Rabbi Yosef Eliyahu Henkin, one of the greatest halakhists of the twentieth century:

> ...but with regard to the nations of the world as well, if they call God "the God of gods" (see the end of Tractate Menaḥot), Scripture gives them favorable mention. It has already been written that the sons of Noah were not admonished with regard to syncretism, and this is the straightforward meaning of Scripture (see the commentary of Rabbi Mecklenberg [in *HaKetav VeHaKabbala* – Ed.]). It was only when they settled in the Land of Israel that they had to give up idolatry completely. However, when they are each in their place, the Sages say of them: "To expel them from the world" – meaning, that their punishment will be in the next world, and we are not responsible for them. Rather, we must seek their peace, and "Beloved is man for he was created in the image of God." This applies even to idolaters (see *Tiferet Yisrael* on Tractate Avot).
>
> All the more so, the nations of the world today are not idolaters (see the commentary of Rabbi Ovadia of Bertinoro

which states that according to Rema, gentiles were not admonished with regard to syncretism. See Rabbi Yaakov Emden's *Mor UKetzia* §224.

57. Editor's note: See *Ḥavot Ya'ir* §185: "For gentiles nowadays are not idolaters, as they were not admonished against syncretism." See also Rabbi Yitzhak Isaac Herzog, "Minority Rights According to Halakha," *Teḥumin* 2 (1981), p. 174 (Heb.).

> to mishna Avoda Zara 1:1), and with the passage of the generations, idolatry has been progressively uprooted from their hearts (and even those who bow down to an image [i.e., a cross – Ed.], perhaps today it has become akin to a mere statue; this requires further investigation). This seems to be the reason why halakhists became progressively more lenient with regard to the laws regarding gentiles, with respect to renting houses, selling animals, deriving benefit from wine, etc. And even if there are some who worship idols, in my opinion, the overwhelming majority is in the category of *ger toshav* (resident alien).
>
> As for the ruling in the Talmud (Yevamot 46, Avoda Zara 64) that a *ger toshav* must accept the seven Noahide commandments before a tribunal of three "in accordance with the command of our teacher Moses, from God's mouth," that applies only with respect to the obligation to provide him with sustenance and [the permissibility of his] residence in the Land of Israel, but insofar as being removed from the class of idolaters is concerned, anyone who denies idolatry and acknowledges that the seven Noahide commandments are obligatory is a *ger toshav*. So it seems to me.[58]

I explained the status of *ger toshav* at length elsewhere,[59] so here I will just briefly touch on a few points. It is clear that every people and every society has elements that give it its unique identity – specific values, practices, and duties – and so others can only be included in that people or society under specific conditions. Each society must preserve its identity, which ensures its continued existence. It is for this reason that nations have immigration laws – each according to its character. Halakha, too, recognizes the status of the *ger toshav* (resident alien): "A gentile who has undertaken not to worship idols, along with the other Noahide laws, but has not been circumcised or immersed [i.e., he has not undergone conversion to Judaism], is accepted, and is among the

58. Rabbi Yosef Eliyahu Henkin, "The End of Days," *HaDarom* 10 (1959), pp. 7–8 (Heb.).
59. *Responsa Si'aḥ Naḥum* §93 (Maaleh Adumim, 2008) and *Yad Peshuta* on *Hilkhot Avoda Zara* 10:7.

pious of the nations of the world. And why is he called a *ger toshav*? Because it is permitted for us to allow him to reside among us in the Land of Israel."[60] The acceptance of a *ger toshav* is up to the discretion of a rabbinical court, but it is practiced only when the Jubilee years are in operation. This idea of "accepting" a *ger toshav* and the power of the court to confer the status of *ger toshav* is similar to the immigration laws that are in force in every civilized country in the world.

However, the law regarding one who does not wish to live in our land is different. Maimonides writes: "Anyone who accepts the seven mitzvot and takes care to observe them is among the pious of the nations and has a share in the World to Come – as long as he accepts and observes them because God commanded them in the Torah…."[61] Nevertheless, it is not necessary to investigate each and every individual to see if he has indeed accepted the seven mitzvot. Rather, his affiliation with a group whose leadership requires adherence to the seven mitzvot and maintains a proper justice system is sufficient. Thus, anyone who observes the seven mitzvot is considered a righteous gentile, or at least a wise gentile. Those who do not observe them will be judged by their peers, for setting up a court system is one of the seven Noahide mitzvot.

We must distinguish between preventative norms and proactive norms. It is obviously forbidden to steal[62] or cause damage to non-Jews, and even to idolaters.[63] On the other hand, no one can care for every person. Man, by nature, lives in social circles: family, community, nation, etc. Proactive norms that bring benefit to others are therefore structured concentrically, with different levels. Since man cannot be commanded

---

60. *Hilkhot Issurei Bia* 14:7.
61. *Hilkhot Melakhim* 8:11. See *Yad Peshuta* ad loc.
62. "Whether one robs a Jew or robs a gentile idolater"; *Hilkhot Gezeila VaAveida* 1:1: "It is forbidden to steal or exploit even a gentile idolater." See also *Commentary on the Mishna* to Kelim 12:7.
63. Editor's note: See *Hilkhot Avoda Zara* 10:1 and compare to Tosafot on Avoda Zara 64b, s.v. *eizehu*; *Hilkhot Melakhim* 9:14 and *Yad Peshuta* ad loc.; Ḥullin 13b, "The gentiles outside of the land [of Israel] etc." and Maimonides' explanation of this statement in *Commentary on the Mishna* to Ḥullin 1:1; *Hilkhot Avoda Zara* 10:7 and *Yad Peshuta* ad loc.

to love all human beings equally, there are some positive commandments that extend only to those closest to us – our families or our people.

It is also clear that some things are unique to the residents of a certain locale or members of a specific nation. These include a shared culture, shared values, particular modes of conduct, and certain duties and privileges. Those duties and privileges cannot be extended to one who is not part of that nation and does not accept its shared values – except under certain conditions.

With respect to a *ger toshav*, Maimonides writes: "Since you are commanded to sustain him, he must be given medical treatment without charge."[64] In *Hilkhot Melakhim*, Maimonides expands on this: "We treat a *ger toshav* with courtesy and kindness, like a Jew, for we are commanded to sustain them...."[65] The source is a Scriptural verse: "You shall support him, stranger or resident alien, and he shall live among you" (Lev. 25:35),[66] even on Shabbat.[67] It seems that the obligation[68] to sustain a *ger toshav* applies only to one who lives among us, such as one who has permission to live in the Land of Israel. It is inconceivable that Jews must seek out all pious gentiles in every corner of the world so that we can sustain them wherever they may be. Certainly, however, if a gentile was accepted as a *ger toshav* and given permission to live in the Land of Israel, then just as we are obligated to give him somewhere to live, so we are obligated to sustain him, for he is our brother since he observes the seven Noahide laws. We can infer from here that anyone who has the status of *ger toshav*, even today, "you are commanded to sustain."[69] This

64. *Hilkhot Avoda Zara* 10:2.
65. *Hilkhot Melakhim* 10:12.
66. *Hilkhot Zekhiya UMattana* 3:11.
67. See Rabbi Meir Dan Plotsky, *Ḥemdat Yisrael* (Piotrkow: 1927/New York: 1965), *Kuntres Ner Mitzva* §52, p. 27 and *Kuntres Sheva Mitzvot* §37, p. 204 and §40, p. 206. Regarding Maimonides' ruling in *Hilkhot Shabbat* 2:12, see *Yad Peshuta* ad loc.
68. Note Maimonides' formulation: "You are *commanded* to sustain him" (*Hilkhot Zekhiya UMattana* 3:11).
69. Often in the course of history, Jews were persecuted by gentiles, and we cannot say that one who persecutes us has the status of a *ger toshav*. Nevertheless, there is also a halakhic obligation to sustain gentile paupers out of concern that we will increase enmity otherwise. See my *Melumdei Milḥama* §43 (Maaleh Adumim, 2004).

includes someone who already lives in the Land of Israel: if he observes the seven Noahide laws, he has the status of a *ger toshav*.

Regarding those who keep the seven mitzvot because they deem it rational, not because they believe in the Creator, it is said: "If they observe the seven mitzvot and say... based on their own thinking that this is what reason demands, or they syncretically added the name of a foreign deity... their only reward is in this world."[70] They deserve reward in this world, so clearly we must treat them with respect and support them.

Maimonides writes of them: "If his observance [of the seven mitzvot] is based on a reasoned conclusion,[71] he is not a *ger toshav* and not among the pious gentiles, but one of their wise men."[72]

Maimonides explains in several places that man has an innate sense of justice:

> For Him, may He be exalted, justice is necessary and obligatory; namely, that an obedient individual receives compensation for all the pious and righteous actions he has accomplished, even if he was not ordered by a prophet to do them, and that he is punished for all evil acts committed by him, even if he was not forbidden by a prophet to do them; this being forbidden by the inborn disposition – I refer to the prohibition against wrongdoing and injustice.[73]

He further explains:

> Inasmuch as it is not made clear in the Torah with regard to the disobedience of the Flood that an envoy of God was sent to them at that time, nor that prohibitions were imposed on them and that they were threatened with destruction, it is said that God was angry with them in His heart.[74]

70. *Mishnat Rabbi Eliezer* §6 (Enelow ed.) (New York: Block, 1933), p. 121.
71. The term "reasoned conclusion" ("*hekhra daat*") is similar to the idea of natural law ("*Lex naturalis*").
72. *Hilkhot Melakhim* 8:11.
73. *Moreh Nevukhim* III:17, p. 470.
74. *Moreh Nevukhim* I:29, p. 62.

Even the generation of the Flood was expected to understand, based on a "reasoned conclusion," that it must refrain from corruption. The seven Noahide laws constitute the minimum standard of natural morality expected of every human being, containing prohibitions that anyone with integrity can comprehend. Yet there are many different gradations of human intellectual capacity. Individuals of superior wisdom are likely to be found even among those gentile nations that are entirely unfamiliar with the Torah, because every person was created in the Divine image and is capable of reaching a lofty moral plane. Therefore, we should develop peaceful and friendly relations with people of other nations, at the very least so that we can fulfill the dictum of the Sages: "What is hateful do you, do not do to your fellow."[75]

Moreover, Maimonides writes at the end of the *Hilkhot Shemitta VeYovel*:

> ...any individual in the world whose spirit moves him; who has understood, in his wisdom, to set himself apart and stand before God, to serve Him, to worship Him, and to know God; who walks upright, as God created him to do; and who has cast away the burden of the many calculations that people pursue – is sanctified with the utmost holiness. God will be his portion and his inheritance forever and ever.[76]

It is consequently clear that one who is scrupulous about the seven mitzvot because of his natural morality, and certainly one whose moral conduct is such that he "walks upright, as God created him to do," is worthy of being saved, even on Shabbat. Is it conceivable that it is forbidden to desecrate Shabbat to rescue one who is "sanctified with the utmost holiness"? Maimonides has written: "The Torah's laws do not bring vengeance to the world, but rather bring mercy, kindness, and peace unto the world."[77]

---

75. Shabbat 31a.
76. *Hilkhot Shemitta VeYovel* 13:13.
77. *Hilkhot Shabbat* 2:3.

Even with respect to actual idolaters, Maimonides rules: "With regard even to heathens,[78] our Sages instructed us to visit their sick, to bury their dead along with the Jewish dead, and to sustain their paupers among Jewish paupers, for the ways of peace, as it is written, 'The Lord is good to all and His mercies are over all His works' (Ps. 145:9), and 'Its ways are ways of pleasantness, and all its paths are peace' (Prov. 3:17)."[79] It goes without saying that this law applies where there is concern for hatred and hostility toward Jews. Moreover, the Sages of the Talmud asserted: "Gentiles living outside of the Land of Israel are not idolaters; rather, they uphold the customs of their ancestors,"[80] and as explained above, most nations of the world have advanced considerably since the talmudic era.

Clearly, from a moral perspective man is expected to conduct himself properly even toward others who are not members of his people. However, we must also be careful not to develop misplaced priorities. It is sometimes easier for one to show concern to those who are distant than it is to show concern for those who are close; this is a distortion of morality. At the same time, one who shows care and concern for his relatives and to his own people, and is thus able to extend that concern to all of humanity, has reached a lofty moral plane.

Torah Study for Gentiles

Another example pertains to the Talmud's statement: "R. Yoḥanan said: A heathen who engages in Torah study deserves death, as it is written: 'Moses commanded the Torah to us, an inheritance' (Deut. 33:4). It is an inheritance for us, not for them."[81]

However, Maimonides writes in a responsum:

> *Question:* The dictum of R. Yoḥanan, "A heathen who engages in Torah study deserves death," is this the law? Must every Jew

78. Maimonides uses the term "*goyim*" here, which he generally uses to refer to idol worshippers. See *Hilkhot Maakhalot Assurot* 11:8.
79. *Hilkhot Melakhim* 10:12.
80. Ḥullin 13b.
81. Sanhedrin 59a.

> refrain from teaching him any of the mitzvot aside from the seven [Noahide] mitzvot, or not?
>
> *Answer:* It is the law, without a doubt.... But it is permissible to teach the commandments to Christians and to draw them close to our religion.... If they were presented with the correct interpretation, perhaps they would recant, and even if they don't recant... it will not be a stumbling block for us, since their scriptures are no different than ours.[82]

We see that the aim of this prohibition is to prevent stumbling blocks from being placed before Jews, but with respect to study that does not entail any risk, and, on the contrary, where there is hope that something positive will come from it, it is permissible to teach Torah to a non-Jew. It seems that the same would apply to the prohibition on non-Jews to observe Shabbat, since Maimonides explains: "The general rule is: We do not permit them to introduce new rituals (*leḥadesh dat*)."[83] Based on this responsum, we can understand why the Sages taught Torah to two Roman commissioners:[84] there was no concern that they would mislead Jews, and indeed, they proclaimed, "We have gone carefully through your Torah, and found it correct...."

Meiri writes:

> Nevertheless, anyone who engages in the [study of the] principles of the seven mitzvot, their details, and their implications, even though this includes most of the corpus of the Torah, is honored, even as much as we honor the high priest, for there is no concern that we will be misled by him, since he is engaged in the study of what belongs to him as well. All the more so if the purpose of his investigation is to arrive at the ultimate perfection

---

82. *Responsa Rambam* §149.
83. *Hilkhot Melakhim* 10:9. The expression used by Maimonides, "*leḥadesh dat*," seems to refer to the performance of mitzvot that are religious rituals, not to the performance of interpersonal mitzvot that express humanity and morality – like giving charity – even if the gentile is motivated by religious consciousness.
84. See Bava Kamma 38a; Y. Bava Kamma 4:3.

of our Torah, to the point that if he finds it perfect, he will recant and convert. And all the more so if he studies and observes the principles of the mitzvot for their own sake, even the ones that are not included in the seven mitzvot.[85]

War and Peace

"R. Yehoshua said: Great is peace, for the name of the Holy One, blessed be He, is called peace, as Scripture says, 'And he called it "the Lord is peace"' (Judges 6:24)."[86] "R. Shimon b. Ḥalafta said: There is no vessel that holds blessing as does peace, as Scripture says, 'The Lord will grant strength to His people; the Lord will bless His people with peace' (Ps. 29:11)."[87] Our obligation is to "seek peace and pursue it" (Ps. 34:15). Accordingly, the prophets longed for the awaited day: "It shall come to pass at the End of Days that the mountain of the Lord's house will be established atop the mountains…and nations will stream toward it… and they will beat their swords into plowshares and their spears into pruning hooks. Nation will not lift up sword against nation, nor will they practice war any longer. Each man will sit under his vine and under his fig tree with none to frighten him" (Mic. 4:1–4).

It is obviously forbidden to wage war without cause, because no sin is more severe than bloodshed. Nevertheless, the Torah does not totally forbid war; indeed, we are commanded and obligated to wage certain wars. The Torah even recognizes and permits "optional" wars under certain conditions. How can we resolve the contradiction between establishing peace as one of the highest values (to the point that *shalom*, peace, is considered a name of God) and the Torah's explicit commandments related to war?

The Sages declared:

> "Its ways are ways of pleasantness, and all its paths are peace" (Prov. 3:17) – everything written in the Torah was written for the sake

---

85. Meiri on Sanhedrin 59a.
86. *Derekh Eretz Zuta, Perek HaShalom.*
87. Mishna Uktzin 3:12.

> of peace. And even though wars are written in the Torah – they, too, were written for the sake of peace.[88]

In a cruel world, where kingdoms attack each other and "a man would swallow his fellow alive,"[89] the law must necessarily provide that "if one comes to kill you, arise and kill him first."[90] A nation that is not prepared to defend itself and its land will not last; it will quickly pass from the world. Preparedness for war is a necessary condition for the building of a society, for the fulfillment of Torah, and for the realization of a vision.

Even the stories that the Torah tells about wars were written for the sake of peace:

> One finds that the Holy One, blessed be He, revoked a decree for the sake of peace. When? When the Holy One, blessed be He, said to Moses, "When you besiege a city for many days…" (Deut. 20:19) etc., and the Holy One, blessed be He, said to him that he must utterly destroy them…. But Moses did not do so, saying, instead, "If I now go to attack, I do not know who has sinned and who has not sinned. Rather, I will approach them in peace," as Scripture says, "I sent messengers from the wilderness of Kedemot…with words of peace, saying" (Deut. 2:26). When he saw that [King Sihon] did not respond in peace, [Moses] attacked him…. The Holy One, blessed be He, said to [Moses], "I said 'Utterly destroy them,' and you approached them in peace? By your life, as you have said, so will I do," as it is stated: "When you approach a city to make war on it, you shall [first] call out to it in peace" (Deut. 20:10).[91]

This has been codified as a halakhic ruling: "We do not wage war against anyone until we have offered peace."[92] The very assertion that we do not

88. *Midrash Tanḥuma, Tzav* §5.
89. Mishna Avot 3:2.
90. Sanhedrin 72a.
91. *Midrash Tanḥuma* loc. cit.
92. *Hilkhot Melakhim* 6:1.

wage war before we offer peace, even if we concede that this rule was not fully developed in ancient times, indicates a general approach – and this certainly is expressed by the manner in which this ruling is articulated by Maimonides.

I have already noted[93] that, to the best of our knowledge, there is no Ancient Near Eastern legal code that placed restrictions on how to wage war. This was an innovation of the Torah. Of course, we must understand the Torah's laws of warfare in the context of those times and the conditions under which war was waged then, but the laws nevertheless reflect certain fundamental principles.

For example, the Torah instructs us that when besieging a city, we must give anyone who wishes to flee the opportunity to do so. It is clear that if we implemented this mitzva nowadays, it would be very difficult to wage war; practically speaking, it stands to reason that this must be implemented differently in every generation, based on changes to life conditions. Still, basic principles emerge from this discussion.

This is an example of primary legislation about a phenomenon that has been part of human history from the beginning: hostility and warfare between peoples. These laws acknowledge the human phenomenon of war but aim to limit its scope. They even express a positive attitude toward all human beings. Some halakhot, including some of the details pertaining to war, are hard to grasp fully given the changes wrought by time. In such cases, it is hard to ascertain the Torah's aims, since we do not always understand the real-life setting of these laws and how they were meant to be carried out. The trend, however, is absolutely clear: even in the most dangerous and acute situations, we must not forget that every man is created in the Divine image.

All the commandments related to war were given in order to restrict the scope of warfare and to replace attitudes that glorify war and its heroes with yearnings for peace. As long as dangerous enemies lurk, we must arm ourselves with swords, bows, and spears. When these weapons grow outdated and impotent, we must equip ourselves with the latest and most effective weaponry. But we must not forget for a moment

93. *Pathways to Their Hearts*, ch. 2, "The Role of the Commandments," section "The Beautiful Captive Woman," pp. 32 ff.

that all of these weapons "are nothing but shameful, as Scripture says, 'They will beat their swords into plowshares and their spears into pruning hooks' (Is. 2:4)."[94]

In this context, it is worth commenting on the concept of an "optional" war ("*milḥemet reshut*"). An optional war does not mean simply that there is a choice whether or not to wage war. Killing others, and placing oneself at risk of being killed, cannot be "optional."[95] A *milḥemet reshut* has fundamentally lofty aims and goals: "To uplift the true religion, to fill the world with righteousness, to break the arm of the wicked, and to fight the wars of the Lord."[96] However, these aims do not generate a temporal or qualitative obligation. It is inconceivable that Israel must, at all times, endanger itself to fill remote locales at the ends of the earth with righteousness. Clearly, then, these aims only justify war when there are immediate needs and weighty political and economic reasons for waging war. Even the goal of "magnifying the prominence and eminence"[97] of the king of Israel means projecting deterrence against hostile elements so that things do not escalate into real conflict, as Moses did with respect to Sihon: "This day I begin to put the dread and fear of you upon the peoples everywhere under heaven, so that they shall tremble and quake because of you whenever they hear you mentioned" (Deut. 2:25).

Nevertheless, when the danger is not immediate – meaning, it does not "help deliver Israel from the hands of its enemies" – the Torah does not permit waging war on the basis of such considerations, except under specific limited circumstances. The assessment of a king or general that the situation calls for war is not sufficient. The consent of the Sanhedrin, which reflects broad public agreement, is required, as is that

---

94. Mishna Shabbat 6:4.
95. See Joshua 7:5–6, which recounts how thirty-six men fell out of a three thousand soldiers, whereupon "Joshua rent his clothes. He and the elders of Israel... strewed earth on their heads." That is, they treated the deaths of a few dozen soldiers like a national tragedy. The Talmud (Sanhedrin 44a) says that Joshua said before God: "Sovereign of the universe! For these shall a [number equal to a] majority of the Sanhedrin he killed?"
96. *Hilkhot Melakhim* 4:10.
97. Ibid. 5:1.

of the high priest. Their consent ensures that wars are not just the adventures of rulers who take lightly the blood of their own citizens – and therefore certainly of members of other nations – as was the case with heathen kings.

The Torah authorized the king, in consultation with the Sanhedrin and others, to decide that there is sufficient cause to wage war. For this reason, such a war is called "optional." However, it is clear that unless there are good reasons why it is necessary, even a *milḥemet reshut* is not permitted in any way.

On a practical level, war is forbidden nowadays unless enemies are attacking us or threatening us, in which case we are obligated to defend ourselves. For this, there is no need for a king, a Sanhedrin, or a high priest. In essence, the reason for waging such a war is to save lives; the duty to wage it devolves upon the Jewish people as a whole and is incumbent upon each and every individual.[98]

Allegiance to our covenant with God creates a difficult dilemma, because it does not exempt the individual or the nation from the vital need to struggle for its survival and its homeland. On the one hand, the Sages taught us that weapons are "nothing but shameful." On the other hand, how can a small nation tucked between rival empires maintain its independence without being willing to take to the battlefield, so that its wicked neighbors understand that it is not worthwhile to try to subdue it? Only one who believes in the covenant between God and His people can make such a calculation. The inclination toward idolatrous determinism, whether in its ancient or modern forms, and fear of becoming "a nation that dwells apart," leads some people to the notion that a small nation cannot survive unless it allies itself with mighty neighbors and tries to curry favor with them. Faith in the covenant thus creates a dilemma for the soul: How can one wage war while yearning for peace?

The moral dilemma of one who believes in God and His Torah should not be treated lightly. When Ammon and Moab attacked King Jehoshaphat, he was terrified, and he turned to God in prayer: "Now

---

98. For a broad halakhic discussion of wars that are a mitzva, "optional" wars, and the mitzva to settle the Land of Israel, see my *Responsa Melumdei Milḥama* §1 (Maaleh Adumim, 2004).

the people of Ammon, Moab, and the mountain of Seir, into whose [land] You did not let Israel pass when they came from Egypt – rather, they turned aside from them and did not wipe them out – these now repay us by coming to expel us from Your possession which You gave us as ours. O our God, surely You will punish them, for we are powerless before this great multitude…" (II Chr. 20:10–12). The verses continue:

> Then in the midst of the congregation the spirit of the Lord came upon Jahaziel… and he said, "Give heed, all Judah and the inhabitants of Jerusalem and King Jehoshaphat; thus said the Lord to you, 'Do not fear or be dismayed…. March down against them tomorrow…. Do not fear or be dismayed; go forth to meet them tomorrow and the Lord will be with you'"…. Early the next morning they arose and went forth to the wilderness of Tekoa. As they went forth, Jehoshaphat stood and said, "Listen to me, O Judah and inhabitants of Jerusalem: Have faith in the Lord your God and show yourselves faithful; have faith in His prophets and you will succeed." He stationed singers to the Lord… ahead of the vanguard. (ibid. 14–21)

There is no victory without faith that war is in God's hands, but if one does not enter the fray of battle, faith will not help him. God accepts praise specifically when it comes from the ranks of the vanguard. However, when Isaiah warned Ahaz with the very same words, "If you do not have faith, it is because you are not faithful" (Is. 7:9), the king and his officers preferred to take the "safe route": "At that time, King Ahaz sent to the king of Assyria for help" (II Chr. 28:16). The end was bitter: "King Tillegat-pilneser of Assyria attacked him and harassed him instead of supporting him" (ibid. 20).

The danger faced by a soldier, even one who is fighting for truth, is not just to his physical life, but also, even primarily, to his spiritual life. Although King David established a correct standard – "With the pure, act in purity, and with the perverse, act with guile" (II Sam. 22:27) – nevertheless, even if it were possible to determine in each and every case who is truly wholesome and pure and who is perverse, the soul of the righteous would be corroded by the very fact that he is meting judgment on the wicked. Maimonides writes about King David himself that even though he was worthy of prophecy and he faithfully tended to every need of his people, since he spent most of his life fighting Israel's wars and tenaciously, courageously, and boldly saving them from their enemies, "we find that he was cruel":

> It is explicitly stated in Chronicles that God, considered him unworthy to build the Temple, as it was not fitting in His eyes, because of the many people David caused to be killed. So God said to him, "You shall not build a house to My name, because you have shed much blood" (II Chr. 22:8).[99]

This seems puzzling. David needed to be hard-hearted so he could win his wars; the failure of his predecessor, Saul, was that, in the moment of truth, he lacked this trait. Yet, Maimonides' description is clear and reflects a dualism. In their praises of the king, the Korahides sang: "Gird your sword upon your thigh, O hero... for the cause of truth and humility and righteousness" (Ps. 45:4–5). However, with respect to that very sword, we are commanded: "If you make for Me an altar of stones, do not build it of hewn stones; for you have wielded your sword upon them and profaned them" (Ex. 20:22). The mishna explains: "Iron was created to shorten man's life, and the altar was created to prolong man's life. It is not fitting to wield the shortener against the prolonger."[100] To save Israel, David had to sacrifice his blood and guts on the battlefield. But that is not all; he made an even greater sacrifice. Even though he yearned his whole life to build God's Temple with his own hands, he had to give up that lofty aspiration, because "it is not fitting to wield the shortener against the prolonger." Even use of the sword to protect God's people is in some way profane, and even the deliverer of Israel may not enter the Sanctuary at will.

It requires constant effort in the face of difficult decisions to engage in war and maintain one's sanctity. This is what our father Abraham was afraid of when he waged war to rescue Lot and the people

99. *Shemonah Perakim*, ch. 7, p. 81.
100. Mishna Middot 3:4.

of Sodom from captivity, until God appeared to him and said: "I am your protector" (Gen. 15:1). The Midrash explains: "R. Levi said: Our father Abraham was growing fearful and saying, 'Among the population that I killed, was there not one righteous man? One God-fearing man?'"[101] If Abraham was afraid of this, what can we say for ourselves? Who could emerge unscathed from such a test?

Yet the Jewish people was chosen to be a kingdom of priests. This national mission cannot be fulfilled in exile, and so the covenant mandated our return to our land time and again: "I will remember in their favor the covenant with the ancients, whom I took out ... in the sight of the nations to be their God" (Lev. 26:45).

Life in exile taught us how to cope and survive under conditions of weakness and powerlessness. We were very nearly exterminated, and the verse that states "You shall perish among the nations" (Lev. 26:38) was almost fulfilled in its entirety. However, we survived due to our covenant with God: "Yet, even then, when they are in the land of their enemies, I will not reject them or spurn them so as to destroy them, annulling My covenant with them" (ibid. 44).

Life in our national home is supposed to teach us how to wield material power – and, at the same time, to control the urge to dominate; we must not flinch from defending ourselves by whatever means necessary – yet we must not glorify war and its accoutrements. Put differently, we must not forget the covenant even when we have the wherewithal to succeed. This idea was articulated well by Nehemiah when he charged the returnees to Zion with a dual mission: "Do not be afraid of them! Think of the great and awesome Lord, and fight for your brothers, your sons and daughters, your wives and homes" (Neh. 4:8), and indeed, as they rebuilt the walls of Jerusalem, "they were doing work with one hand while the other held a weapon" (ibid. 11). During that same era, the prophet explained the meaning of this charge: "Not by might, nor by power, but by My spirit – said the Lord of Hosts" (Zech. 4:6).

This task is almost too great to bear, all the more so when it is charged to an entire nation. When one is exposed to murderers and must therefore stand at the ready, day and night, strategizing how to strike

101. Genesis Rabba 44:4.

them and defend against them, how can war not become a goal in itself? For many nations, war is indeed considered a goal in itself, and it brings those who engage in it successfully the highest accolades and honors. A military career often paves the way to national leadership. On the other hand, a nation that recoils from war is at risk that its soldiers will flee the battlefield – and of course, defeat would soon follow.

A society whose role models are fighters and killers, even lawfully, can easily sink into a moral abyss. Yet if these heroes are not considered exemplars and are not shown the proper gratitude and reward, who will protect the public in a time of need? Still, placing successful generals in positions of leadership can have a destructive influence on society.

The educational challenge is massive. The Sages were very concerned that militarism, so prevalent among other nations, would take root in Israel. To prevent this mistake, they went against the plain meaning of Scripture and expounded verses that describe military feats as referring to the "war" of Torah, the thrust and parry of argumentation in the talmudic tradition,[102] thereby removing the glory of actual warfare and reinforcing the severity and undesirability of bloodshed, which is nothing more than a necessary evil. The valiant warriors who risked life and limb for God and His people are recast by the Sages as having accomplished great feats in other, non-military contexts, all but ignoring their military efforts, so that they can be honored properly and treated as models for emulation. It was not Joshua's military prowess that made him worthy of leading Israel; the Sages found other merits to explain his worthiness:

> He would arrive early and stay late at your [Moses'] study hall, arranging the benches and spreading out the mats. He will take the reins of leadership, in fulfillment of the verse: "He who tends a fig tree will enjoy its fruit" (Prov. 27:18).[103]

This is a Jewish accolade for an outstanding soldier!

---

102. Editor's note: See Yitzchak Blau, "Ploughshares into Swords: Contemporary Religious Zionists and Moral Constraints," *Tradition* 34:4 (2000), esp. pp. 42–46.

103. *Yalkut Shimoni, Pinḥas* §776.

Sometimes the weary soul longs for a bit of tranquility, and at those times the dream of peace in the Middle East, or a regional, EU-like economic union, can seem very enticing. Giving in to these temptations ignores the fact that it is impossible to duplicate and accelerate processes that took almost two thousand years in the West to the point where the Arab world can undergo the same transformations in just sixty years, so that the wolf will be ready to lie down with the lamb.

Without realizing the internal contradictions, the people with this dream make the opposite claim as well: in the long term, there is no hope of overcoming the demographic power and nationalist strains of the Arab world, which will overwhelm us. We therefore must reach an agreement – any agreement – quickly. Add the moral claim that constant war drains the soul and undermines justice, which is the basis for our connection to this land, and you have the perfect recipe for immediate national surrender.

It is possible, though, that this nightmare sprouted from other, more hidden roots. Buried deep within the recesses of all human beings is a spark of faith. Maimonides made us aware of this marvelous phenomenon when he explained that even idolaters are motivated by the drive to believe, which is characteristic of all who were created in the Divine image. It is precisely those who fight so passionately against religion who most fervently and blindly cling to their faith in the power of "revolution" to repair the world, without realizing their own inconsistencies and contradictions.

Human beings want to believe, and no person can live without faith of some sort. But faith in the Torah is frightening and intimidating, because it leads inexorably to the conclusion that each individual human being bears the heavy burden of responsibility before the Creator for the choices he makes. In contrast, faith in materialism's god of progress is tantamount to the enthronement and deification of man. Since progress is ostensibly assured, for historical processes are imagined as ironclad laws, if we would only channel our energies in accordance with the signs that indicate the phases of the process, we could easily cure all that ails the different nations in the region. A bit of political vision, a dash of investment capital, and *voila*, all sorrow and sadness will disappear.

Many people have innocently been led to believe that hatred for Israel can be transformed into adulation and cooperation by means of flexible diplomacy. All we need to do is lay aside our spiritual identity and merge with the secularist mainstream, which, with historical inevitability, will overwhelm the entire region.

It is likely, however, that if the social, economic, and spiritual successes of the State of Israel become apparent to all, along with its enduring military strength, this may challenge, persuade, encourage, and ultimately spur and guide its neighbors to adopt democratic values without any active intervention on the part of Israel. We cannot manipulate such processes or rush them artificially. Perhaps, just as Islam drew fundamental ideas from Judaism in the past, it will happen in the future. Perhaps, just as major Christian denominations have drawn closer to their Scriptural sources, Islam may one day change its attitude toward the Bible and toward history in general. This would be a fulfillment of the verse: "All the families of the earth shall be blessed through you" (Gen. 12:3).

Although the return of the Jewish people to its homeland is of major significance for the nations of the world, especially the surrounding nations, we cannot and must not try to peer behind the curtain to ascertain the Almighty's plans. On the other hand, there is one thing we know for certain: without strong dedication and determination that stem from our steadfast faith in the Redeemer of Israel, we will not last long.

Realization of the Torah's peaceful goals does not depend on us alone. As long as we live among "the wicked of the nations, who are compared to wolves and leopards, as Scripture says, 'A wolf of the desert plunders them; a leopard lies in wait at their cities' (Jer. 5:6)";[104] as long as hatred of the eternal nation prevails, we are powerless to establish peace among the nations. The goal remains beyond us, for now, but the day will surely come, "for the mouth of the Lord of Hosts has spoken" (Mic. 4:4).

---

104. *Hilkhot Melakhim* 12:1.

People of the Covenant

The return to Zion is a critical milestone, and not only for the Jewish people. The history of the Jewish people is of enormous significance, with ramifications for the entire world. Even nations that were not influenced by Christianity and Islam – certain African countries and the Far East, for instance – are now being exposed to Israel's influence. And the new light shining from Zion is also directed toward nations that have absorbed fragmentary ideas and partial truths from the Torah, as contained in the teachings of Christianity and Islam. We must raise high the banner of Israel, as a beacon for the nations.

The kingdom of priests' awareness of its mission and consciousness of the covenant are the distinguishing marks of Jewish identity. The mission of the Jewish people is to imbue all of human history with meaning. The return of the Jewish people to its land begins a new chapter in biblical history, and, of course, the primary challenge is ours: we must fulfill our duties in accordance with the covenant. Our Torah has proven itself through its power to preserve us through thousands of years of wandering and exile while radiating its light far and wide.

Since the Jewish people endures by virtue of the covenant, it follows that the Jewish state exists by virtue of the covenant as well. The State of Israel is supposed to embody the divine promise that God will not abandon His people, and we are enjoined to fulfill our duty to sanctify God's name in the world by means of this state. This is the arena where the significance of Jewish history and all of human history are manifest.

Our task demands openness to all human suffering and all human potentials. When a baby learns to speak, his father teaches him two verses – in essence, two words – that are the key to all of Judaism: "Torah" and "*Shema*."[105] These two words point toward unending horizons. The first – the challenge to achieve moral excellence, to accept the divine command, and to be willing to work to improve the world;

105. *Hilkhot Talmud Torah* 1:6: "When he begins speaking, he teaches him 'Moses commanded the Torah to us, an inheritance…' (Deut. 33:4) and the first verse of the *Shema*."

the second – broadening and deepening our understanding to its very utmost limits; and they depend on each other. Scientific and technological progress enables the production of immense resources, which in turn can improve society and human life. One who has nothing cannot be charitable, and when the land does not give its produce, famine is inevitable. Yet without consciousness that man is subject to divine command, scientific and cognitive progress can lead, God forbid, to devastation. Human knowledge and understanding can be deeply problematic when not anchored in the awareness that one was created by God, who will hold him accountable for his actions.

Just as an individual must balance between the pride brought about by the realization that one was created by God Himself and the true humility of one who recognizes his fleeting temporality, so too the state must find the golden mean that combines the ancient paths that cross all of human history with the narrow, winding, ascending route of a small nation, whose entire existence hinges on God's grace. On the one hand, only a people infused with faith in its historic mission and its importance for all mankind will gather the strength to stand firmly against the forces of destruction all around. On the other hand, only a nation that stands before the Creator and demands nothing but light is worthy of this mission.

Unprecedented historical processes are unfolding before our eyes, and the prophet implores us to observe what is happening: "Raise your eyes and look around; they have all gathered and come to you" (Is. 49:18). It has been foretold: "I the Lord, in My grace, have summoned you, and I have grasped you by the hand. I created you, and set you as a covenant of the people, a light of nations" (ibid. 42:6). This, in essence, is the definition of the Jewish people and the purpose of the State of Israel: the people of the covenant, a symbol of the covenant between the Creator and all mankind. And where are the attentive ear and the heart of flesh that can hear the question of all questions: "Why, when I came, was no one there? Why, when I called, would none respond?" (ibid. 50:2)? Despite the waves of antipathy and loathing, large countries like China and India want to collaborate with Israel. We cannot grasp why, but the answer was given long ago. We need only pay attention:

"Listen to Me, My people, and give ear to Me, My nation, for teaching shall go forth from Me, and My justice will become, in a moment, a light for peoples" (ibid. 51:4).

We must only recall the covenant in order to comprehend what is happening to us and understand the magnitude of the task ahead. The word of God reverberates through the eternal heavens: "I am about to do something new; even now it shall flourish... the people I formed for Myself that they might declare My praise" (ibid. 43:19, 21).

Chapter 12

A Dialogue Between Rabbi Rabinovitch and Rabbi Lord Jonathan Sacks*

A Model Society

Rabbi Sacks: Allow me to begin by the asking the question of questions: The Jewish people has returned to being a sovereign, self-governing nation. What, ideally, do you think the Torah would be telling us to make of this society? This is the first time in twenty centuries that we have had a chance to create a society founded on Jewish values. What should our aspirations for this society be, according to the Torah?

* Rabbi Lord Jonathan Sacks (1948–2020) served as Chief Rabbi of the United Hebrew Congregations of the Commonwealth from 1991 until 2013, has authored dozens of books and articles, and is known as one of the most important thinkers of our time. He studied under Rabbi Rabinovitch in England for over a decade. See the introduction to his book *The Great Partnership: Science, Religion, and the Search for Meaning* (New York: Schocken, 2014) and the English introduction to the second volume of *MiBirkat Moshe* (Maaleh Adumim: Me'aliyot, 2012), a collection of articles on Maimonides in honor of Rabbi Rabinovitch.

This chapter is an edited version of a conversation that took place in 2014.

Rabbi Rabinovitch: It seems to me that the real goal of any kind of society is the blessing of *shalom* – of peace. There must be a genuine sense of peace among all sections of the population, in spite of the natural differences that inevitably exist between people. It is very important to cultivate a sense of communal responsibility. At the same time, it is also very important to ensure the expression of a range of opinions, because that develops a greater sense of responsibility and a greater awareness of the question of which version of the truth is guiding us.

In Israel, we are still far from these goals, and, unfortunately, sectionalism and disputes of various kinds are very acute. We have yet to overcome the endless disputes and rifts that have characterized the Jewish people since ancient times, as described in Tanakh and throughout history. Until we overcome them, we can expect hard times.

But on the other hand, I think there is a growing awareness that we are witnessing the realization of the divine promise that the Jewish people cannot and will not be, God forbid, eliminated. Throughout history, we have survived under abnormal circumstances. Toynbee, among others, thought that we were fossils, and one can understand where he was coming from given his time and his frame of reference. I don't know what he would say today, but it's clear that this "fossil" has come to a very exciting stage of life. Who would have thought that we would get to where we are today? We just celebrated the anniversary of Jerusalem's reunification. The city's population has never been this large. In the Land of Israel as a whole, the Jewish population today is close to seven million. It never reached that high a number in antiquity.

We need to learn how to disagree and yet be loyal to each other, to disagree and cooperate with each other, and that is a difficult task. The Diaspora had many effects upon us, but I think that one of the worst possible effects is the divisiveness which still haunts us. Much of that divisiveness comes from the Diaspora.

Rabbi Sacks: It's true. In the nineteenth century, the Jews of Europe were faced with a terrible dilemma. Non-Jewish society offered them participation and integration, but on condition that we would stop being Jewish, at least in public. This created a fracture, expressed in one way in Western Europe and in a different way in Eastern Europe, but it shattered the Jewish people into a lot of different denominations and sects and ideologies. In a sense, we are still living with the consequences of that nineteenth-century crisis.

Rabbi Rabinovitch: That, it seems to me, is a correct analysis.

Rabbi Sacks: So if I could just break this down a little bit. First of all, what binds us together? When I visit the US, I am struck by how there is a general American narrative, an American story, and new immigrant groups take that story and make it their own. In many respects, this is the Jewish story. It's the story of the exodus from Egypt, only instead of Egypt, it's England, and instead of the pharaoh, it's the king. Replace the Reed Sea with the Atlantic. Somehow or another, American presidents, from Washington and Jefferson until today, talk about this story of the journey to the land of promise, almost as though it is the promised land – can we do the same here in Israel? After all it was our story to begin with. Is there a collective narrative that can bring people together despite all the divisions?

Rabbi Rabinovitch: I hope there is, but there must be a willingness on the part of all the different segments of the population. The reality is that almost all of us are immigrants, children of immigrants, or maybe grandchildren or great-grandchildren of immigrants. There are very few whose families have been here for centuries, so in a sense we all have a common history as "returnees from the Diaspora." Yet somehow the sense of identity is not defined by that, and the divisions, whether cultural, religious, or political, are not subsumed under the unifying conception that we are all immigrants, all *olim*.

Rabbi Sacks: Do you think the religious leadership is doing all it can do, or all it should do, to bring a sense of togetherness?

Rabbi Rabinovitch: I think that much of the religious leadership is aware of the fact that there is a problem, and that is one of the reasons for the proliferation of Yeshivot Hesder and Mechina programs which teach and act with respect for all segments of society, along with promoting Torah study and working to spread Torah throughout society. God willing, these institutions will change the climate of the Torah world in Israel. However, we must be careful not to adopt simplistic solutions that do not address the root of the problem. Simplistic approaches are liable to deepen divisions even further.

Rabbi Sacks: One thing has always intrigued me. We have been able to handle *maḥloket,* disagreement, in very creative ways. I think Judaism is the only civilization whose canonical texts are all anthologies of arguments. So you get Abraham arguing with God, Moses arguing with God, Jeremiah; in the Midrash you have statements like "*Shiv'im panim laTorah*" ("The Torah has seventy faces"); and in the Mishna you have Rabbi X says this and Rabbi Y says that. We were the world's experts in arguing and yet staying together. What did we lose that made us pull apart?

Rabbi Rabinovitch: I think that is a question for psychologists and sociologists. I certainly cannot see an imminent solution to the problem of groups' unwillingness to recognize that there is something in the other group's position that I can live with, or that we must try to work things out together.

Rabbi Sacks: And yet the Gemara says explicitly that the views of Beit Hillel were accepted against those of Beit Shammai because, among other things, they taught the views of their opponents, and they taught the views of their opponents before they taught their own. Where did we lose that one?

Rabbi Rabinovitch: I am concerned that we have in fact lost it to a very large extent. Even in the specific area of halakhic decision-making, there are very few rabbis who are willing to accept that "*Elu ve'elu divrei Elokim ḥayim*" ("These and those are the words of the living God"). Additionally, there is a fear of making decisions. And some of the halakhic questions that require decisions today are new issues with no clear historical precedents. There is a fear of setting precedents.

The Establishment of the State and the Messianic Vision

Rabbi Sacks: Do you see the State of Israel today as part of a messianic process?

Rabbi Rabinovitch: I don't know what a messianic process is. We need to be aware of the fact that we have witnessed miracles, but no one can know where this process will lead. In the early Second Temple era there were prophets who sought to comfort the people and to reassure them that the salvation they had experienced was real. And it was real, but it did not lead to the Messianic Era. But it is clear that, thank God, our generation has been privileged to witness the kind of historical developments which disprove for now and forever the theory that Judaism is a fossil. *Am Yisrael ḥai*! Each of its limbs and parts is alive and well. This is something fundamental. One of the messages of our prophets is that the Jewish people cannot and will not be eliminated, God forbid. If proof for this principle was ever needed, we have seen it in our lifetime. We were almost annihilated. The decree almost reached the entire people of Israel. And we have come out of it in a manner that nobody in his right mind could have even contemplated seventy-five years ago. No one could have thought of this possible outcome.

Rabbi Sacks: I have a strong suspicion that were Theodor Herzl to come back to life today, he would have made both a "*SheHeḥeyanu*" and "*Al HaNisim*," because even he didn't envision anything as remarkable as the current State of Israel.

Rabbi Rabinovitch: Indeed.

Rabbi Sacks: Let's take this piece by piece: with the return of Jewish sovereignty, we would expect a return of the *malkhut*, the monarchy. I imagine you see the democratically elected Knesset as this *malkhut*.

Rabbi Rabinovitch: Correct.

Rabbi Sacks: Do you see democracy, a democratic State of Israel, as a religious value? As a Jewish value?

Rabbi Rabinovitch: I think this is the essence of the Jewish concept of the state, although, of course, the word "democracy" doesn't appear in our rabbinical literature or historical sources.

Rabbi Sacks: The Greeks tended to have names for things, and we tended to actually have them without necessarily naming them.

Rabbi Rabinovitch: Indeed. A general rule of the Torah is that any major decision has to be accepted by the community, and if the community doesn't accept even an enactment of the Sanhedrin, it has no validity. The same thing is true of political appointments. This is part of our heritage, but nowadays it is often not part of our practice. Today, in certain religious communities, there is a sense of piety or *Ḥasidut* that obliterates the role of the community and elevates the role of the leader, the *rebbe*, to a level that he never enjoyed in antiquity.

Rabbi Sacks: Do we have prophets today? That is, if a prophet, a *navi*, is someone who sees God in history, then we can understand why, after Haggai, Zechariah, and Malachi, we did not have any prophets – because we weren't full, independent agents in history. But now that we have returned to history, do you expect the return of prophecy?

Rabbi Rabinovitch: God willing, that's part of the promise. Part of the promise of the restoration of the Jewish people to the Land of Israel is that the Almighty says, "Your sons and your daughters shall prophesy" (Joel 3:1).

Rabbi Sacks: Do you see the first flickering of this?

Rabbi Rabinovitch: Unfortunately, I do not have the ability to identify prophecy, but I certainly feel that God's promise is much closer to realization than ever before.

Rabbi Sacks: We were talking about the messianic process, slow, gradual or whatever, and the return of *malkhut*, of sovereignty, as the beginning of the return of prophecy. What about *kehuna*, the priesthood? Do you have a strong view about how the Third Temple will look and what will be offered there?

Rabbi Rabinovitch: We have to trust the Almighty. What He has done for us, what I have seen with my own eyes, is ample proof that He has demonstrated beyond all doubt, that "*Am Yisrael ḥai.*" With God's good grace, we hope He will help us see the rebuilding of the Temple. What will it look like? We will have to wait and see. I think we just need to trust the Almighty.

Rabbi Sacks: I am curious – you have spent a lifetime writing an extraordinary commentary to Maimonides' *Mishneh Torah,* and I imagine that in many ways, you have been shaped by his views. How do you read Maimonides' view of sacrifices, both regarding the past and the future?

Rabbi Rabinovitch: That is an important question. It is clear that Maimonides held that *korbanot,* animal sacrifices, are not the most desirable and efficient mode of worshipping God, and it may very well be that in his view most personal *korbanot* will no longer be offered. But apparently he held that communal offerings will be restored in the future Temple.[1] Again, I hope we will be fortunate enough to see for ourselves.

Rabbi Sacks: Which I imagine would have been his answer as well, really. He said we wouldn't understand what this means until we're actually there.

Rabbi Rabinovitch: Indeed. We have to leave certain things for the Almighty.

Rabbi Sacks: If the prophet Amos were to visit us, would he criticize the way our economy functions?

1. For a treatment of Maimonides' view, see "Society and History: The Uniqueness of Maimonides," in my *Studies in the Thought of Rambam* (Jerusalem: Me'aliyot, 2010), pp. 214–27 (Heb.).

Rabbi Rabinovitch: There are things in the economy that need to be criticized, but who would have thought that a small nation in a tiny country that is bereft of most natural resources could reach the level of prosperity that we, thank God, have been blessed with? Now, it's true that there are poor people, and not everybody is well off. That is all true, but even though there are many poor people today, here we stand before a *Shemitta* year, and I don't think anybody could imagine poor people going out to the fields to pick whatever grows naturally in the seventh year. Such abject poverty no longer exists. This is testimony to the wonders of the Creator.

Rabbi Sacks: There's no doubt that in Israel, as well as all economies in the world right now, the gaps between rich and poor are increasing. What would be a Jewish response to that? Is there something intrinsically wrong with some people being so much wealthier than the poorest, or is that to be dealt with by means of *tzedaka* and voluntary giving?

Rabbi Rabinovitch: Look, I'm not a politician, and I don't understand much about economic development, but it seems to me that if proof was needed as to whether imposing absolute equality by law and strictly enforcing it is a recipe for failure, that has been proven now several times over, with the Soviet Union and with other countries. I think that anyone who still holds onto Marxist ideas of what makes an ethical society is not living in the real world.

Rabbi Sacks: So what then would the Torah say about the demand that everybody in Israel should be provided with an education, health care, and other basic necessities?

Rabbi Rabinovitch: Education, health care, and basic sustenance are in fact essential needs, and society should ensure that people have them and do not sink into poverty. Additionally, society must prevent the concentration of too much economic power in the hands of individuals. The key question is what constitutes "too much," which is not simple.

Rabbi Sacks: I was very struck that the UN and the international community actually created something called Jubilee 2000, in order to mitigate or cancel third world debt. You had one of the major international economic policies of our time actually motivated by the idea of *Yovel* (the Jubilee year).

Rabbi Rabinovitch: That was a real accomplishment. And it shows that it is possible to apply the central ideas of mitzvot without creating a socialist nightmare.

Rabbi Sacks: Would it therefore be correct to say that we have responsibilities as Jews toward humanity as a whole?

Rabbi Rabinovitch: Most certainly.

Rabbi Sacks: What is the source of that responsibility? Is it the verse: "All the families of the earth will be blessed through you"? Or perhaps: "It is your wisdom and understanding in the eyes of the nations"?

Rabbi Rabinovitch: It's more than that. Before the giving of the Torah, God charges the people of Israel to be "a kingdom of priests and a holy nation," "*mamlekhet kohanim vegoi kadosh.*" What does it mean to be a "kingdom of priests"? Rabbi Avraham, the son of Maimonides, explains that Israel is to be the priesthood for mankind. Just as the priests are responsible for teaching Israel and mediating between the people and God, so too Israel is charged to be the priests of the world at large. The responsibility to all nations is fundamental. It's part of the hope and the dream of the Messianic Era.

Rabbi Sacks: So when the world is very critical of Israel, how do you interpret that?

Rabbi Rabinovitch: I think that even when the world is unfairly critical of Israel, it's not enough to say "Well, we're being picked on." We must also say that the world expects us to act in a manner worthy of a *mamlekhet kohanim.*

Rabbi Sacks: How do you understand the relationship between Israel and the Jews of the Diaspora? Should we be telling everybody to make *aliya* immediately? Is there a role for Jewish communities outside of the Land of Israel?

Rabbi Rabinovitch: I'm not quite sure that I can even suggest a direction for an answer. I think you are more familiar with the structure of Jewish life in the Diaspora, but it seems to me that, on the one hand, it's not likely or reasonable to expect that all Jews throughout the Diaspora will come to Israel, and all the communities in all the world will, God forbid, come to an end. But on the other hand, it's not at all clear to me how Jewish communities can continue to grow and flourish and act as a *mamlekhet kohanim* when they are in the Diaspora all the time.

Religious Legislation, Religion and State

Rabbi Sacks: How do you envisage the relationship between religion and state? It's a big question, but surely a central one. To what extent do you feel that an Israeli government would be justified in imposing Torah norms on a society, a large section of which might be very secular?

Rabbi Rabinovitch: First of all, I don't think the imposition of Torah norms is a proper thing to do. Worse than that, the mere fact that it is imposed creates an automatic backlash. Earlier you mentioned the disputes of Beit Shammai and Beit Hillel. At one point in the history of their disputes, things reached such a fever pitch that it was declared: "One who wishes to act in accordance with Beit Hillel may do so, and one who wishes to act in accordance with Beit Shammai may do so." Not every disagreement needs a quick resolution. Sometimes it is preferable to avoid coming to a clear decision, and at times even generations have to pass before certain decisions can be taken, so it's a very complicated issue.

There are some things which are best not written in the law books, and if written, best not enforced by the state or the powers that be. There are things that are commanded in the Torah that are directed to individuals to enforce on themselves. The less there are governmental or other instruments to enforce certain kinds of laws, the more successful these laws are in their application. It sounds paradoxical, but I think it's absolutely true.

Rabbi Sacks: Did you derive this from Maimonides' approach to history, which views human beings as evolving very slowly?

Rabbi Rabinovitch: Indeed.

Rabbi Sacks: Not every halakha is meant to be legislated. In that case, what is the role of the religious public in the State of Israel? Are you suggesting that maybe it should be more focused on shaping societal attitudes through education rather than legislation?

Rabbi Rabinovitch: Yes. I would like to see less religious legislation, and more religious education. And I think, and I hope, that we are moving in that direction.

Rabbi Sacks: I suppose this would be consistent with a liberal democratic philosophy, which gives individuals freedom within the law but allows those who are interested in doing so to have a moral education and maintain a strong religious commitment.

Rabbi Rabinovitch: I think that this is what God wants from us. Let's not forget that the whole purpose of the institution of lawful government coercion is, as Maimonides makes a central theme, to prevent transgressors from going free. If there is no legal remedy, chaos ensues, and everybody goes after his baser urges. So there has to be a certain amount of prevention, and prevention is the important part of public legislation, not the penalty.

Rabbi Sacks: So you see law as having an educational force.

Rabbi Rabinovitch: Indeed.

Rabbi Sacks: Would you be in favor of an active campaign to convert people to Judaism?

Rabbi Rabinovitch: Yes. I think one of the problems that we have today, which has not been dealt with adequately yet – but I hope will be before it's too late – is the absorption of much of the Russian *aliya*. There is a lack of distinction between Jews and non-Jews, and this is the kind of issue that could cause very serious rifts in society, God forbid.

Rabbi Sacks: And would you feel that our current attitudes toward conversion are excessively restrictive?

Rabbi Rabinovitch: Not only are they excessively restrictive, I think they are beyond the norms that halakha prescribes for us. It is not enough to say that they are restrictive. They are potentially a destructive force on our whole society. I hope things change.

Rabbi Sacks: If you were Prime Minister for a day –

Rabbi Rabinovitch: Heaven forbid.

Rabbi Sacks: If there is one thing that you would do to make Israel more cohesive or more in the spirit of Torah – where should one begin? With Shabbat? The school system?

Rabbi Rabinovitch: Well, I think both Shabbat and the school system are lasting contributions of the Jewish heritage to the whole world. It's well known that most of the civilized world has not had a school system for more than two centuries, whereas we already had it two thousand years ago.

Rabbi Sacks: England only had compulsory universal education from 1817, which is quite odd given that the British flag was flying over one quarter of the earth's land surface. So Judaism was really millennia ahead of its time.

Rabbi Rabinovitch: Indeed, and the same thing is true of Shabbat. Today there likely isn't a single place on earth where the seven-day week is not the standard. It's not a natural standard; it's not based on any scientific or natural fact or cause. It derives from the concept of the

Shabbat, a day of rest every seventh day. In fact, the word Shabbat has entered into most civilized tongues.

Rabbi Sacks: Yes, like the word "sabbatical." Twice they tried and failed to abolish it: during the French revolutionary assembly and in the League of Nations.

Rabbi Rabinovitch: The League of Nations I am not aware of, but the communist regimes tried and failed. That says something about the nature of both schooling and Shabbat as the fundamentals of society and civilization. We therefore should take responsibility for making sure that these institutions thrive and flourish. We should cultivate their relevance for all of mankind. There is no need for us to submit to ideas, such as the one recently propounded in Tel Aviv, that in some areas businesses can be kept open seven days a week. This can not only destroy our civilization but can negatively affect other civilizations as well, because we know that the institution of Shabbat is such a powerful force in the development of civilization everywhere.

Halakha and Morality

Rabbi Sacks: Have you ever sensed a conflict between halakha and morality?

Rabbi Rabinovitch: It seems to me that if there is a conflict between halakha and morality, then something is wrong either with one's moral sense, or with his understanding of the halakha, or both. Theoretically, such conflict should not be possible. Unfortunately, though, sometimes people's moral sense is distorted and, on the other hand, people often have a distorted understanding of halakha.

Rabbi Sacks: When you issue halakhic rulings, do you often find yourself guided by broader ethical imperatives?

Rabbi Rabinovitch: I think that the rulings of a *posek* who is not guided by broad ethical imperatives, as you describe them, are not worth the paper they are written on.

Rabbi Sacks: In other words, you see halakhic rulings as the translation of an ethical vision into the details of conduct?

Rabbi Rabinovitch: Into the details of conduct and of life. In life, many principles need interpretation in order to be applicable, and without the proper interpretation, what you think is right may be all wrong.

Rabbi Sacks: Let me take the specific example of the mitzva to eradicate Amalek. Is that still applicable, or do we say about that since Sennacherib mixed up the peoples, it no longer applies?

Rabbi Rabinovitch: Already in the days of King David Amalekites could be left alive. The young man who brought news to David of Saul's death describes himself as the son of an Amalekite "*ger*." Some medieval commentators explain that the father was a convert, and others that he was a resident alien ("*ger toshav*"). In either case, even when there was a distinct people of Amalek they could escape their status by becoming *gerim*, or *gerei toshav*. Moreover, Maimonides rules that before attacking Amalek we are to offer them peace, and if they accept, we do not attack. It is also clear from Maimonides that there no longer is a trace of Amalek. It's interesting that the Gemara says that Haman's descendants taught Torah in Bnei Brak.

Rabbi Sacks: In Tanakh there are other commandments to wage wars that appear to be wars of annihilation against whole nations. Now the question that I imagine many of us ask is how does that accord with the principle that our patriarch Abraham articulates, and God agrees to, that if there are ten innocent human beings, the whole of Sodom should have been spared? How do we reconcile that insistence on individual justice, and, on the other hand, what looks like collective punishment?

Rabbi Rabinovitch: I'm not sure that it's something that I can reconcile or that needs reconciliation. I think, first of all, one should bear in mind that the approach of the Torah in all the commandments is developmental. In other words, history determines when certain values can be applied and when the world is not yet ready for their application. Maimonides makes this very clear with respect to certain mitzvot; for example, the mitzvot dealing with slavery. The Torah abolished the status of slavery as it was practiced throughout the ancient world by giving the slave an independent identity. It restricted the slave owner through mitzvot like Shabbat and other mitzvot. With respect to war as well, I don't know of any other ancient literature where there are laws of proper conduct in war. According to the Torah, there are mitzvot governing how to engage in war. Women and children must not be killed in a war. When you besiege a city, you must leave one side open for those who want to flee. I don't know if there is a parallel to such laws of war in antiquity. I don't know of any.

Rabbi Sacks: At the time of Tanakh, I believe there in fact were not. However, the laws of just war did grow up in late antiquity, in the early centuries of Christian Rome, partly due to Roman law and partly biblical in inspiration. There is no doubt that no one before the prophets Isaiah and Micah saw peace as an ideal and took the romance out of warfare. I am referring to the discussion in mishna Shabbat (6:4) about whether one can carry weapons on Shabbat. The Sages say it is shameful, quoting the verse from Isaiah about swords being turned into plowshares as a prooftext that weapons are a badge of shame rather than a badge of honor. That goes completely against the ethics of antiquity, because even in Greece and Rome to be a heroic warrior was the highest of all honors. So I think peace enters Western civilization as an ideal with Isaiah and Micah, and it doesn't resurface until Immanuel Kant in the eighteenth century, when he writes his essay *Perpetual Peace*, which is the first time the modern West sees war as not an ideal. It seems, then, that this conception of human moral development was found in Judaism at a very early stage. According to Maimonides in *Hilkhot Melakhim*, Joshua was not allowed to wage any one of his thirty-one military campaigns without first offering peace.

Rabbi Rabinovitch: Maimonides based himself on a gemara: "Joshua sent three letters" (Y. Shevi'it 6:1).

Rabbi Sacks: Maimonides was criticized for introducing a historic developmental element into the discussion of mitzvot, and this remains a serious question today. Are there any limits to the possible historical development of Judaism? Once you introduce this historical dimension, where do you stop?

Rabbi Rabinovitch: I hope you don't stop before the development reaches its maximal limit, which is in the distant future. But, indeed, it's very important to recognize that historically there has never been a successful attempt to impose a social and political structure that was beyond the ability of people given their time and their economic reality. If you make demands that can only be realized in the distant future, at best they remain unrealized aspirations; at worst, they simply become negated.

Rabbi Sacks: So your view is then that all those laws of war in Numbers about Midian and in Deuteronomy were very specifically for that age?

Rabbi Rabinovitch: They were specifically for that time and place, and even within that reality the Torah prescribed limits to what can be done. The surrounding nations recognized this. We find that when the army of Ben Haddad of Aram was routed by the Israelites, his servants urged him to beg for mercy from the king of Israel, "for they are kind kings" and don't kill prisoners (I Kings 20:31). The practice among other nations was to kill prisoners, and already in those early times it was known that Israel does not engage in this practice. This must be of concern to us today as well.

In Conclusion

Rabbi Sacks: Let us turn back to contemporary Israel. We have a state, a religious public, and synagogues. Synagogues in Israel tend to be different from those abroad. In Israel they are places to pray, whereas in the Diaspora they are also about building community. Do you think that is something that's important to bring back to the State and Land of Israel – the community-building function of shuls and of the rabbinate?

Rabbi Rabinovitch: I'm not much of an expert in sociology, but it seems to me that there is an important function to communities, and there seems to be some positive development in this direction. Let's not forget that we're dealing with a public that's new. The whole country is new. The creation of communities means that people in a certain local area can join together to create a whole community. This is something that requires time and development. We're still in the process of building what one can call a pre-community. But there are already communities in many places. Certainly the smaller settlements are essentially communities. And even in the larger places, the cities, there are some communities. It takes time to develop that sort of thing.

Rabbi Sacks: You've spent much of your life training rabbis. I am your student. What is it that you most want your students to do when they go out into the world?

Rabbi Rabinovitch: It's not just my students – I want everybody to join together to sanctify God's name publicly. This means creating the kind of environment in which the values that God teaches us become the norm for our society at all levels – individual, family, society, and community. These are not easily attainable at all levels, but the Almighty seems to be helping us, and for that we thank Him.

Rabbi Sacks: Do you sense a greater openness to Judaism among the secular public in Israel than there was in the early years of the state?

Rabbi Rabinovitch: I think so, yes. I think there is a real awakening among many, many people. Some of the secular public has begun to realize that there is more to true Jewish living than secular values.

Rabbi Sacks: What would you recommend for your students to focus on? To go out and teach Torah? To build communities? Engage in acts of kindness? Are all the rabbi's areas of activity a seamless web, or do you have sense of the priority of right now? Is there a crisis right now, an issue we should be facing?

Rabbi Rabinovitch: I don't think that concentration on one issue is a healthy state of affairs, though there are issues that arise and must be addressed more urgently. Above all, we have to be concerned about the fact that we are building a new society, and any new society must incorporate and even create fundamental social structures that will reflect its principles.

Rabbi Sacks: To conclude, I would like to return to the subject we began with. When you reflect on Jewish history, given that the Jews have excelled in so many fields, why was it that we were unable to prevent those divisions and rifts that you spoke about earlier, which brought about the destruction of the Second Temple and, in a sense, the First Temple as well, because of the division of the kingdom? Why were we so unsuccessful at handling self-government?

Rabbi Rabinovitch: That's a very good question. What do you think?

Rabbi Sacks: What do I think? I think that we didn't read the instructions. I'm very struck by the fact that if you read the Torah at a simple, literal, straightforward level, you know that there is Isaac and there's Ishmael. We know that Isaac will be the carrier of the covenant of the Torah, and Ishmael will not. Yet the Torah practically forces us to empathize with the plight of Hagar and the plight of Ishmael when he's dying of thirst. It confronts us with the pathos of Esau in that great scene when he comes in and realizes that Jacob has taken his blessing. He and Isaac weep together, and we sympathize. It's almost as if God is saying yes, you are My chosen people, but don't forget that other people are also created in My image and are also My children. I think that is what He is telling Jonah at the end of the book that bears his name. I think we've failed to realize how deeply God wants us to understand the people who are not like us. Or have I got that wrong?

Rabbi Rabinovitch: No. I think that is absolutely true. That's fundamental, but that is a challenge which, unfortunately, we have not always been able to live up to. In many instances, when we look back on the historical record, we can identify cases where people failed to understand their responsibility toward those they disagreed with. But does it help us face that challenge in our own times and in our disagreements and in our own confrontations? That's the crucial issue, and there, unfortunately, it is not always so easy to make the correct decision.

Rabbi Sacks: Isaiah Berlin used to quote something that the Russian thinker Alexander Herzen said about Slavs: They have a great deal of geography, but very little history. Berlin would then add that the Jews have exactly the opposite. We have very little geography, but a great deal of history. It seems to me that the commandment "*Zakhor*!" – Remember! Commemorate! Invoke! – appears in Tanakh, in some form or another, an overwhelming number of times. That verb appears one hundred sixty-nine times in Tanakh. The Almighty is saying to us: Please learn from history if you want to avoid repeating it. And I think that is what I learned from you.

So if I may, thank you not only for your comments now, in this conversation, but for the values that guided me when I had the privilege of being your student and which I have tried to take into the world, not least, through my own students. I thank you for your words, for your inspiration, and for your vision, and I pray that we may be worthy of all of them.

Rabbi Rabinovitch: I thank you very much for what you're saying, but you know, the Sages say, "*Umitalmidai yoter mikulam*." I have learned more from my students than from anyone else. So here we are, I have to be grateful to you – which I am.

Rabbi Sacks: I think that what we really learn when we study Torah, study Gemara, is that it's the multiple voices that enlarge our imagination and our sensibilities.

Rabbi Rabinovitch: That is really the crux of the matter.

Rabbi Sacks: Thank you so much.

Rabbi Rabinovitch: Thank you.

Epilogue: The Song of the Redeemed

Hallel: The Song of Jewish History

The Gemara explains with respect to the recitation of Hallel:

> Now since there is the Great Hallel, why do we recite [the regular Hallel]? Because it includes [a mention of] the following five things: The Exodus from Egypt, the splitting of the Sea of Reeds, the giving of the Torah, the resurrection of the dead, and the birth pangs of the Messiah. The Exodus from Egypt, as it is written: "When Israel came forth out of Egypt" (Ps. 114:1); the splitting of the Sea of Reeds, as it is written: "The sea saw and fled" (ibid. 3); the giving of the Torah, as it is written: "The mountains skipped like rams" (ibid. 4); the resurrection of the dead, as it is written: "I shall walk before the Lord [in the land of the living]" (ibid. 116:9); the birth pangs of the Messiah, as it is written: "Not for us, O Lord, not for us" (ibid. 115:1), and R. Yoḥanan said: "Not for us, O Lord, not for us" refers to the subjugation of the [foreign] kingdoms. Some say that R. Yoḥanan said: "Not for us, O Lord, not for us" refers to the war of Gog and Magog.[1]

The "Great Hallel" (Ps. 136) contains twenty-six verses of praise for God, each of which concludes, "for His kindness endures forever." Even

1. Pesaḥim 118a.

though this psalm alludes to several different episodes of salvation, and even though it invokes the Tetragrammaton, which refers to God's attribute of mercy, it is nevertheless evident that if we are to sing songs of praise in every generation, we choose to recite our Hallel (i.e., the regular Hallel) because it contains these five elements, which encompass all of Jewish history, from the moment of its inception. It even contains a song in praise of the future world, which will be wholly good: "I shall walk before the Lord in the land of the living."

When Israel sings songs in praise of God, it must begin with the Exodus, when not only were the power and might of the Almighty revealed, but Israel's virtue was as well. It is for this reason that the psalmist emphasizes, "When Israel came forth out of Egypt," evoking the words of the prophet: "I remember you, the devotion of your youth, your love as a bride – how you followed Me in the wilderness, in a land not sown" (Jer. 2:2). They knew that they were headed into a desolate wilderness, that they faced scorching hot days and frigid nights. They were well aware that dangers lurked along the way, in addition to the natural fear of famine and drought. What would sustain such a large people in a barren land? Where would they find food for the children, water for the weary? They did not ask. They were not concerned. They went out of Egypt on the strength of their robust faith, and many generations later the prophet declared that the merit of their faith would endure forever, even after all their other merits would be used up. "I remember you, the devotion of your youth... how you followed Me in the wilderness." Therefore, "all who consumed [Israel] were held guilty" (Jer. 2:3), for all generations.

When we sing Hallel, we rely on the merits of such ancestors. "When Israel came forth out of Egypt" because of the devotion of our youth, "Judah became His holy one" (Ps. 114:2), God's eternal people!

Clearly it is also fitting to mention the splitting of the Sea of Reeds, when even a maidservant witnessed what the greatest of prophets would not see at other times.[2] Why so?

2. See *Mekhilta DeRashbi* on Exodus 20:15.

> R. Meir said: When the Israelites stood by the Sea of Reeds, the tribes strove with one another, each wishing to descend into the sea first. Then the tribe of Benjamin sprang forward and descended first into the sea.... For that reason the righteous Benjamin was worthy to host the Almighty, as it is said: "He dwells between his shoulders" (Deut. 33:12). R. Yehuda said to [R. Meir]: That is not what happened; rather, each tribe said, "I am not entering the sea first." Then Nahshon, the son of Aminadav, sprang forward and descended first into the sea.... Concerning him it is stated in Scripture: "Save me, O God, for the waters are taking my life. I sink in deep mire, where there is no standing" (Ps. 69:2–3).[3]

Whether it was Nahshon or the tribe of Benjamin who entered the sea first, it is a great credit to Israel! Who had ever walked into the sea and emerged? They knew full well where that path led. This attests to the character of this nation, whose every action is for the sanctification of God's name. Even the depths of the sea do not discourage Judah and Benjamin. We say of the forces of nature that they are "faithful workers who do their work faithfully" because "they do not alter their functions."[4] And Israel? With their eyes wide open, they saw that the time was ripe to sanctify God's name. He commanded, "Go forward" (Ex. 14:15), and they followed. "Draw me after You! We will run!" (Song. 1:4) – even unto the depths of the sea!

There is no need to explain at length why the giving of the Torah is mentioned in Hallel, as it is entirely to Israel's credit that they declared, "We will do, and we will obey" (Ex. 24:7). It was for the sake of that day, on which Israel accepted the Torah and reached lofty spiritual heights, that the entire world was created – on behalf of Israel, which is called "first," who received the Torah, which is called "first."[5]

---

3. Sota 36b–37a.
4. Sanhedrin 42a.
5. See Rashi on Genesis 1:1.

The Endurance of Israel's Faith in the Exile

Another aspect of the Gemara in Pesaḥim poses a difficulty, though. The Exodus, the splitting of the sea, the giving of the Torah, and the resurrection of the dead are all invoked explicitly in Hallel; even children who read these verses understand them well. But the Gemara's statement, "The birth pangs of the Messiah, as it is written: 'Not for us, O Lord, not for us,'" requires explanation. What does the verse have to do with the Messianic Era? Likewise in R. Yoḥanan's statement that this verse refers to the subjugation of foreign kingdoms or, according to the alternative explanation, to the war of Gog and Magog, the connection between the verse and the message derived from it is unclear. It is, in fact, very puzzling!

However, one who contemplates the history of our people, which has known so many troubles, will quickly recognize that our willingness to give up our lives to sanctify God's name has always been part of our heritage. In every generation, enemies rise against us, and in every generation, we have cultivated Nahshons willing to jump into water or fire for the sake of God's name. Even during the cruelest persecutions, a Jew could always choose to sanctify God's name.

The enemy was a blasphemer whose entire purpose was to mock: "Who is the Lord that I must listen to His voice?" (Ex. 5:2). If a Jew had no means of escape, at least he had a choice, and he chose to sacrifice his life for the sake of God. It is the merit of this faith that has stood by us in every generation. Neither the most sophisticated lures and temptations of wealth and honor nor the most demonic threats of death and torture could separate Israel from its Father in heaven. Tens of thousands chose burning at the stake over renunciation of their faith. Even young children instructed by their enemies to prostrate themselves before an icon would show their scorn and stretch out their necks in honor of God's great name. Their righteousness endures forever. Even during the harshest persecutions, our ancestors remained free, at least in the sense that they were free to sanctify God's name in their deaths.

The Holocaust

This was true of the distant past. In our generation, however, an unprecedented darkness descended upon the world. Not only were death and destruction decreed upon us, but the devious and accursed enemy invaded the most precious recesses of our soul. Not only did he take our lives, but he even stole our self-sacrifice. A Jew could always choose to sanctify God's name. We are the first generation that was not given the choice. The wicked enemy did not want the Jew to deny his Creator and did not care to see him bow before an idol. Anything that bore the name of Israel, even the grandchild of an assimilated Jew, who knew nothing of Judaism, was swept away by the evil torrent.

In every generation, the condemned Jew knew that his death would increase the honor of God and that he would merit having sanctified God's name. Even this small comfort was stolen by our nemesis in our generation. It made no difference whether the Jew could withstand the test, because there was no test! All were condemned to death. The righteous man ready to give up his life and the coward alike were led together like sheep to the slaughter.

All of this was foreseen by the psalmist when, in the dark terror, he screamed bitterly: "Not for us, O Lord, not for us." This time, we have no merit. When Nahshon leapt into the sea, even if the sea had not split, the merit he accrued would have endured for us. But "not for us." The despot took that from us, too. We can no longer give glory to Your name. You are alone: "Give glory to Your own name."

In his wondrous vision, the prophet stood dumbfounded: "Can these bones yet live?" (Ezek. 37:3). And the prophet sees the dry bones join other bones, become covered with flesh, and come back to life. These dry, desiccated bones heeded the word of God and became an enduring symbol. But in Treblinka, not even bones remained. Everything went up in smoke. Can even a prophet address ashes? Can the ashes be gathered so that they may hear the word of God? "Who is she who comes up from the desert like columns of smoke?" (Song. 3:6).

There was no sage, no prophet, no prophetic vision or dream. The flames erupting from the chimneys of Treblinka did not ascend to the heavens. They undermined the very foundations of creation. All hope was lost, and who could know if these were the birth pangs of the Messiah?

The Rebirth of Israel

Yet after the darkness, the dawn broke. The radiance of morning illuminated the sky, and a new light shone on Zion. Who, more than us, is enjoined to sing Hallel? And is there any song that expresses the essence of our generation's soul more than Hallel? Our generation is an ember saved from a furnace; we have seen what courageous heroes who were absolutely loyal to God were never privileged to see. "It is not for us" to ask why. It is not for us. The heart aches when we recall the flames that consumed our people, for even Moshe Rabbeinu hid his face from fear of peering at God's attribute of justice.[6]

Indeed, God has remembered us, and so we will praise Him before all the nations, declaring loudly and clearly that our choice has been restored to us, and we now eagerly and knowingly sing: "It is good to trust in God" (Ps. 118:8).

Seventy years of independence have not been easy. We have paid a price in blood for every inch of our ancestral homeland that we have redeemed, and a wall of hostility still divides us from our neighbors. Time and again we have been astonished to see the fulfillment, in us, of the verse, "No weapon formed against you shall prosper" (Is. 54:17). A scroll of independence, written by God Himself, has unfurled before our eyes:

> I made you as a covenant of the people, to restore the land and bequeath its desolate estates; to say to the prisoners, "Come out," to those in darkness, "Show yourselves." (ibid. 49:8–9)
>
> Look! These are coming from afar, those from the north and west. (ibid. 12)
>
> Raise your eyes and look around; they have all gathered and come to you. (ibid. 18)

6. See chapter 1 above, pp. 13 ff.

> For the Lord has comforted Zion, comforted all her ruins; He has made her wilderness like Eden, her desert like the Garden of the Lord. Gladness and joy shall be found there, thanksgiving and the sound of music. (ibid. 51:3)

Choosing to Accept the Yoke of Heaven

Now that we have been granted independence – renewed power of choice on a broad scale, as individuals and as a nation – we must not forget that the power to choose comes with a price. We have the freedom to choose, but we have no guarantees that we will choose intelligently or wisely. Freedom of choice demands that the utmost attention be given to every action and full responsibility taken for its consequences. A free person cannot evade the duty to accept the yoke of the kingdom of Heaven and to take all suitable actions to advance that noble goal. He cannot shirk his obligation with the futile claim that it is best to remain passive. If one does not rise to the needs of the hour, and certainly if he takes actions that have ruinous consequences – even if he claims that his intentions were good – he will be held responsible. When it comes to the desecration of God's name, whether intentional or otherwise, one is always held to account.[7]

This applies to everyone, but especially to public officials, elected representatives of the people, party leaders, and heads of government. If one's proper exercise of choice in his own life is praiseworthy, then it is certainly so when others are under his influence. Maimonides taught us as follows:

> "Be not like a senseless horse or mule [whose movement must be curbed by bit and bridle]" (Ps. 32:9) – that is, what curbs their wildness is something external, like a bit and bridle. A person should not be like that. Rather, he should be restrained by his soul, that is, his human form, which, when perfected, will keep

7. Kiddushin 40a.

> him away from anything that will prevent his perfection...and spur him toward things that will lead to his perfection.[8]

May it be God's will that we understand how to unite our hearts in His worship out of our own free will. May we be privileged to spread Torah to the masses and to inspire people – and they, too, will return from their own free will, without bit or bridle. Rather, the light of Torah will bring them back, and the redeemer shall come to Zion speedily in our days. Amen.

> A voice rings out: "Clear in the wilderness a road for the Lord! Level in the desert a highway for our God! Let every valley be raised, every hill and mount made low. Let the rugged ground become level and the ridges become a plain. The glory of the Lord shall appear, and all flesh, as one, shall behold that the Lord Himself has spoken." (Is. 40:3–5)

---

8. *Commentary on the Mishna*, Introduction to the Tenth Chapter of Sanhedrin (*Perek Ḥelek*), p. 139.

Appendix

Sources of Essays

Much of this book is based on articles that were originally published in a variety of venues. We are grateful to the editorial boards of these books and journals for permitting their republication. Each article underwent significant revision. Some articles appear in this book as complete chapters, as they were initially published, in which case we used titles similar to the original titles. In cases where the articles are not preserved intact, we have not preserved the titles of the original articles.

The following is a list of articles and their publication information:

English Articles

"A Halakhic View of the Non-Jew," *Tradition* 8:3 (Fall 1966), 27–39.

"The Religious Significance of Israel," *Tradition* 14:4 (Fall 1974), 20–28.

"The Way of Torah" (trans. Joel Linsider), *The Edah Journal* 3:1 (2003), 1–34. Earlier versions of this article appeared as: "On Religions and Politics in Israel," in *Orthodoxy Confronts Modernity*, ed. Jonathan Sacks (Hoboken: Ktav, 1991), 123–35; and "The Torah Way," in *Religious Zionism after 40 Years of Statehood*, ed. S. Spero and Y. Pessin (Jerusalem: Mesilot, 1989), 277–308.

Hebrew Articles

"הלכות מדינה כיצד?", אור המזרח כד, תשרי תשל"ה, ניו יורק, עמ' 108-116.

"עדות ה' נאמנה", שנתון הציונות הדתית, תשמ"ד, עורך: ש. בורשטיין, מסילות, ירושלים, עמ' 26-34.
"דרכה של תורה", מעליות י, תשמ"ח, מעליות, מעלה אדומים, עמ' 8-42.
"לבחינת דרכה של יהדות התורה", גוילין ג, טבת תשנ"א, מעלה, ירושלים, עמ' 54-62.
"ציונות מול בג"ץ", קובץ הציונות הדתית, תשנ"ז, עורך: שמחה רז, הסתדרות המזרחי הפועל המזרחי – המרכז העולמי, ירושלים, עמ' 332-344.
"על דת ופוליטיקה", מעליות יח, תשרי תשנ"ז, מעליות, מעלה אדומים, עמ' 109-128.
"על השואה ועל התקומה", מעליות כא, תשנ"ט, מעליות, מעלה אדומים.
"שירת גאולים", חזון למועד, עורך: יהודה שביב, מפעל רבנים ובני תורה שליד התנועה העולמית של המזרחי, מהדורה חדשה מורחבת, ירושלים תשס"ב, עמ' 156-159.
"קווים למדיניות כלכלית על פי התורה", צדק חברתי ומדיניות כלכלית במדינה יהודית, עורכים: אליעזר דון־יחיא, אלה בלפר ושמואל סנדלר, רמת גן, אוניברסיטת בר־אילן, תשס"ד, עמ' 15-24.
"עם זו יצרתי לי", דברים ושברי דברים: על יהדותה של המדינה הדמוקרטית, עורכים: אביעזר רביצקי וידידיה צ' שטרן, תשס"ז, ירושלים, המכון הישראלי לדמוקרטיה, עמ' 671-721.
"האישה – בין חזון למציאות", מורשה קהילת יעקב – חידושי תורה ומאמרים לכבודו של הרב יעקב צבי זקס, עורכים: הרב שמואל סיימנס והרב מיכאל פולק, ארה"ב תשע"ד, עמ' קסג-קפו.

For a complete list of the author's books and other publications, see (in Hebrew):

מברכת משה: קובץ מאמרים במשנת הרמב"ם לכבודו של הרב נחום אליעזר רבינוביץ, עורכים: צבי הבר וכרמיאל כהן, כרך ב, מעליות תשע"ב, עמ' 995-1007.

The fonts used in this book are from the Arno family

Maggid Books
The best of contemporary Jewish thought from
Koren Publishers Jerusalem Ltd.